How To Change Your Spouse
(Without Ruining Your Marriage)

How to Change Your Spouse
(Without Ruining Your Marriage)

H. Norman Wright &
Gary J. Oliver, Ph.D.

VB
VINE
BOOKS

Servant Publications
Ann Arbor, Michigan

Vine Books is an imprint of Servant Publications especially
designed to serve evangelical Christians.

All Scripture quotations unless otherwise noted, are from *The
Amplified New Testament,* copyright © 1958 by The Lockman
Foundation, La Habra, California. Used by permission.

Published by Servant Publications
P.O. Box 8617
Ann Arbor, Michigan 48107

Cover design and page layout by Diane Bareis
Cover illustration by Patrick J. Powers

Printed in the United States of America
ISBN 0-89283-872-8

Contents

For Joyce and Carrie

So much of what we know about
understanding emotions, appreciating differences,
growing through conflict, experiencing love, patience, and joy,
we have learned in our relationships with you.

You have been steadfast in your love,
support, and encouragement.
Your thoughtfulness, selflessness, graciousness,
concern for others, and love for the Lord
continue to be a source of motivation and inspiration.

Thank you for your faithful love,
gentle confrontation, and constant encouragement.
Thanks for being your unique self.

While we are still growing,
God has used you more than you will
ever realize to help change us
and become more of the kind of men
He would have us to be.

Apart from our Lord Jesus Christ,
You are God's greatest gifts to us.

CHAPTER ONE

Can You Change Your Spouse?

H. Norman Wright

"When I got married I was told, 'Don't even think of trying to change your partner.' I bought that statement hook, line, and sinker. Whenever my spouse's attitude or behavior bothered me and I wished for something different, I felt a twinge of guilt. I guess I stuffed my feelings pretty deep and then became resentful. Maybe that's why we drifted apart. Now, a year after our divorce, I still wonder if it wouldn't have been better to bring up those issues. Maybe my partner would have made some changes. The more I think about it, the more I think I got some bad advice. It may be possible to change a spouse. After all, I changed; I reacted to what my partner did. I didn't want to stop loving, but I did."

After reading these words, perhaps you're wondering, *Can* my spouse change? *Will* my spouse change? Is it *OK* to try to change another person? I want you to know you can change another person. Before we discuss how to do that, let's take a look at some more stories. As you read, see if any of them sound familiar.

"I've tried. Only God knows how I've tried to get her to change. There isn't one method I haven't used. I've talked, pleaded, begged, threatened, pouted, exploded, withdrawn, shown compassion, sensitivity, indifference… nothing has worked. She's entrenched in doing things her way. No person or approach will ever get her to change.

It's futile. I've just got to let her be the way she is and do things the way she wants."

"I want my husband to change some of his habits. It's not that they're destructive, just annoying. They cause me more work and they're a poor example for the children. And I think he knows it. That's what's so irritating. He won't consider changing, and when I want to talk about it, he cuts me off. I'm stuck. I've just got to learn to live with this problem."

"I actually got her to change. It took time, but she finally realized that doing it my way was the best. Resistance? Oh, yeah, there was plenty of that. But in time my persuasion wore her down. She just didn't have good reasons for running the house the way she did. It's true that I'm a neat freak, but that's the best way to live. When you keep after a person, in time they will learn from you. And even though she hasn't said it, I think she feels better about the way the place looks, too."

"I knew John and I were different the moment we began to date. I seemed to carry the social calendar for both of us. That was OK, but after ten years of marriage I'm tired of it. I enjoy talking and being with people. John says it drains him and he'd rather work on his computer than get together with friends. He's told me it's our personality differences and because I'm an extrovert and he's an introvert. I don't buy that. He can change and be outgoing if he weren't so stubborn. If John spends more time with others he'll learn to be more outgoing. He can change if he really wants to."

"Jean has told me on several occasions that I've changed her. Amazing! I didn't think it could be done, but she's right. And she's changed me. We've shared this with other people and some of them have even tried to rephrase our statements for us. They seem uncomfortable with what we say. For a while, I wondered why it bothered them so much. I think it's because they've struggled with their own desires to see their partners change. At the same time, they believe it's not possible to change another person. Then we come along and prove it can be done. A few people ask us how we did it. It's fun to tell them how."

As you've read these comments, did you find yourself identifying with any of them? Are you reacting to some? Probably. Most people would. But what about it? Is it really possible to change another person? Yes, it is! Contrary to what you may have heard or been taught over the years, it is possible. It's not wrong to want another person to change for the good of the marriage relationship. Furthermore, trying to change another person doesn't have to destroy the marriage relationship; it can even help it to flourish.

FOR THE GOOD OF THE MARRIAGE

I think we're afraid to say we want our spouses to change, especially in the Christian community. We may say, "I'd like you to respond in a different way," or "I'd like you to alter your way of reacting a bit," but we hesitate to state our desire directly.

A few months ago I heard a well-known Christian speaker say on the radio, "We don't change other people and we can't change them. But we do influence them." Yet the whole purpose of influence is to bring about change!

The author of a book on gender stated that a woman should not try to change a man nor try to improve him. Yet later in the book he cites a letter his wife wrote to him about how she felt when he spent too much time at work and how he appeared not to value her feelings. Even though she didn't say, "I want you to stop working so much and spend more time with me and the children," that was the intent and purpose of the letter. We all have times when we want our partners to modify their behaviors or attitudes. I will even go so far as to say not trying to change your partner could be destructive to your marriage. If something about your partner causes you to distance yourself or feel resentment, then change is necessary.

Change is an important part of a healthy growing marriage. If we didn't change, it would imply that we're perfect and have no need to grow. And we all know the response to that. In fact, it's impossible to remain the same if you're married.

One woman said to me at a seminar, "My husband is the same person he was when I married him. He does things the same way, and all his annoying behaviors are still there. If anything, he's even more extreme in what he does now than twenty years ago. It's as if he's refined and perfected those tendencies. And oh, did I try to change him. I tried every approach in the book. Nothing worked."

My response to her was, "Didn't it work? It sounds as if it did."

"What do you mean?" she asked.

"Well," I replied, "you've just told me he *did* change. He became more set in his ways. He changed, but not in the way you wanted."

Too often the changes we desire don't happen, but the behaviors we'd like to see go away merely increase. Could it be that we're the catalysts causing our partners to change in a way we don't want? Unfortunately, that can be true. But it doesn't have to be that way.

One reason we'd like our partners to change after we've been married a few years is because they aren't the same people we fell in love with. A somewhat different person has emerged. Why? Think back to your own experience.

Most couples enter marriage while they're in the romantic rather than the realistic stage. Maybe this happened to you. Your partner seemed perfect, and if there were any noticeable flaws you discounted or ignored them.

Infatuation can color our perception and cause us to overlook even significant differences. You assume the romantic high will continue far into the future. You see your partner in an unrealistically positive light, often referred to as the "halo effect." You feel complete because of the presence of this other person in your life. You've found the one to complement what you already have and supplement what you think is missing. But with time, the shine on the halo tarnishes and the real person begins to emerge. I've heard many people say, "Where's the person I fell in love with?" Oh, they're there all right!—in our imaginations. The greater the halo effect, the more we will want to change our partners later. But there's another reason for wanting to change our partners.

I've seen many cases in which, prior to marriage, the man was sensitive, open, communicative, vulnerable, and a listener. But sometimes those behaviors, even within the first month of marriage, all but disappear. I've listened to husbands say that before marriage their wives took an interest in their hobbies and sporting events and even participated in them. But once they got married, the interest waned. In both cases the spouses felt cheated and abandoned. They married their partners because of the way they perceived them. And of course they now attempt to change their partners back to the way they were in the pre-marriage state.

A desire for change is normal, healthy, and universal. When a marriage relationship changes, it's because the people in that relationship have changed.

NO MARRIAGE IS COMPATIBLE

The book *Questions Women Ask in Private* was based upon the results of a survey from seven hundred professional counselors and ministers. They were asked to identify the five most frequently asked questions by women in counseling. Do you have any idea what the most frequently asked question was? "How can I change the man in my life?"

More women than men seem to voice concern over seeing their spouses change. And that seems to be obvious as reflected in the numbers of books written for women on how to understand, figure out, and get along with a man. A few of the titles I've seen recently are *How to Love a Difficult Man, How to Light His Fire, Men: A Translation for Women, What Every Woman Should Know about Men, How to Keep a Man in Love with You Forever,* and the list goes on.

If you think you're one person who doesn't try to change your spouse, consider these requests:

Please hang up your clothes when you take them off.

Pull your car forward in the garage so I can park in the driveway.

Take a shower before you come to bed.

Wash out the tub when you're finished with your bath.

Don't share intimate things about us when we're with friends.

Call me if you're going to be late.

Don't call me that name in public.

Turn off the TV when we're talking.

Let me know in the morning if you want sex that night.

Pick up the house before I come home.

When I spank Jimmy, please don't joke about Mommy abusing him.

Why do individuals or couples come for marriage counseling or attend a marriage enrichment seminar? They want their marriages to be better. In other words, they want their marriages to change. Underneath this desire is the hope their partners will be different. In some cases they see the need for change in their own lives, too.

You've got to change or your marriage will fail, since *no couple who marries is compatible.* This is the shocking statement I share with every couple in the first session of premarital counseling. When they recover from the shock, they're ready to hear the rest. I suggest that it will take the first five to ten years to learn to be compatible. And this means each person will need to change and learn to complement his or her partner.

The founder of the "Recovering Hope in Your Marriage" program wrote:

> It's always a mistake to depend on your partner magically changing after marriage. Everybody changes. But basing a marriage on the hope that helpful change will just happen is a dangerous hope. Many people marry believing that intolerable conditions will improve. Those conditions do improve if there is a sufficiently strong commitment to the marriage. However, things often get worse before they get better. This time of getting worse happens because we are so reluctant to make waves—disclose our feelings, confront ourselves, and face our situation. The hope that the problems will just effortlessly go away is an enticing fantasy that is hard to let go.[1]

People do change and they will change—especially when you care about them changing. But perhaps change happens for reasons other than those you would expect.

CHANGE FOR THE BETTER

Recently my brother and I made a quick overnight trip to my place at Lake Arrowhead so he could see the new addition we had made to our home. This was one of the few times my wife, Joyce, wasn't with me.

As my brother and I prepared to leave the next morning, I went through a very set routine of cleaning and getting everything in order for several couples who were coming to use the place that weekend. As I left, it struck me that I had just cleaned the house the way Joyce would have! A few years ago I wouldn't have done it that way or even thought of doing it that way. What happened? Joyce taught me. I learned from her. I was doing it her way. I had changed.

There's a faster way to recognize change. Try this simple experiment to see how you can affect the way other people react to you. Go into a store and determine in advance how you're going to behave toward the salesperson. Do this three different times with three different salespeople and keep notes of their responses.

With the first one, appear as though you're discouraged, depressed, and defeated. Look at the person, then look away, sigh, and say, "You probably don't have what I'm looking for either. Nothing has gone right today."

With the second one glare and say in an angry tone, "I sure hope you can help. I'm getting ticked off at the inefficiency I've found so far today."

With the third one, smile, ask how they are, and in a pleasant voice say, "You know, I'm sure you'll be able to help me. You look as if you know what's going on."

This is not a foolproof experiment, but in most cases you'll find that the first salesperson responds with empathy and concern. The second is either subdued or defensive, and the last one is cordial. What caused the difference? You did, with your different overtures. Your behavior was a major factor in how they responded to you. You brought about a change in each one.

I see people change all the time through counseling. Often I say, "Is what you're doing now working for you? If not, perhaps there's a better way of responding." I like to suggest to couples that they help one another change by listing specific, loving behaviors they would like their partner to do for them. Each partner lists twelve to fifteen behaviors important to him or her, many of which are absent from the relationship. They exchange lists, and it's up to each partner to take personal responsibility to act on the various requests. What they do is not dependent upon what the partner does. And it works. Changes do happen. (We'll discuss this in detail in chapter 12.)

We've all been changed by others. But just your presence won't change the other person. Neither will time. However, there are specific ways to bring about change. Think about it for a moment. Over your life span, who has taught you? Influenced you? Challenged you? A parent, minister, teacher, counselor, coach, friend? How were you changed by them?

Before we discuss this, let me clarify one thing. Wanting your partner to make some changes from time to time has nothing to do with your level of commitment to your partner. Commitment means you accept your partner without waiting for change to make him or her more acceptable.

You commit to another person because of the depth of your love and because being with that person fulfills you. You commit knowing the other person's faults. Even if you had doubts about your partner's differences and behaviors, your love said, "In spite of those differences and behaviors, I commit to you." Any marriage is two imperfect people making a commitment to accept one another.

If this is true, how does the desire to change your partner fit into this expression of commitment? Doesn't it violate it? No. Whether your partner changes or not has no effect upon your commitment, nor should it make your love diminish. But change can enhance, strengthen, and enrich your marriage.

WHAT DOES THE BIBLE SAY ABOUT CHANGING OTHERS?

Consider these verses:

And when (Apollos) wished to cross to Achaia (most of Greece), the brethren wrote to the disciples there, urging and encouraging them to accept and welcome him heartily. Acts 18:27, AMPLIFIED

I entreat and advise Euodia and I entreat and advise Syntyche to agree and to work in harmony in the Lord. Philippians 4:2, AMPLIFIED

Let the word (spoken by) the Christ, the Messiah, have its home (in your hearts and minds) and dwell in you in (all its) richness, as you teach and admonish and train one another in all insight and intelligence and wisdom (in spiritual things, and sing) psalms and hymns and spiritual songs, making melody to God with (His) grace in your hearts. Colossians 3:16, AMPLIFIED

But we beseech and earnestly exhort you, brethren, that you excel (in this matter) more and more. 1 Thessalonians 4:10, AMPLIFIED

Therefore encourage (admonish, exhort) one another and edify— strengthen and build up—one another, just as you are doing.
1 Thessalonians 5:11, AMPLIFIED

What are we to exhort one another to do? What are we to teach or encourage one another to do?

The word *exhort* in these passages means "to urge one to pursue some course of conduct." It looks to the future. Exhorting one another is a three-fold ministry in which a believer urges another person to action in terms of applying scriptural truth, encourages the other person with scriptural truth, and comforts the person through the application of Scripture.

In Acts 18:27, the word "encourage" means "to urge forward or persuade." In 1 Thessalonians 5:11 it means "to stimulate another person to the ordinary duties of life."

Consider the words found in 1 Thessalonians 5:14, "And we earnestly beseech you, brethren, admonish (warn and seriously advise) those who are out of line—the loafers, the disorderly and the unruly; encourage the timid and fainthearted, help and give your support to the weak souls (and) be very patient with everybody— always keeping your temper."

Scripture uses a variety of words to describe both our involvement with another as well as the actual relationship.

Urge (parakaleo) means "to beseech or exhort." It is intended to create an environment of urgency to listen and respond to a directive. It is a mildly active verb. Paul used it in Romans 12:1 and in 1 Corinthians 1:4.

The word *warn (noutheo;* "admonish," KJV) means both "to warn" and "to confront" at the same time. It is an active verb. It refers to creating a confrontational environment for the purpose of producing a change in direction or behavior. It is also meant to be used with a strong-willed person who is running out of control.

The word *encourage (paramutheomai)* means "to console, comfort," and "cheer up." This process includes elements of understanding, redirecting of thoughts, and a general shifting of focus from the negative to the positive. In the context of the verse, it refers to the timid ("fainthearted," KJV) individual who is discouraged and ready to give up.

Help (anechomai) primarily contains the idea of "taking interest in," "being devoted to," "rendering assistance," or "holding up spiritually and emotionally." It is not so much an active involvement as a passive approach. It suggests the idea of coming alongside a person and supporting him. In the context of 1 Thessalonians 5:14, it seems to refer to those who are incapable of helping themselves.

Take a moment now and look back over these words from Scripture. Can you think of an example from your own life for each one? Were you on the receiving or giving end? In either case, what happened?

BEWARE OF REFORMING!

In marriage, each partner is to be an encourager rather than a critic, a forgiver rather than a collector of hurts, an enabler rather than a reformer.

This kind of person helps others become all that it is possible for them to become. He makes things easy or possible.

Too often people discover that marriage stifles and limits, rather than frees them to become all they can be. Often this is because the spouse adopts the role of critical reformer. Reformers try to get their spouses to meet their standards or even become a replica of them. An insecure person wants his mate's behaviors, beliefs, and attitudes to be just like his own, and he is threatened by any real or supposed differences. This is not a healthy request for change.

Some spouses seem to have an almost irresistible urge to reform or improve their partners in some respect. It's constant; there's never any satisfaction. A wife may want to make her husband more socially acceptable, or to get him to take more responsibility around the house. A husband wants his wife to be a better housekeeper, or to be more organized. Sometimes even the tiniest habits seem to require corrective action: the way one dresses, the way one walks, the way one squeezes a tube of toothpaste.

All of us need to change and grow in hundreds of different ways. But it's a problem when a husband or wife appoints himself or herself a Committee of One to see that the necessary change is enacted, and in doing so says, "You must change; I can't really accept you as you are until you get busy and do it." The result is that grace is smothered and all genuine desire for love-motivated change is undercut.[2]

There's the difference! A demand confines; a request gives freedom.

Paul urged the believers in Ephesus to be "living as becomes you—with complete lowliness of mind and meekness, with patience, bearing with one another and making allowances because you love one another" (Eph 4:2, AMPLIFIED).

The changes we want in our partners generally fall into two categories: refinement and correction. *Refinement* changes are small and are part of the process of learning how to be compatible. Every couple needs to experience refinement changes in order for intimacy to develop in the relationship. Sometimes refinement changes happen immediately, sometimes over a period of years.

However, if you keep silent about your desire for change, your partner may believe everything is all right. This happened to Tom and Lisa:

Lisa: Tom, I wish you would stop taking food off of my plate. It's my food and I want it to be my food.

Tom: Look, I don't like to waste money. I only eat food off your plate when we're out at a restaurant. You never eat it all anyway. We save money this way. I can order less and finish yours. Why gripe about it now? I've been doing this for years. It didn't used to bother you.

Lisa: I don't like it; I feel rushed. And I don't like being watched by a vulture waiting to pounce on my leftovers. I feel like every bite I take is a bite out of your mouth. And it has bothered me for a long time. I've made comments before but you've ignored them.

Tom: I just don't like wasting food. What if I don't just take it but ask you first?

Lisa: I'd prefer it if you didn't ask or even expect it. If any is left I'll take it home. Please order enough for yourself. There are times when I've eaten everything and you were bothered.

Tom: Well, what if I never said anything and waited until you offer it? That way there's no pressure. I don't know why it's such a big deal with you. I don't care if you take food off my plate but if it's important to you, I'll go along with you. Next time it would help to know sooner. Otherwise, how would I know it's a problem?

Ever been in this situation? Fortunately, this one worked out fairly well.

Corrective changes are more difficult because they involve issues that can seriously erode or destroy a marriage relationship. These issues include communication, sex, neglect, abuse, financial irresponsibility, or various compulsions and addictions.

Years ago I discovered a wise quote:

> We try to change people to conform to our ideas of how they should be. So does God. But there the similarity ends. The way in which we try to get other people to conform is far different than the way in which God works with us. Our ideas of what the other person should do or how he should act may be an improvement or an imprisonment. We may be setting the other person free of behavior patterns that are restricting his development, or we may be simply chaining him up in another behavioral bondage. The changes God works in us are always freeing, freeing to become that which He has created us to be.[3]

Whatever change you seek needs to be advantageous for both you and your partner, as well as for the relationship. It's not our responsibility to take on the job of reformer. The Holy Spirit can do that much better than we can. Our task is to request change with our spouse and provide an atmosphere of acceptance and patience that allows God freedom to work. Then we must learn to trust God to do the work.

Scripture does *not* say that in order to bring about change in another person we are to criticize, tear down, put down, undermine self-esteem, or find fault. Consider these passages:

> Do not judge and criticize and condemn others, so that you may not be judged and criticized and condemned yourselves. For just as you judge and criticize and condemn others you will be judged and criticized and condemned, and in accordance with the measure you deal out to others it will be dealt out again to you.
>
> **Matthew 7:1-2** AMPLIFIED

> Then let us no more criticize and blame and pass judgment on one another, but rather decide and endeavor never to put a stumbling block or an obstacle or a hindrance in the way of a brother.
>
> **Romans 14:13,** AMPLIFIED

> Fathers, do not provoke or irritate or fret your children—do not be hard on them or harass them; lest they become discouraged and sullen and morose and feel inferior and frustrated; do not break their spirit. **Colossians 3:21,** AMPLIFIED

If you're a faultfinder, you will drive your spouse away from you.

Too often, legitimate requests get swallowed up by faultfinding.

Here are several reasons why faultfinding is so destructive in the marriage relationship:

Faultfinding deeply wounds your partner. Constant verbal and nonverbal criticism says, "I don't accept you for who you are. You don't measure up, and I can't accept you until you do." In more than twenty-five years of counseling I've heard multitudes of people in my office cry out in pain, "My spouse's criticism rips me apart. He makes me feel like dirt. I don't feel accepted. And right now I'm still looking for someone who will tell me I'm all right." A wounded spouse becomes afraid or angry and retaliates through overt or covert withdrawal, resentment, or aggression.

Faultfinding really doesn't change your partner. Though your spouse may appear to change behavior in response to your criticism, the heart rarely changes. Some spouses simply learn to cover their inner attitudes with external compliance.

Faultfinding is contagious. A faultfinding spouse teaches intolerance to his partner. Thus, both of you learn to be critical and unaccepting of yourselves as well as each other.

Faultfinding accentuates negative traits and behaviors. When you pay undue attention to your partner's mistakes or irresponsible behaviors, you tend to reinforce instead of eliminate them.

Satisfying marriages have a common ingredient—mutual education. Mutual education means that both partners must become skilled teachers as well as receptive learners. The reason for this is to develop a greater degree of compatibility. If you neglect this education process, your relationship could be in jeopardy.

Mutual education is a gentle process. It involves positive modeling of the desired attitudes or behavior, gentle prodding, sensitive reminders, encouragement, believing your spouse can succeed, and not blaming or rebuking. It focuses on the positive, and you want to manage that change so the end result is positive.[4]

We're sure that's what you want, too.

HOW'D THEY DO IT?

For several months, Gary and I talked with people and distributed hundreds of surveys. People's reactions were interesting. They either believed they couldn't change their partners or they hadn't been able to change them over the years. But when we explained what we've expressed in this chapter, they began to realize that change is possible.

We've selected responses to our survey that were thorough and would give you the opportunity to learn from another's experience. Hopefully these stories will encourage you to reach out and assist your spouse to grow. You will find a similar story at the conclusion of each chapter. The last chapter is a compilation of many such stories. Here's the first one.

"When I married my wife, we both were insecure and she did everything she could to try to please me. I didn't realize how dominating and uncaring I was toward her. My actions in our early marriage caused her to withdraw even more. I wanted her to be self-assured, to hold her head high, and her shoulders back. I wanted her to wear her hair long and be perfect at all times. I wanted her to be feminine and sensual.

"The more I wanted her to change, the more withdrawn and insecure she felt. I was causing her to be the opposite of what I wanted her to be. I began to realize the demands I was putting on her, not so much by words but by body language.

"By God's grace I learned that I must love the woman I married, not the woman of my fantasies. I made a commitment to love Susan for who she was—who God created her to be.

"The change came about in a very interesting way. During a trip to Atlanta I read an article in *Reader's Digest*. I made a copy of it and have kept it in my heart and mind ever since.

"It was the story of Johnny Lingo, a man who lived in the South Pacific. The islanders all spoke highly of this man, but when it came time for him to find a wife the people shook their heads in disbelief. In order to obtain a wife you paid for her by giving her father cows. Four to six cows was considered a high price. But the woman Johnny Lingo chose was plain, skinny, and walked with her shoulders hunched and her head down. She was very hesitant and shy. What surprised everyone was Johnny's offer—he gave eight cows for her! Everyone chuckled about it, since they believed his father-in-law put one over on him.

"Several months after the wedding, a visitor from the U.S. came to the Islands to trade and heard the story about Johnny Lingo and his eight-cow wife. Upon meeting Johnny and his wife the visitor was totally taken back, since this wasn't a shy, plain, and hesitant woman but one who was beautiful, poised, and confident. The visitor asked about the transformation, and Johnny Lingo's response was very simple. 'I wanted an eight-cow woman, and when I paid that for her and treated her in that fashion, she began to believe that she was an eight-cow woman. She discovered she was worth more than any other woman in the islands. And what matters most is what a woman thinks about herself.'

"This simple story impacted my life. I immediately sent Susan flowers (I had rarely if ever done that before.) The message on the card simply said 'To My Eight-Cow Wife.' The florist (who was a friend of mine) thought I had lost my mind and questioned if that was really what I wanted to say.

"Susan received the flowers with total surprise and bewilderment at the card. When I returned from the trip I told her that I loved her for who she is and that I considered her to be my eight-cow wife, and then I gave her the article to read.

"I now look for ways to show her that I am proud of her and how much I appreciate her. An example of this involved a ring. When we became engaged I gave Susan an antique engagement ring that I inherited from a great-great aunt. Susan seemed very pleased and I never thought any more about it. But I had come out cheap, and that's how she felt. After twenty years of marriage she shared with me how she felt about the hand-me-down wedding ring. We had our whole family get involved in learning about diamonds. Susan found what she liked. It was not the largest stone nor the most expensive. I would have gladly paid more. I bought it and gave it to her for Christmas. 'To my Eight-Cow Wife, with all my love!' But what this did for our relationship is amazing.

"First, it changed me! My desires began to change. My desire now is for Susan to be all that God has designed her to be. It is my responsibility as her husband to allow her that freedom.

"It also changed her. Susan became free. She learned who she is in Christ. She has gained confidence and self-assurance. She is more aware of her appearance, her clothes, hair, and makeup, because she is free to be who she is.

"Susan rarely buys clothes for herself. Last year for Christmas I told her this year I would buy her an outfit or some type of clothing each month. This has boosted her confidence in her appearance. She looks great because she wants to!

"Susan really is an Eight-Cow Wife of whom I am very proud. We have been married now since 1971."

TAKE ACTION

1. How did you see your parents change one another?

2. What teaching have you heard over the years about changing others?

3. How have you changed during your marriage?

4. What three changes would you like to see in your partner?

5. What three changes would you like to see in yourself?

CHAPTER TWO

Roadblocks to Change

Gary J. Oliver

"**W**hy should I be the one to change? I'm not that bad. I know a lot of people who are worse than I am."

"You know, you're not so hot yourself. Who are you to think your way is the right way?"

"I'll never be able to change; it's just the way I am. My father and grandfather were the same way. I was born this way and it's too late to do anything about it now."

"You can't teach an old dog new tricks."

For most of us, hanging onto familiar habits, even though they hurt us, is not a conscious choice. Few people say to themselves, "Gee, I think I'm going to choose to stay stuck, play it safe, stagnate." For most of us, avoiding change is a reflex action, an unconscious and automatic response.

What little sense of safety and security some of us have feels threatened by change. We hope that if we wait long enough, our problems will take care of themselves. And who can blame us for wanting a perfect and preferably painless solution to our problems? However, as Tom and Connie discovered, problems won't go away unless we become involved in their solution.

"When we were engaged Tom made me feel like I was the most wonderful, unique, intelligent person in the world," Connie said somewhat wistfully. She and Tom had been married for fourteen years and, like many couples, had slowly drifted apart. She continued in a voice that reflected as much hurt as frustration, "He was eager to see me, anxious to talk with me, excited about what I had to say. Now it seems as if he doesn't see me even when he's looking at me. Instead of talking with me he talks to me or at me. And rather than being excited about what I have to say he seems to endure it."

Although some of what Connie said hurt Tom, there was enough truth in her statements to break through his defenses. "Early in our relationship Connie complimented me on how I looked, on what I did, on who I was. She made me feel like I was someone special. I didn't just love her for who she was. I also loved her for how she made me feel when I was with her." Now Connie was listening. Tom continued, "But it didn't take long before I couldn't do anything right. I didn't dress right, I didn't keep our room right, I worked too long or too hard, I didn't talk enough or didn't say the right things when I did talk. It's as if she was trying to change me into a totally different person. Over time I began to feel like a failure."

I've heard similar conversations from hundreds of couples. Have you ever had feelings similar to those of Tom or Connie? When we get married we have dreams and expectations. It usually doesn't take very long for the reality of our differences to hit the fan and we see our dream of this "ideal" relationship with this "special" person begin to fade.

Now what do we do? Most people attempt one of three options. They pretend the differences do not exist and go on as if nothing has changed; they sell out on who God has called them to be, trying to placate their partner, hoping they can be happy; or they go on a campaign to attempt total personality reconstruction and "change" their partner. The good news is: There's a fourth option.

HOW DO WE GROW UP?

I can't remember when I first came across this particular quote. I know it was many years ago, but it has had a tremendous impact on my life.

"God loves us just the way we are, but He loves us too much to leave us that way."

There aren't any big words in it. It doesn't contain any deep or convoluted theological concepts. Yet there's power in its simplicity.

I grew up in the sixties when the mottoes were "Live and Let Live" and "Do Your Own Thing." Individualism was the order of the day. If you really loved someone you would accept that person just the way he or she was. You wouldn't try to change people. You would encourage them to stay the way they were—to fulfill their individual destinies. You were responsible only for yourself.

On the one hand these aren't bad ideas. We do need to respect the God-given uniqueness He's built into each of us. However, you don't have to read very much of the Bible to realize that one of God's primary goals for us as Christians is to grow.

The Bible has a lot to say about growth, change, and becoming mature. While God loves us just the way we are, He loves us too much to leave us that way. Because He loves us He wants to see us "become conformed to the image of His son" (Rom 8:29). Because He loves us He wants to help us "grow up in all aspects into Him, who is the head, even Christ" (Eph 4:15).

In 1 Corinthians 3:1 Paul expressed concern over the Corinthian Christians because they hadn't grown. He writes, "And I, brethren, could not speak to you as to spiritual men, but as to men of flesh, as to babes in Christ." The writer of Hebrews expressed concern that the readers hadn't changed, they hadn't deepened or matured (Heb 5:11-14). He begins chapter six by exhorting them to "press on to maturity" (6:1). What he was really saying was, "Hey folks. It's time for you to make some changes. It's time for you to grow up."

Our willingness to change, to learn, to grow is God's love language. It tells Him we believe in Him, we trust Him, we want to be who and what He wants us to be. Openness to change is our way of taking His hand and following Him. He will never give us more than we can handle (1 Cor 10:13); He can cause all things to work together for good (Rom 8:28); and He will supply all of our needs according to His riches in glory (Phil 4:19).

How do we grow up? How do we mature? How do we become who God wants us to be? How do we learn to honor one another, to serve one another, to prefer one another as more important than ourselves?

In 1 Peter 1:7, Peter uses a powerful word picture to describe this process. He compares our lives to gold that is purified by fire. The refining process involves several different "firings" to bring the alloys and impurities to the surface so that the goldsmith can remove them. The refining process takes time, hard work, and at times can be painful, but the product is worth it. The end result is pure gold.

God uses many people and experiences to refine our lives. For those of us who are married, one of the most effective refiners is our spouse. Through the frustrations, discouragements, disagreements, and hurts of the marriage relationship we learn to have the love of Christ, the patience of Christ, and the forgiveness of Christ. Each time the gold of our lives is reheated, different alloys and impurities come to the surface. At each step of the process the gold is a bit different than it was before. The gold is *changed*.

In a healthy, growing marriage we struggle to accept our differences, to value our partner's uniqueness, to make peace with each other. Unfortunately some have interpreted this to mean that if you really love your spouse, if you truly accept them for who they are, you will never ask them to change.

For years I bought into the idea that one person couldn't change another. Early in my ministry I remember reading Cecil Osborne's excellent book, *The Art of Understanding Your Mate.* In this book he wrote that there is a universal law of mind and spirit, in three parts.

1. I can change no other person by direct action.

2. I can change only myself.

3. When I change, others tend to change in reaction to me.[1]

In some ways that's true. We can't "make" anyone change. We need to change ourselves first. And then—maybe—our spouse will change. The only problem is that no matter how hard you work at changing yourself, it may or may not lead to change in your partner. Over the past twenty years I've seen many individuals make personal changes that didn't produce any change in their partner.

I've also seen people who have worked on changing themselves to become who God would have them to be. They've become sensitive to many of their partners' preferences. They've learned how to share their own needs and concerns with their partner in ways that led to increased sensitivity and awareness, growth, maturity, and, yes, change.

Time after time, I've seen spouses who did things that over time led to constructive, positive changes in their partners. I'm convinced that it's practical, realistic, and wise to try to help each other change for the better, for the good of the marriage, and for our spiritual growth.

God has not called us to lives of isolation. He has called us to love, honor, build, encourage, nourish, cherish, serve, rebuke, and exhort one another.

When we focus only on changing ourselves, our perception is limited. We can become so focused on ourselves that we fail to see how God would like to use us in the lives of others. If we're afraid to share our needs, concerns, and preferences with those we love, they will, over time, cease to know who we really are. If we're afraid or unwilling to "speak the truth in love," we may have quenched the Holy Spirit and limited God's ability to use us as a tool in others' lives.

"Tom," I asked, "what does it mean to you when Connie asks you to change something?" Tom's response was immediate. "It means something is wrong with me. I've failed." Tom's answer reflects a common misunderstanding many people have about change. In seminars and workshops around the country we've asked hundreds of people to complete the sentence "Change is... "

Here are some of the most frequent responses:

exciting	scary
positive	necessary
stressful	uncomfortable
an attitude	awkward
a lot of work	essential for maturity
hard	refreshing
threatening	the opposite of death
a crossroads	like walking through a mine field
easier for some than others	opportunity for self-examination
painful	easier to require in others
unavoidable	a tremendous source of fear

The word *change* means to make different, to give a different course or direction, to replace one thing with another, to make a shift from one to another, to undergo transformation, transition, or substitution. However, to most people change is negative, something that implies inferiority, inadequacy, and failure. No wonder so many people resist the idea of change. Who wants to feel inferior and inadequate?

"Tom," I asked, "What would it feel like if Connie encouraged you to... ?" and then I shared with him some of the words listed below. As you read through this list of words, be aware of your response. Is it positive or negative? Is it encouraging or discouraging?

become	expand	develop	enlarge	swell
augment	supplement	extend	mature	advance
bud	shoot up	progress	thrive	bear fruit
prosper	flourish	luxuriate	bloom	blossom

Each of these words is a synonym for *grow,* a word that describes positive change. Most people's response to the word *grow* is much more positive than it is to the word change. Yet without change there is no growth.

I remember hearing Warren Wiersbe say,

We can benefit from change. Anyone who has ever really lived knows that there is no life without growth. When we stop growing we stop living and start existing. But there is no growth without change, there is no challenge without change. Life is a series of changes that create challenges, and if we are going to make it, we have to grow.[2]

CHANGE IS THE PATHWAY TO GROWTH

People are a lot like trees; they either grow or die. There's no standing still. A tree dies when its roots become blocked. God has made us in such a way that we become mentally, spiritually, and eventually, physically dead when we choose to allow the circumstances of our lives to keep us from growing. Pastors, physicians, and psychologists spend their lives trying to help individuals and institutions that have chosen to stop growing.[3]

What's the opposite of growing? Consider these words:

stagnant	stale	sluggish	lethargic
passive	lazy	dormant	dead
lifeless	deteriorated	degenerate	in a decline
gone to seed	vegetative	atrophied	decayed

What's your first thought after reading that list of words? Mine was "Yuck!" I don't think anyone would like to be described as lethargic, stagnant, deteriorated, and atrophied. Yet that's what we choose when we choose not to grow.

Tim Hansel tells a great story about what it's like to be around people who've chosen to play it safe, to stay stuck, to not grow:

A close friend of mine was asked back to his forty-year high school reunion. For months he saved to take his wife back to the place and the people he'd left four decades before. The closer the time came for the reunion, the more excited he became, thinking of all the wonderful stories he would hear about the changes and the accomplishments these old friends would tell him. One night before he left he even pulled out his old yearbooks and read the silly statements and the good wishes for the future that students write to each other. He wondered what ol' Number 86 from his football team had done. He wondered if any others had encountered this Christ who had changed him so profoundly. He even tried to guess what some of his friends would look like, and what kind of jobs and families some of these special friends had.

The day came to leave and I drove them to the airport. Their energy was almost contagious. "I'll pick you up on Sunday evening, and you can tell me all about it," I said. "Have a great time."

Sunday evening arrived. As I watched them get off the plane, my friend seemed almost despondent. I almost didn't want to ask, but finally I said, "Well, how was the reunion?"

"Tim," the man said, "it was one of the saddest experiences of my life."

"Good grief," I said, more than a little surprised. "What happened?"

"It wasn't what happened but what didn't happen. It has been forty years, forty years—and they haven't changed. They had simply gained weight, changed clothes, gotten jobs... but they hadn't really changed. And what I experienced was maybe one of the most tragic things I could ever imagine about life. For reasons I can't fully understand, it seems as though some people choose not to change."

There was a long silence as we walked back to the car. On the drive home, he turned to me and said, "I never, never want that to be said of me, Tim. Life is too precious, too sacred, too important. If you ever see me go stagnant like that, I hope you give me a quick, swift kick where I need it—for Christ's sake. I hope you'll love me enough to challenge me to keep growing.[4]

Let's face it. When you boil the Christian life down to the basics the name of the game is change. Those who want to learn, who are willing to look at themselves in the mirror before grabbing the binoculars to look at others, those who refuse to stay in a rut, those who make time to listen for the still, small voice of the Holy Spirit, those are the ones God is free to use, to bless, to honor. Those are the ones who know what it means to "be more than conquerors" (Rom 8:31).

WHY IS IT SO HARD TO CHANGE?

If change is valuable, necessary, and essential for growth, why do so many people avoid it? Whenever we've asked groups to complete the sentence "Change is… " we've also asked them to list what they consider to be the most significant barriers to change. Here are some of the most frequently listed barriers:

obligations	fear of failure
pride	security
fear of unknown	lack of role models
family ties or messages	admitting wrongdoing
limited emotional tool-kit	need for control
denial	easier to do it the old way
fear of self-examination	easy to say no to a new idea
we don't know how	we've tried before and failed

While the pace of change around us has accelerated dramatically in the past twenty-five years, that's not the major barrier to change. Time and time again we've found that, of all the reasons why "it's too hard to change," there is one that stands head and shoulders above the rest.

Before I tell you what it is, I want to ask you a question. What do you think of when you hear the word *crazy?* Someone who believes he is Napoleon Bonaparte or Abraham Lincoln? Someone who has conversations with trees? Someone who has a severely impaired reality orientation?

How's this for a definition? *Crazy* is to find out what doesn't work and keep on doing it. Think about it. If you saw someone flick a light switch two or three times, you wouldn't think a thing about it. However, if you saw someone flicking the same light switch for a half-hour, you would know something was seriously wrong with their thought processes.

Everybody wants to be different but few people want to change. Does that sound a bit crazy? It is. But it's the truth. I've worked with hundreds of couples who have spent twenty and thirty years doing the same dysfunctional dance with each other, refusing to grow, refusing to change, refusing to budge. They want to have a different kind of marriage but neither one is willing to change. They're stuck in a personal and relational rut. And you know what a rut is don't you? A rut is a grave with both ends kicked out.

How does this happen? How can something that seems so simple be so difficult? Why do some couples choose to endure a mediocre relationship when they could significantly increase mutual satisfaction in their marriage?

It's simple. We are creatures of habit. We get used to seeing things a certain way. After awhile it's hard to see it any other way. As we grow up we develop a grid—a way of looking at life and the way things should be. It's hard for us to understand why others can't see things the same way we do, but usually we attribute it to lack of training, lack of opportunity, or lack of intelligence. The opinions we have about the way things should be become the way everyone should see things.

When Christ came in fulfillment of the hundreds of prophecies concerning the Messiah, those who knew the Scriptures the best were the ones who didn't recognize Him. Not only did they miss Him, they crucified Him. Why? Because He didn't come in the manner they thought He would. He didn't fit their "model" of what the Messiah would look like. They were expecting a mighty and powerful king who would annihilate the Romans and free them from their bondage. They weren't expecting a baby, born in a manger, who took the form of a servant so that He could die on a cross.

Throughout history people have chosen to stay stuck in the rut of the safe and familiar. In the sixteenth century, Galileo struggled with people stuck in such a rut. He challenged his day's accepted theory about the solar system by inventing a telescope to prove Copernicus' claim that the sun was the actual center of celestial movement instead of the earth. Galileo took the leading scientists of his day to the top of the Tower of San Marco to look through his newly perfected telescope to share his exciting discovery that the earth went around the sun.

His peers were so threatened, so antagonized by his shocking assertion that he was threatened with torture if he didn't retract his position. Over time, of course, his idea won out. But what kept these "experts" from admitting what they had seen with their very eyes?

We all have opinions of how things are and how they should be, and the respected scientists of the sixteenth century were no exception. These opinions or "models" are useful. They are like filters that screen the information that comes into our minds. They establish boundaries, show us what's important and what isn't, help us solve problems, and define what is normal or abnormal, healthy and unhealthy.

The only problem is that sometimes our "models" of reality can become *the* model, the only way to do things. We get stuck in the rut of seeing things the way we have always seen them. Anything different threatens us and makes us feel uncomfortable. Most of us tend to see ourselves the way we want to be, should be, or are expected to be, rather than the way we really are.

Tom and Connie grew up with a "model" of what it meant to be a husband and wife. They learned different habits and ways of doing things. But from their individual perspectives, their own way was the right way.

Their "models" of how things should be kept them from seeing areas that needed change—from seeing new creative opportunities. Sometimes, even in the face of overwhelming evidence that something we're doing isn't working, we choose to stay in the rut of the safe and familiar rather than venture into that which has some risk but also the possibility of leading us to maturity and growth. Our perspective becomes paralyzed by our limited perception. It doesn't matter how bright or talented we are. All of us suffer from this tendency.

For over one hundred years Swiss watchmakers set the standard for excellence in watchmaking. In 1968 they had 65 percent of the world's market share, and according to expert estimations over 80 percent of the profits.

However, only ten years later their market share plummeted to below 10 percent. In the next three years they had to let go over half of their sixty-five thousand watchmakers. Who is the world leader in watchmaking today? Japan.

In 1968 Japan had virtually no share in the watch market. A "Japanese-made" watch was no comparison for a "Swiss-made" watch. What changed? The totally electronic, quartz-movement watch. It is one thousand times more accurate than the mechanical watches it replaced, and it can run for several years on one little battery.

Do you know who invented the quartz-movement watch? The Swiss. That's right. It was invented by Swiss researchers in laboratories in Switzerland. But when it was presented to the Swiss watchmakers in 1967, they rejected it. They said it would never work. After all, it didn't have a mainspring, bearings, or gears. These watchmakers were so confident in their opinions that they didn't even protect their idea with a patent.

When those same researchers displayed their invention to the rest of the world at the annual international watch convention, representatives from Seiko and Texas Instruments took a look at it and the rest is history.

Why didn't the Swiss see the incredible potential for this new invention? Why didn't they even take the simple precaution to patent their idea? It didn't fit their model. They were blinded by their old filters, their old way of looking at things, their idea of what a watch should be.

Let's look at a more current example. For years church leaders knew that it was almost impossible to get men involved in ministry. Thousands of churches across the country had women's ministries, but only a handful had men's ministries. Why? Because no one would come. Well, maybe for a Father and Daughter banquet or a Sweetheart Dinner, but that was about it.

A couple of men in Boulder, Colorado, believed that God wanted to do a special work with men. They gathered a few more men who fasted and prayed. Out of this came the vision for a national men's ministry that would include a yearly conference.

At first there were many skeptics who said "Don't waste your time." The perception was that men don't read books, they don't want to grow, they aren't willing to change, and they certainly wouldn't show up for a national men's conference. But these men had the faith to believe it was time for a change. They believed that men were willing to dare, willing to believe, willing to learn, willing to grow... willing to change.

In 1991 the first conference was held and over four thousand men attended. In 1992 the second conference was held and over twenty-two thousand men attended. And in 1993, over fifty-four thousand men showed up at the third conference from every state in the union and many foreign countries. Today Promise Keepers is a national ministry that is influencing hundreds of thousands of men across the country and around the world, helping them to change.

LOOKING AT THE WORLD
THROUGH DIFFERENT EYES

While doing research for this book I came across a letter allegedly written over 150 years ago from Martin Van Buren to President Andrew Jackson.[5]

January 31, 1829

President Jackson,

The canal system of this country is being threatened by the spread of a new form of transportation known as railroads. The federal government must preserve the canals for the following reasons.

One, if boats are supplanted by railroads, serious unemployment will result. Captains, cooks, drivers, hostlers, repairmen, and lock tenders will be left without means of livelihood, not to mention the numerous farmers not employed in growing hay for horses.

Two, boat builders would suffer and towline, whip, and harness makers would be left destitute.

Three, canal boats are absolutely essential to the defense of the United States. In the event of the expected trouble with England, the Erie Canal would be the only means by which we could ever move the supplies so vital to waging modern war.

As you may well know, Mr. President, railroad carriages are pulled at the enormous speed of fifteen miles per hour by engines which, in addition to endangering life and limb of passengers, roar and snort their way through the countryside, setting fire to crops, scaring the livestock, and frightening women and children. The Almighty certainly never intended that people should travel at such breakneck speed.

Sincerely yours,
Martin Van Buren
Governor of New York

When I first read that letter I was incredulous. Looking through today's eyes his concerns are unbelievable. In fact they're absurd. But in 1829 those views didn't seem quite so weird.

Change can come packaged in all kinds of shapes and sizes. It's easy to see how a major change or one that involved some kind of setback might be difficult to deal with. However, even positive changes such as a promotion, a new house, or a bonus can produce stress and anxiety. They cause us to do something differently, and that takes some work. Sometimes unlearning an old habit, no matter how small or insignificant, can take a lot of emotional, mental, and even physical energy.

Recently one of my patients told me about a struggle he was having with his golf game. "I've played golf for close to twenty years. I love the game and I play several times a week. But over the years I've developed some bad habits." Because of his love for the game and his desire to become a better player, he decided to take some lessons from one of the top golf pros in Denver.

"I couldn't believe how difficult it was to change a few simple aspects of my game. Unlearning unhealthy and automatic ways of swinging my club was a lot more work than I thought it would be." He had to spend hours and hours working on some new techniques. "At first I felt kinda silly doing some of the exercises he made me do. And after the first few practices my arms ached." I could tell by how he talked about it that it really had been painful. "But now," he said with a smile, "it doesn't hurt me at all." His smile got even bigger and with a tone of pride he added, "And, I've lowered my handicap by six strokes."

Now, I don't golf. But I know enough about the game to know that dropping your handicap by six strokes is a significant accomplishment. How did he do it? What brought about his growth? What led to his increased sense of confidence and competence? How was he able to improve on habits he had practiced for over twenty years?

His desire to grow, improve, and increase his skill and competence made him willing to risk some pain, look awkward, confront some feelings of inadequacy, and to take on the challenge of change. He took the risk, paid the price, and won.

REAL CHANGE IS WORTH IT

Charles Swindoll writes:

Change—real change—takes place slowly. In first gear, not overdrive. Far too many Christians get discouraged and give up. Like ice skating or mastering a musical instrument or learning to water ski, certain techniques have to be discovered and developed in the daily discipline of living. Breaking habit patterns you established during the passing of years cannot occur in a few brief days. Remember that. "Instant" change is as rare as it is phony.[6]

It's true. Change takes time, and it can be hard, painful, discouraging, and difficult. But think of the option. What is the cost of not changing?

Have you viewed change as positive or negative? Remember that change doesn't always involve losing old things. It often means adding new things. Growth or development can enrich. Where you had only one way to respond, now you have two. Where you had only one way of looking at things, now you have several. Where you had only one tool to work with, now you have an entire tool chest. Change has helped you "become equipped for every good work" (2 Tm 3:17, NASB).

Is your goal to become what you, society, or others want? Or is your goal to become the man or woman God wants you to become? When you have a biblical view of who you are in Christ, when your significance and security is based on His completed work for you on the cross, not on your performance or some perceived need to be right all of the time, you will be more open to healthy change. You will have a desire to learn and grow and become more of whom God would have you to be. You will also experience an increased openness to pleasing, honoring, and serving your spouse.

And that's called maturity. It's worth the price.

HOW'D THEY DO IT?

This isn't about changing my wife. It's actually about how she changed me. During the early years of our marriage, I was fairly sloppy when it came to hanging up my pajamas in the morning. I took care of most of my other clothes, but in the morning when I took off my PJ's I gave them a fling toward a hook in the closet where they were supposed to go or else they stayed on the bed. I know I was reminded about it numerous times and I'd give verbal assent, but somehow the message never took hold.

One day when I was seated on the couch reading the newspaper, Joyce sat down next to me and waited until I turned toward her. I noticed that my pajamas were neatly folded on her lap. She put her arm around me, looked me in the eye and said, "Norm, I just know that a man of your organizational ability and your attention to detail and results would have such a sense of satisfaction going to work each day knowing that your pajamas were hanging neatly on the hook in the closet eagerly awaiting your return at night. Thank you for listening." And with that she walked out of the room and I sat there with my mouth hanging open.

I didn't even realize it until a couple months later that since that day I had been hanging up my pajamas. She got my attention in a new way and I guess I finally heard her.

TAKE ACTION

1. What is your partner's filter or "model" for viewing change?

2. If you could change any one thing about yourself what would it be?

3. If your spouse could change any one thing about you what would it be?

4. If God could change any one thing about you what would He change?

5. What are some of the major and minor changes you have experienced in the past two years? Include things like job changes, moves, promotions, children's graduations or other accomplishments, a major illness or surgery, a divorce, or the death of a family member or close friend.

6. What are some of the positive and negative ways these changes have affected your life? Many people are surprised to discover that positive change can have some negative effects and negative changes can have some positive effects.

7. How have these changes affected your emotions? What kinds of feelings have you experienced? Anger? Sadness? Helplessness? Discouragement?

8. How have these changes affected how you feel about your relationship with God?

9. How have you dealt with these emotions and the changes that prompted them?

CHAPTER THREE

Creating a Climate for Change

H. Norman Wright

Stubbornness. We've all seen it in children, men, women, dogs, horses, mules. When change is the subject, we tend to dig in our heels. And it's not just the other person we'd like to change who resists; we may resist trying to get them to change!

I've talked to spouses with fairly healthy marriages as well as those with distressed marriages. They all struggle with the same belief: Things cannot get any better. They think that if a spouse won't change, the relationship won't change. This belief becomes a self-fulfilling prophecy. It cripples motivation, thwarts desire, and destroys hope. Let's consider some of the beliefs that keep us from asking for change.

My spouse isn't capable of change. I've heard this belief many times, yet I've never found it to be true. A spouse may appear entrenched in his or her lifestyle and way of responding. But it's usually because the partner hasn't yet discovered the right combination to unlock his or her resistance. I've had counselee after counselee tell me, "My spouse would never come in for counseling." But he did. I've had counselees tell me, "My spouse would never change." But she did. They may not be willing to change at first. But that's all right. The potential is there.

Nothing could happen to improve my marriage. Really? In counseling, the first step is to identify exactly what you would like to see happen. Once you know that (and it is a reasonable expectation), you then develop a well-thought out plan to achieve your goal.

However, the criteria you use to measure success may need some adjustment. One wife wanted her husband to spend fifteen minutes a day talking with her. This was both a reasonable and a necessary request for their marriage to grow. When she came in for her next counseling session two weeks later, she complained that her husband sat down to talk with her on only four of the last twelve days. To make matters worse, on three of those days he talked for only ten minutes instead of fifteen.

My response shocked her. I said, "That's fantastic. It's excellent. Didn't you tell me during our first session that he wouldn't change and nothing would improve your marriage?" She replied with a hesitant yes. I continued, "Look what's happened! That's change! That's improvement. If you have a 20 to 25 percent improvement this soon, that's incredible. I know you wanted to talk every day, but that can be a future goal. You must have done something positive and encouraging to get him to make this much change. What did you do?" The whole tenor of our conversation took a positive turn.

By the way, in your own marriage, do you spend your energy looking at the good times or the difficult times? When I work with couples in marriage counseling, too often they focus only on the problems. I know I've frustrated some by limiting the amount of time they can talk about problems. Instead, I ask them to describe the times they get along or feel the relationship is more positive than negative. If they resist this, I may ask, "Why are you here?" They usually say, "We want our marriage to be better." Then I say, "If that's the case, wouldn't it be better to talk about what's working?"

Talking about and focusing on the good times or the exceptions to the problems may solve the problems. When your spouse makes a slight change, concentrate on that. When you hit a rough spot in your marriage, don't allow it to distort your thinking. Looking for the exceptions to the problems creates optimism.

When I hear counselees use words such as, "I never, we never, he always, we always," I gently challenge those absolutes and soon they are substituting the words "Sometimes I, sometimes we." Once we've identified an exception to a problem, we can discover what made it happen and what can be done to make it recur.

One author pointed out that when you identify the fact that there have been exceptions, the problems seem smaller. When you choose to look for the exceptions (and it is a choice), it gives you hope that your partner is capable of changing. One counselee came to see me with a list of exceptions. He went on to tell me that he had analyzed what preceded the exceptions and discovered what steps to take to keep the exceptions recurring.

Identifying and looking at exceptions will point you toward solutions. And when you look for exceptions, your partner will feel like you're giving him a break. You're seeing him through the eyes of hope rather than condemnation. In addition, you end up feeling that you're getting credit for some of the good things you've done.

How do you identify the exceptions to the problems? Look for them. Expect them. Think about what you will do to make them happen. Discover how you can make them happen again and again.[1]

If I try something different, it may make matters worse. I don't want to lose what I have now. Sometimes spouses have experienced so much disappointment and hurt that it's too painful to continue to make an effort at change. They'd rather remain numb.

Trying something different won't necessarily make matters worse. With new information, new understanding, and new approaches there's a greater possibility that change can happen. If you pay attention to the smallest changes—the slightest improvement on your spouse's part—you can find hope again. Learn to identify and counter your negative thinking. If your next attempt at change doesn't succeed, you may be tempted to think, "See, I knew it wouldn't work. It isn't worth it." Challenge this thinking. Tell yourself, "All right, it didn't work this time, but at least I tried. Let's see how I can change my response for the next approach."

Our marriage is too far gone for all this time and effort. The damage is too great. I've seen some marriages restored that surprised even me. From a human perspective some relationships look hopeless. Even as believers we sometimes neglect to invite the Holy Spirit to be the change agent in our lives as well as our marriages.

Most individuals or couples use ineffective methods or approaches in trying to change their partners or improve their marriages. Frequently, I see someone in counseling who says "Our marriage is over. I've tried and nothing has worked. We've decided that divorce is the only solution." I don't attempt to persuade them not to divorce. Instead I ask, "If you were to divorce at this time, could you say that you gave a 150 percent effort and tried every approach possible? If you can, then no one can fault you on your intentions and responses. But if not, could you commit yourself to three months of intense work using some new approaches? At the end of three months, if there hasn't been any improvement, then you decide what direction to take with your lives."

In many cases, when a spouse or couple takes this approach, the marriage not only survives, it thrives.[2]

What keeps a person from trying to change his partner and his marriage? Fear—of the unknown, of failing, of rejection. But we haven't been called to live in fear. "For God did not give us a spirit of timidity—of cowardice, of craven and cringing and fawning fear— but of power and of love and of calm and well-balanced mind and discipline and self-control" (2 Tm 1:7, AMPLIFIED).

When change happens in a spouse's life, words like *encourage, motivate, persuade, confront, sensitivity, timing, modeling,* and *teaching* are part of the process.

Take a risk and do something. It's worth it.

UNDERSTANDING RESISTANCE

Everyone resists change at one time or another. We resist attempts to change our behavior, the way we perform at work, how we relate to others, our lifestyles, our plans, beliefs, opinions, and daily habits. We resist change even when the change would be for our benefit! Unfortunately, when another person resists our requests for change, we slap labels on them such as inconsiderate, self-centered, stubborn, or bullheaded. We think it's a lack of concern on their part, but it usually isn't. What is the person thinking when he or she refuses to change? And what are some classic forms of resistance?

Some people *refuse to listen*. Fred told me in a counseling session, "You want to know why I don't listen? I'm afraid if I do, Jean will think I'll make the change once I've heard her. That's not what I want."

Another way of resisting is *agreeing to change without having any intention of changing*. A person will say, "I'll see to it," "I understand what you mean, and I'll change." But the listening and response is just a way to get the requester off their case. It's a way of buying time and putting off making any changes.

Some resist by *responding in a hurt manner,* throwing the focus of responsibility back onto the requester. "How in the world could you say that about me? I can't believe you would think that." This is a way to activate your guilt and detour you from your goal. You end up feeling bad for even making your request.

A classic response is a *direct counterattack* such as, "Well, what about you?" Frank told me this in a counseling session. "When I bring up something I'd like Sandy to change, she turns it around and says I'm the one who needs to be different and who needs to change. And it doesn't stop there. The history lesson begins and she brings up stuff she's logged into her mind over the last five years. It's unbelievable. Then I start to get defensive and we go nowhere." Turning the issue back on the requester is an effective means of getting out of the spotlight.

One of the worst forms of resistance is for a spouse to *increase or intensify the very thing the partner is asking them to change.* Children and teenagers are not the only ones who do this. Adults can respond with this discourteous and humiliating kind of resistance. It's as though the person not only refuses to change, he or she declares it in a very obvious way. It's a radical form of saying "No way."

All five forms of resistance have as their goal the hope that you will abandon your effort. Have any of them ever happened to you?[3]

When you are asked to change, how do *you* feel? Accepted or threatened? Hopeful or fearful? Affirmed or criticized? Good or bad? We all resist change for a number of reasons. Sometimes we label our resistance to change as "good reasons not to" and our partner's resistance as "excuses."

Why are we so reluctant to change?

Habit. Gary alluded to this in the previous chapter. Day in and day out we maintain a fairly predictable routine. Inside we have a selection of comfortable responses that make us feel secure. We don't have to think about or work at new ways of responding. But the habits that make us feel secure may be an irritant to others. Habit is probably the most frequently used form of resistance. Why? Because it works so well.

Have you ever used or heard these excuses? "I've always done it this way." "After twenty-eight years, it's too late to change now." "Why change? I'm comfortable. This way works." "How do I know the new way is better? I don't have to think about this one. I just do it."

Perhaps you live with a man who is messy. He does not pick up after himself, put items away, hang up his clothes when he comes home from work, change into old clothes before he does a messy chore, pick up the paper and magazines he dropped on the floor, clear his own dishes away from the table.

You may have tried to correct him by begging, pleading, threatening, or letting the mess accumulate for days or even weeks, but nothing has worked. Probably your husband was accustomed to having people pick up after him while he was growing up. If this is the case, perhaps he developed the belief that he's special and deserves to be waited on. When his wife says, "Pick up after yourself," the message he hears is, "You no longer deserve to be catered to." Thus his self-esteem is under attack. The way he thinks about himself has been challenged. This is the real reason why he resists. If he changes he will have to change some of his self-perceptions. (In chapter 13 you'll discover a number of suggestions on how to handle this problem.)

Ignorance. "I didn't know that's what you wanted." "I don't know how to do that." "Who do you think you married? Superman?" Ignorance can be an effective tool because it puts the person making the request on the defensive. He begins to question whether he's expecting too much.

Control. If someone asks me to change, I may not comply for fear of losing control. We don't like others determining how we are to behave. The request for change may not be a control issue, but that's the way we interpret it.[4]

Fear of domination. Time and again I've made a suggestion to a husband or wife during a counseling session and they've responded with, "That's a good idea; I'll give it a try." But their partner almost erupts with the response, "I can't believe it. I've been telling you that for years and all you've done is ignore me. Now he suggests it once and you're ready to do it. Why do you listen to him and not to me?"

The only explanation I can offer is that as a counselor I'm a safe person. It's less threatening when I ask than when the spouse asks, because there's no fear of being dominated by me.

Unwillingness to take blame. Perhaps this is best expressed by one wife's response: "If I make this change and do it in this different way, it's as though I'm admitting I was wrong all this time. That's a terrible admission and I'm not about to make it."

Feeling of futility. A spouse may believe his or her partner's need for change is insatiable. The fear could be, "If I give in now, the requests and demands will never end." If the spouse is a perfectionist, the partner may feel that he or she can never meet the demands, no matter how much effort goes into it. If the requesting spouse has overly high standards, is compulsive, or has a low tolerance level for perceived failures and inefficiency, no wonder the partner feels a sense of futility.

Uncertainty or anxiety. "How will this change affect me?" "Will I be capable of changing?" "Will people still respond to me in the same way?" "What if I can't please you?" Any perceived threat to our self-esteem results in resistance.

ARE YOU DEMANDING CHANGE?

When you're considering the possibility of assisting your spouse in the change process, ask yourself, *Why do I want my partner to change? For whose benefit is it? One of us? Both of us? For the sake of the marriage relationship? Am I trying to recapture something I once had? Am I trying to make up for a lack in my childhood? Who will feel better if this change occurs?* When you understand your own reasons for wanting your spouse to change, it will help you to make change a reality.

Sometimes our request for change is prompted by our own expectations and the need to fulfill them. When your needs go unfulfilled and your expectations unmet, frustration and anger often result. The higher the level of expectation (especially unexpressed expectation), the more you will find yourself blocked. We all have a different flashpoint at which anger comes rushing in, but when we're unfulfilled, it's a fairly predictable visitor.

Eventually, unfulfilled expectations evolve into demands. This is when major problems arise. A spouse will sense a demanding tone and be offended by it. Restating the expectation as a demand often helps to define it. I've often asked those I've counseled to do this. There's quite a difference between a request and a demand. For example:

"I demand that he start the dinner each night, since he arrives home first."

"I demand that she always be at home when I arrive after working all day."

"I demand that she dress the way I've suggested in order to please me."

Most of us are unaware of the demands we make on our spouses to behave in a certain way. We're only aware of the feeling of anger or annoyance we experience when our demands aren't realized. That feeling is so strong that we think it's not only justified, it's unavoidable. We also believe that the emotion is caused by our spouse's failure to meet our expectations. This is because we focus more on the failure than the demand.

Demandingness is a major barrier to mutual growth in marriage. The person making the demand is likely to spend most of his or her time and energy in self-pity, blowing things out of proportion. Little creative energy is spent in planning ways to develop the relationship.[5] Since every behavior of a spouse elicits a responsive behavior from the other spouse, you can imagine the result. In most cases, when one partner reacts negatively, the other one responds by behaving equally negatively. This creates an endless cycle of demandingness leading away from growth and development of the relationship. Many spouses discover the only time they can truly give to their partner is when it isn't being demanded.

In most cases, when we marry, each of us demands little but receives much. In the glow of some very intense feelings, we respond to our partner's needs. But in time this changes. Where previously most of our attention was focused on our spouse's needs, our attention begins to focus on the fulfillment of our own needs. Each of us moves into the stage of giving less and expecting more. Thus, needs become a source of conflict, because each of us wants our own needs met. One counselor described the problem in this way:

To be able to balance one's own needs along with all that is required of one, to remain attuned to another's needs, to be able to give when one feels more like getting, to be able to protect one's own interest, all these require a certain level of maturity. Many who enter marriage are often looking for a way to resolve unmet needs and are handicapped in their capacity to give. The normal stresses of a changing relationship affect these people more intensely.[6]

ARE YOU EXPECTING TOO MUCH?

Sometimes our unmet need is for security or attention. At times we get our need met, but soon the emptiness returns. Then we place an unrealistic demand on our partner to get the need met again. We begin to see our partner as someone to be used.

No one can meet all the wishes of another. The notion that we deserve to have what we want is nothing but self-centeredness. I'm not saying you shouldn't expect some of your desires to be met; some expectations are both legitimate and appropriate. The difficulty arises when expectations exceed realistic possibilities (what is realistic varies from person to person).

Some people are raised in an atmosphere of neglect. They never received the attention they needed in their developmental years. A man from this type of background may lack the capacity to feel important. Sometimes he's unable to feel concern for others and how they feel. He may run from one person to another, hoping the next relationship will supply what he's missing. He's perpetually dissatisfied with people, including his spouse.

He longs for a close, intimate relationship, but his need is so deep that he craves to be parented. He has an excessive need for warmth, love, and attention. Even if his wife were able to get that close, he would be afraid to let her. He would be unable to accept the attention he needs. (This is also true of some women.) These unfulfilled needs are often referred to as frozen needs.

Another possible reason for unrealistic expectations is when a spouse is either a controller or a perfectionist. He or she doesn't know what it means to make a request or to accept things as they are. Everything is a demand, and the person's appetite to have things go his or her way is insatiable. (We'll discuss this in detail later.)

TAKE OUT THE GUESSWORK

Sometimes I've asked couples if they've ever shared with their partner exactly what their needs are and how they would like (not demand) their partner to meet those needs. Usually they haven't. I then ask them to list their needs under five categories: emotional, social, sexual, intellectual, and spiritual. Then they identify in writing how they would like their partner to respond and they exchange requests. In a sense, this becomes a road map for change and usually is quite acceptable to each spouse. Here's what one woman shared:

EMOTIONAL

My Needs	How Ken Can Meet Them
To feel loved, cherished	Call me, prepare me for sex, hold me, kiss me, look at me with a glimmer in his eye, take naps so he will feel refreshed to be with me.
To feel supported, believed in	Pray for me in my hearing and in secret as well. Challenge me, praise me, see my potential in specific situations.
To feel comforted	Hold me, let me cry on his shoulder, feel my hurt with me, be gentle and sensitive to my moods, let me know he notices them.
To feel not alone	Share my daily joys and sorrows, enter into the conversation about my day, be interested in daily details that help him understand me.
To feel free to be myself, to be genuine	Be himself, be genuine, see through my masks, let me know it. Know that I love him deep down so he can take my present anger. Accept my goofy antics as me but when he doesn't like them, let me know gently what he prefers instead and give me the opportunity to change it.

Sharing specific lists can take the guesswork out of marriage. It's important to let your partner know that you would like a change, what it is you want changed, and the reason for the change. By doing this, you avoid manipulation.

But don't most people resist when they know someone wants them to change? Of course. You do and I do. So did Ted.

RESPONDING TO RESISTANCE

Kathy was forty-two and had been married to Ted for fifteen years. She described her marriage and part of her frustration. "I just don't understand why Ted has to be so stubborn. I don't think what I'm asking is unreasonable. But he always has to resist my suggestions. For once I wish he would just consider what I want and not put up such a fuss."

I'm not sure Kathy was ready for my response. I simply said, "Ted's resistance is normal. It's what I would expect from him, from you, and from me. Most of us resist a request to change. Perhaps in your heart and mind you could give him permission to resist the change initially and that would take some of the pressure off of you."

When someone resists, let them. You can't stop them. I continued on with Kathy. "Do you ever tell yourself that Ted is stubborn?" She admitted she often thought it. "And do you ever tell Ted that he's stubborn?" She nodded. "And has it made him less stubborn?" I already knew the answer to that, but now Kathy was beginning to realize her approach wasn't working. She had fallen into the trap so many couples do after being married for a number of years.

I've seen couples say they were attracted to one another during dating because one was easygoing, tolerant, spontaneous, and fun-loving. The other seemed to be confident, directed, self-assured, and goal-directed. Years later the terminology had changed to, "lazy, irresponsible, passive" and "pushy, critical, controlling." Each time you use a negative label, you reinforce your expectations that your spouse is that way. This soon leads to rationalizing your behavior as well as beginning to think of divorce as the answer.

I suggest that a person reframe—see in a different light—what they perceive as negative qualities. Often character qualities that attracted a person to his partner during courtship have been distorted by the use of negative labels.

Changing your attitude toward your partner's behaviors or traits by relabeling them will bring out more positive responses as well as create a greater climate for change. For example, controlling behavior can be relabeled as decisive, assertive, and influential. Critical behavior can be relabeled as sharp, discerning, successful, or not intended as hurtful. Lazy can be relabeled as laid-back and easygoing. Passive can be relabeled as relaxed, accepting, stress-free.

Reframing negative labels may diminish some of your partner's resistance to change.[7]

IF YOUR PARTNER RESISTS CHANGE...

Do you really think all your requests for change should meet with instant compliance? If your partner resists your request for change, do you become angry, despondent, perplexed, stubborn? Can you see any value in resistance? Probably not. But consider the possibilities.

If your partner resists your requests, perhaps you need to consider why you want the change, how intensely you want it, and how committed you are to pursuing the change. What does your commitment level to this change tell you about your own needs?

Perhaps resistance will help you to be more specific about what you wish changed. Have you considered your mate's resistance as a unique form of communication? Is your spouse telling you something new about what he or she values or about what elements are involved in building self-esteem? If the person's resistance is too strong, you may be convinced to try another approach.[8]

Over the years I've talked with numerous married individuals who sincerely wanted their partners to make some legitimate and necessary changes but also believed there was nothing they could do to make it happen. In each case they had accepted the situation as less than they desired or than it could be. Somehow they coped. You may think that coping is a good solution, but it can be costly and more detrimental than finding creative ways to encourage your spouse to change.

UNHEALTHY RESPONSES TO ANOTHER'S RESISTANCE

Do you know how people usually cope? Unfortunately, many simply *resign* themselves to the situation. They sigh, "I guess I'll just *have to learn to live with this."* The statement flows out of a sense of impotence or powerlessness. And in time it begins to affect their sense of self-esteem. When we think less of ourselves, we tend to think less of our partner, which creates a downward spiral for the marriage. When you think less of a person, your love, care, and commitment to the relationship erode. Learning to live with something can undermine a relationship. As one husband said, "I'm afraid that my learning to live with it was my first step in learning to live without her."

When your desire for change conflicts with the feeling that nothing can be done, it's easy to end up feeling like a *martyr*. In addition to learning to live with it, a martyr learns to get some mileage out of it. You remind your partner of what you have to put up with at every opportunity.

A martyr is often an exacting scorekeeper who focuses more on what he or she has to put up with rather than what the spouse has to endure. A martyr becomes deaf to the spouse's needs and usually tends to withdraw or ends up questioning the value of the relationship.[9]

Revenge is another way of responding—making them pay in a direct and obvious manner. Revenge may be expressed in both invisible and blatant ways. Not only is the action against the other person, it's a slap against the relationship as well. Keep in mind that an act of revenge often comes from the hurt, anger, and resentment that develop over not being able to change behaviors in a partner. Does revenge ever work to bring about the desired change? No, but it does reinforce the negative behavior and frequently triggers the spouse's anger and resentment as well.

Perhaps the most direct way of coping is just to *withdraw*. After all, it's the most common of all coping responses. It can include physical withdrawal, silence, separation, or divorce.

These methods of coping simply do not work, nor do they satisfy. There is one other choice, however. Learn to work for change in a way that is likely to succeed. Make a *request*.

THE PACKAGE MAKES ALL THE DIFFERENCE!

Very few people enjoy hearing complaints from their spouses. They feel judged, criticized, attacked, unaccepted, and condemned. If that's the case, wouldn't it be better if we just eliminated all complaints, since they rarely work and they do so much damage? No. The problem is not the complaint; many complaints are legitimate. It's the package they come in. It's possible to phrase a complaint in such a way that your partner will keep from raising defensive barriers. He or she will listen and consider what you are saying. Note the difference between a complaint and a request:

COMPLAINT

"I get so repulsed when you eat with your mouth open and then try to talk at the same time."

"This house looks like the place where the buffalo roam."

"You're never affectionate anymore."

"You're so sloppy. I don't know why you don't listen to me. You're making me into your mother, you know."

"All you do is live for work, work, work. It's your mistress, and I resent it!"

"You're so inconsiderate and rude when you get on my case in front of the kids."

REQUEST

"I'd appreciate it if you would chew with your mouth closed. It does wonders for my response to you."

"Let's talk about what can be done this week to clean and straighten up the house. I think we'd both feel better about it."

"I would appreciate it if you could give me a kiss and a hug once a day."

"It would help if you would take your dishes to the kitchen when you're through. Thanks for helping me in this way."

"I would like to spend a few minutes with you each day. Can we talk about how we can work that out?"

"I'm upset when you criticize me in front of Tina and Mary. I'd like to hear what you have to say in private."

What guidelines create a climate for change? Your request needs to be reasonable and attainable. In other words, is it something that's possible for your partner to change? If you want to see a basic personality change, forget it. An extrovert will always be an extrovert and an introvert will remain an introvert. But responses can be modified.

If you want a person's attitude to change, don't count on it. If you want your spouse to "feel what you feel" and with the same intensity, you're reaching for the impossible dream. However, you can ask for a change in behavior that can affect personality expression, attitudes, and feelings. Your request should give you an affirmative response to the question, "Will this request enhance our relationship and create a greater depth of intimacy?" This is the fundamental purpose for change.

The authors of *Two Friends in Love* give us some insightful guidelines:

> When change is needed in our traits and personalities, it is only in the realm of the man-inspired, man-prompted characteristics. Those that are God-given do not need touching up. They are fine the way they are. They only need to be acknowledged and appreciated. However, in the man-related realm, when there are characteristics that should be reworked because of the harmful effect they're having on the marriage, exercise great care in the way you handle change.[10]

To create a climate for change, you will need to be both persistent and patient. You'll need to keep trying in a creative, sensitive, and loving manner even when it doesn't seem to work. And you will need to be realistic and not expect too much. That's patience.

Will your request for change help your partner as well as you? Will he or she become a stronger person? Will it increase Christian growth and maturity? Or is the request not that important after all? If you ask yourself these questions, you can become a skilled teacher, and both of you can assist each another in the growth process.

When I conduct premarital counseling, I ask a number of confrontational questions. In the initial session I ask, "What passage of Scripture would you like your fiancée to implement that will make him or her an even stronger and more mature person?"

You can imagine some of the responses. About half of the individuals need a week to think about the answer. After they select a passage, I share my reason for the question. I tell them it's helpful to run a request for change through the grid of Scripture to see if the Word of God has anything to say about it. (Even if Scripture is silent on the subject, the request may still be legitimate.) Consulting Scripture can help a person refine his requests for change.

For example, if we want our spouses to change something in their character, Galatians 5:22-23 is the ultimate model of the qualities we can encourage our spouse toward. We should desire the same qualities for ourselves!

> But the fruit of the (Holy) Spirit, (the work which His presence within accomplishes)—is love, joy (gladness), peace, patience (an

even temper, forbearance), kindness, goodness (benevolence), faithfulness; meekness, (humility), gentleness, self-control (self-restraint, continence). Against such things there is no law (that can bring a charge). Galatians 5:22, 23, AMPLIFIED

Remember: The message in your request is, "I care for you. My request is something I believe will benefit both of us and it will mean so much to me. It's worth considering."

HOW'D THEY DO IT?

"I guess Virginia had a different upbringing and understanding about sex than I did. I was interested, and she seemed to be at times, and then other times she could take it or leave it. I'm fairly easygoing and compliant, and I'm not the best conversationalist. My attempts to talk about it didn't seem to go over that well. So I figured I needed some help.

"I went to a Christian bookstore and looked through the books on sex. Some looked great but others were pretty unrealistic. I bought one called *The Gift of Sex* by the Penners, a husband and wife team. I wrapped it up and took Virginia out to dinner. While we were there I gave her the package with a note that said, 'Remember when you were very young? Your parents probably read you some bedtime stories. I'd like to resurrect the practice by reading this book out loud for both of us at bedtime. I hope this meets with your approval and it could be a new adventure for us.'

"She seemed delighted with the card and ripped open the package just as the waitress walked up to the table. Virginia looked at the title of the book, which was in big print, and said, 'This looks fascinating.' The waitress saw the title, grinned, looked at both of us and said, 'Shall we cancel dinner so the two of you can leave now?' I didn't intend for anyone else to see it. Virginia said I turned red.

"Well, in spite of being the talk of that restaurant, it's been worth it. Virginia has really changed and it was worth the risk of trying something different."

TAKE ACTION

1. What expectations did you have when you married?

2. What are your expectations for your marriage now?

3. What needs would you like fulfilled to a greater extent by your spouse? How will you make these known?

4. What behaviors could you reframe?

5. What type of behaviors do you or your spouse use to resist change?

6. What passages of Scripture would you like to see your spouse implement into his or her life?

7. What passages of Scripture would your spouse like to see you implement into your life?

CHAPTER FOUR

We Are Different, Aren't We?

(Part One)
H. Norman Wright

"I just don't understand him!" "I just don't understand her!" Have you ever heard these statements? Have you ever made one of these statements?

Gender differences are puzzling, baffling, and one of the reasons for marital discord. We're attracted to a person of the opposite sex but have a difficult time understanding and accepting the differences between us. Many relationship problems would be resolved if our perceptions weren't colored by negative value judgments and criticism. And it would be easier to help our partners to change if we tailored our approach based on gender differences.

Perhaps the best way to illustrate the process is to assume you're going to visit a foreign country. When you arrive you're immediately confronted with a new language, customs, history, and values. They're not bad, they're just different. You're uncomfortable with them and perhaps feel at odds because of your own unique culture. You have a difficult time talking, interacting, and relating. But in time, as you begin to learn and understand this new country, it becomes easier to communicate. And the citizens of that country are understanding you better as well. You're becoming bilingual.

You make similar adjustments when you relate to and influence the opposite sex. Before most us will even consider a request for change, we need to be approached as if we were someone from another culture, not an alien from another planet!

Gender differences exist. Personality differences exist. God created us male and female. Sometimes we wonder why he did it the way he did! Those who attempt to close the gender gap and say the differences are learned and not innate are off course. There's a basic need to identify ourselves by gender. Even young children create separate gender worlds to give themselves an identity. Differences need to be understood, accepted, honored, and respected.

GETTING A PERSPECTIVE ON GENDER DIFFERENCES

Several years ago I had an experience that dramatically portrayed gender differences in both thinking and communication style. Joyce and I were visiting historical Williamsburg in Virginia. It's a fascinating and charming setting that preserves colonial history.

One day we decided to take the tour of the old governor's mansion. Our tour guide was male. As we entered the large entry door, he began to give a factual description of the purpose of the room as well as the way it was furnished. He described in detail the various ancient guns on the wall and pointed to the unique display of flintlock rifles arranged in a circle on the rounded ceiling. When he said there were sixty-four of them, some originals and others replicas, I immediately began counting them. Our guide was very knowledgeable and he gave an excellent detailed description as we went from room to room. He seemed to be very structured and focused.

We had to leave before the tour was complete to meet some friends for lunch. Since we both enjoyed the presentation so much, we decided to return the next day and take the tour again. What a difference! Our guide was a woman. We entered the same room and she said, "Now, you'll notice a few guns on the wall and ceiling but notice the covering on these chairs and the tapestry on the walls. They are..." And with that she launched into a detailed description of items that had either been ignored or just given a passing mention the day before. And on it went throughout the tour.

It didn't take much to figure out what was going on. It was a classic example of gender differences. Our first tour guide was speaking more to men and the second one more to women. Actually, we ended up with the best tour imaginable because we heard both perspectives. What a benefit it would be for the guides to incorporate both of their perspectives into their presentations.

Over the past twenty years I've asked a seemingly harmless question in our marriage enrichment seminars. The women meet in small groups as do the men, and they are asked to discuss the question, "What frustrates you about the opposite sex?" The decibel level climbs immediately as though a door were thrown open and all their pent-up frustrations vented. After a few years I could predict what each group would say because the issues never seemed to change.

Each group believes what they are saying is factual rather than just their observations or opinions. It's as though both the men and women are saying, "Why can't you be like me? It would be better if you would." The message seems to be, "The way you are isn't that good. My way is better."

What have I heard from women? For one thing they say men do not share sufficient information and details. But there are other frustrations as well.

"They don't share their feelings or emotions enough. It's like they grew up emotionally handicapped."

"They seem to go into a trance when they're watching sports or when I bring up certain subjects. They're not able to handle more than one task or subject at a time."

"Men seem to think they can do things better, even when they can't. And they won't take any advice, even if it helps them."

"They don't listen well. They're always trying to fix our problems."

"Men need more intuition—get off the factual bandwagon."

"Men need to learn to enjoy shopping like we do. They just don't know what they're missing."

"Men need more sensitivity, concern, compassion, and empathy."

"I wish men weren't so threatened by women's ideas and perspectives."

"They're so over-involved in their work and career. They want a family but they don't get involved."

"Sex—that's the key word. Don't they think about anything else? They're like a microwave oven. Push the button and they're cookin'. Their 'on' button is never 'off.'"

"I'd like men to learn what romance and intimacy really mean."

"A lot of men don't know what manners are. They think the home is the locker room!"

"I wish they were more sensitive."

If you, the reader, are a woman, do you identify with any of these? Are there others you would add? Here are some other responses that were recorded in a group setting:

"Men think too much. There's more to life than thinking."

"I wish he didn't think he always had to define everything. I feel as if I've been talking to a dictionary. Every week for the past year my husband has said, 'What do you mean? I can't talk to you if I don't understand your words. Give me some facts, not those darn feelings!' Well, sometimes I can't give him facts and definitions. Man shall not live by definitions alone!"

"I don't think men understand the difference between sharing their feelings and what they think about their feelings. They tend to intellectualize so much of the time. Why do men have to think about how they feel? Just come out with it unedited. He doesn't have to respond like a textbook or edit everything he shares. I wonder if the emotional side of a man threatens him? Of course you can't always control your emotional responses. So what?"

"My husband is an engineer and you ought to be around when his engineer friends come over. The house is like a cerebral, cognitive conference! All logical facts. They walk in with their slide rules and calculators, and it's as though the house were swept clean of any emotional response. They talk but they don't disclose. They share, but on the surface. They're safe and secure. Sometimes I have this urge to come into the room and start sharing emotions with all sorts of emotional words and then start crying and see how long it would take for some of them to bolt out the door, jump out the window, or hide their face behind a magazine. Why, I could threaten ten men inside of a minute. I never realized what power I had. I think I'll do that next time they're over."

What about men? What frustrates them about women? It's generally the opposite of what women say:

"They're too emotional. They need to be more logical."

"How can they spend so much time talking? When it's said, it's said. So many of them are amplifiers. I wish they would get to the bottom line quicker and at least identify the subject!"

"They're too sensitive. They're always getting their feelings hurt."

"Why do they cry so easily? It doesn't make sense to me."

"I think most women are shopaholics. Their eyes glaze over when they see a shopping mall."

"They're so changeable. I wish they'd make up their minds and then keep them made up."

"Maybe they think they can read minds, but we can't. I don't think they can either."

"What's wrong with the sex drive? Sex is great, only they don't have that much interest. It takes forever to get them interested."

"They think they have the spiritual gift of changing men. They ought to quit. We can't be fixed and we don't need to be."

"They're so involved with other people and their problems."

"Women are moody and negative. You can't satisfy them."

"I wish they would leave some things alone. They're always trying to fix something that isn't broken."

What about it? If you, the reader, are a man, do you identify with any of these? Are there any others you would add? Here are some additional responses men have shared in seminars:

"I understand her need to talk about us and our relationship. I happen to think that there is a right and a wrong way to talk about those things. If you're not careful, the whole thing can get out of hand. It's best to be as rational as possible. If you let it get too emotional, you never can make any good decisions, and if it gets too personal, someone could get hurt. A little bit of distance goes a long way where a lot of these things are concerned."

"It's important first to set out clearly what the issues are. I don't think women do this very well. They latch on to the first thing that comes to mind, get totally emotionally involved in it. The next thing you know, you're arguing about everything under the sun, and no one is happy. I believe in a clear definition of the problem at the outset. If she can tell me exactly what is bothering her, we can deal with it logically. If she can't do that, then there's no sense even talking about it."

"She expects me to have all these reactions right at my fingertips and be able to call them up on the spot. Well, I can't do that. I don't operate the way she does. I need a little more time to think things through. I don't want to say something I'm going to regret later on. Somehow she has the idea that wanting time to think is not being open and honest with her. That's ridiculous. I'm not trying to hide anything, I'm just trying to be sure in my own mind before I talk to her about it. What's wrong with that?"

"Men are just more rational than women. We prefer to deal with things in a thoughtful, rational way. Women are emotional, and that's the way they want to deal with things. Just because a man prefers to discuss things logically doesn't mean he is any less involved than a woman who wears her emotions on her sleeve. Women could profit a lot from thinking things through instead of just reacting off the top of their hearts all the time."[1]

Men have been asked why they don't share their feelings with their wives. In survey after survey, the responses are similar. Many are defensive:

"She knows—or should know—how I feel. I really don't need to tell her."

"I don't really feel the need to talk about this."

"That's just the way I am. And that's just the way most men are. Women are different and they're just going to have to get used to that fact. So I don't reveal a lot of the stuff inside of me. That doesn't mean I don't love her. It's just me."

"I didn't realize she was interested, that she wanted to know about it."

"I really want to tell her, but I just can't find the right time to share this with her."

"I'm not certain how she's going to handle what I say. And I don't want her getting upset or having to talk about this for the next hour. It's easier to keep quiet."

"She just wouldn't understand. And that leads to more and more questions and I get tired of talking about work. I want to leave it there."

"I'll tell you what would help me share more with my wife. For me to open up, there has to be no risk. I can be honest but I don't want to be hassled. I don't want to be judged for what I share and I want to share for as long as I want—and then have the freedom to quit when I need to."

As we consider some of the unique characteristics of men and women, we need to keep two things in mind. First, there are generalizations that pertain to most men and women. But there will always be exceptions in varying degrees. Second, the way men and women are is not negative. It is not a fault to be this way. Some of the characteristics will be more pronounced in some than others because of personality types as well as upbringing. The problem arises when people feel they are always right or that the way they do things is the only right way. They don't care about understanding and accepting the opposite sex the way they are. The more flexibility each can develop the more their marriages will benefit.[2]

WHEN THE BRAIN TAKES SIDES

Much of the mystery is solved when you understand the less obvious physiological differences between men and women. When Scripture says that God created them male and female, he really did create us differently. And much of the unapparent differences are found in the brain.

Our brains are the most complicated part of our bodies and account for many of the gender differences and conflicts. If you looked at a brain you would discover that it is divided into left and right hemispheres. It's like a walnut and each side can operate independently of the other. The two sides are connected by nerve fibers and each has its own tasks and assignments. If you lift your right foot off the floor, the left side of your brain controlled that function. And the right side of your brain controls lifting your left foot off the floor.

The two sides of the brain have more to do than just control our movements. They are responsible for the way we think. Each is quite specialized. Part of your brain is verbal. (I've heard some say all of their spouse's brain is verbal!) The left hemisphere controls language and reading skills. It gathers up information and processes it logically in a step-by-step fashion. When is the left brain used? Every day when you read a book or article, play a game, sing, write, balance your checkbook, and weigh the advantages and disadvantages of buying an item on time versus paying cash.

If you're planning your day's schedule, you may tell yourself it would be a good idea to leave ten minutes early to drop off the video you rented the night before. You will have planned how to get there to be in the right direction to park in front of the store. How did you make these decisions? By using the left portion of your brain. It wants to keep your life sensible, organized, and on schedule.

And then we have the right side of the brain. That portion of your brain comes into play when you work a jigsaw puzzle, look at a road map, design a new office, plan a room arrangement, solve a geometrical problem, or listen to musical selections on the stereo. The right half of your brain does not process information step by step like the left portion. Instead, it processes patterns of information. It plays host to our emotions. It has been called the intuitive side of the brain. It will link facts together and come up with a concept. It looks at the whole situation and, as though by magic, the solution appears.

The thinking pattern of the left side of your brain is positive, analytical, linear, explicit, sequential, verbal, concrete, rational, and goal-oriented. The right side is intuitive, spontaneous, emotional, nonverbal, visual, artistic, playful, holistic, and physical.

If you are more right-side oriented and your spouse is left-side oriented, how will you communicate? It's as though you speak different languages! And you probably do.

Have you ever been in a class or even a church service where the speaker focused on dry, detailed facts? If he was inflexible, he was annoyed by interruptions to his train of thought. So after each distraction he would return to the beginning and review. The speaking was monotonous and step-by-step with little emotional expression. If so, you were listening to a person who was an extreme—and I mean extreme—left-brain dominant.

As I presented this in a seminar one evening a woman blurted out, "That's right. You're describing Wally. That's him to a tee. Now that you've described him, tell me what I can do to change him." (And Wally was sitting right next to her. In fact, he had a panicked look on his face until he heard my response.) I said, "Nothing. There is absolutely nothing you nor anyone can do aside from a brain transplant. This is the way God created Wally and he will always be this way. Wally can work on being more flexible, putting more expression into his presentations, and use some visual aids to liven them up. If he desired, he could work on activating and using his right side more, but the left will always be dominant. This is an expression of who he is. And all the other left-brain dominants love to listen to him. With a little work Wally could appeal more to right-brain people, but perhaps the best you can do is accept this characteristic of Wally, appreciate these features, and whenever he shows hints of any right-brain expressions, praise him."

If you listen to a speaker or someone in a conversation who rambles from topic to topic, relies on his or her own opinion and feelings, is easily led away from the point, leaves gaps in the presentation to give the conclusion, uses emotional language and hunches, you're in the presence of the extreme right-brain dominant. The left side wants to know. "What's the bottom line?" and the right side travels around the barn a few times to get there. And as you'll see in later chapters, personality differences will affect how a person responds, too.

Remember when you were in school? You probably ran into individuals who excelled in math or reading but flunked playground! Why? They were functioning with a highly advanced left brain but the right brain was less developed. We shift back and forth between these two sides of the brain as we carry on our daily activities.

A man who is a highly proficient chemist also enjoys social activities and goes out dancing twice a week. Which portion of his brain is he using for these tasks? He is using the left side for his work that must be careful, accurate, and logical. When he's out dancing, he feels the steps by shifting to the right side of his brain. The chemist may be more comfortable using his left side but he's able to make a switch for some right-brain activities.

It may take a husband longer to shift sides than his wife expects or wants or thinks he can. And remember, we will constantly reinforce our dominant side because it's easier to go that route than to break new ground by using the less dominant side.

Some men do make dramatic shifts during their lifetimes from the use of one side of the brain to the other. In middle age, some men shift to more right-brain interests and activities as they allow themselves to explore a previously unknown and even threatening side of their lives.

Our twenty-sixth president, Theodore Roosevelt, was studious and reclusive as a child. He had highly developed scholarly left-brain skills and this was seen in his writing in the field of wildlife, politics, and history. In domestic policies his reasoning ability showed that his left side was in charge, yet in his foreign policies he was noted for being intuitive and adventuresome, reflecting the influence of the right side of his brain.

A male's brain is organized with a high level of lateralization. Men tend to shift farther left or right than women do. And there are some who make equal usage of both sides, since neither side is dominant.

Is there a genetic right-brain/left-brain difference between men and women? Yes. This is part of the answer to why men and women are the way they are. At birth the cortex of the brain is more highly developed in women than in men. As infants, girls respond more to the sound of the human voice than do boys. Women are left-brain oriented and tend to be more verbally skilled. Men are not. A woman's left brain develops earlier than a man's (this gives her an edge in writing and reading). This is why many little boys do not read or write as well as little girls. A boy can build a complicated model but cannot read as well as the girl who is a year younger. The male's right brain develops earlier than the female's, and all through life men tend to use this side of their brain more skillfully in the spatial area.

Men use the right side of their brains more efficiently than women. And a man's brain is more highly specialized. If I am a typical man, I will use the left side of my brain for verbal problems and the right side for spatial. This latter area tends to help men excel over women in a sport like baseball because a man can better perceive the relationship between ball and bat. If I am putting together a new barbecue grill which came in pieces, I use my right brain to visualize the end result. Thus I shift from one side to the other. I am seeing how it fits together in my mind. If my wife Joyce comes to discuss who we are having over for dinner, I respond out of my left, verbal side.

Personally, I feel we men do not use all the abilities of the right side as much as we could. The emotional, intuitive side in men is often stunted, partly due to a lack of socialization training and encouragement and partly because of our tendency to use one side of the brain or the other at a time but not as much in conjunction.

A woman is different in the way she uses her brain. And it gives her an advantage over men! A woman's brain is not specialized. It operates holistically. A man shifts back and forth between the sides of his brain. He can give more focused attention to what he is doing. But a woman uses both sides of her brain simultaneously to work on a problem. The two parts work in cooperation. Why? Because some of the left-brain abilities are duplicated in her right brain and some of the right brain in the left. Women have larger connectors between the two sides, even as infants, and can integrate information more skillfully.[3]

In addition, women have 40 percent more connectors between the left and the right sides of the brain.[4]

Women can tune in to everything going on around them. A wife may handle five hectic activities at one time while her husband is reading a magazine, totally oblivious to the various problems going on right under his nose. She can juggle more items but can be distracted more easily. He can focus on one task better but can lose sight of other aspects. He has to stop one activity in order to attend to another.

The result causes women to be more perceptive than men about people. Women have a greater ability to pick up feelings and sense the difference between what people say and what they mean. Women's intuition has a physical basis. A woman's brain is like a computer that can integrate reason and intuition.

This drives some men crazy. I've heard numerous stories in which a couple was out socially and the wife said to her husband, "I think there's a problem there or something is going on." Her husband responded with, "How do you know? Where are the facts?" And his wife said, "I don't have any facts. I just sense it." He responds, "You don't know what you're talking about." But a week later, when he finds out she was right, he's amazed and even more puzzled.

It could be that women pick up more information than men do since their sensitivities such as hearing, eyesight, sense of taste, and smell are more heightened than men's.

I've heard wives complain their husbands are too loud and husbands say their wives don't speak loudly enough. Well, it's probably true, and there's not too much that can be changed. There is a difference between male-female hearing and their vocal cords. Men don't hear as clearly as women do. You won't change these differences between men and women, but you can be sensitive to them and adapt. A husband can lower his voice when speaking with his wife and she may need to speak up when talking with her husband.[5]

WHEN DIFFERENCES COLLIDE

When it comes to approaching and solving problems, women use both sides of the brain and are able to create an overview. Men tend to break down the problem into pieces in order to come up with a solution. A man goes through steps 1, 2, 3, and 4 and has a solution. He uses a linear approach. A woman tends to go through steps 1, 3, 2, 5, and 4 and come to the same conclusion. If she arrives there before the man does, he probably won't accept her correct answer because he hasn't completed Steps 1, 2, 3, and 4 yet. He's not ready for her answer.

A woman tends to feel that her husband isn't listening. He is, but he's not ready. A wife complains, "It's obvious, why can't you see it?" He can't see it because that's not the way he thinks.

A husband says, "Just take it one step at a time. You can't approach it that way." But she can. Neither is wrong—just different. Can you imagine what a couple could accomplish if they learned to use each other's creativity and strength?[6]

Men like structure. We like to put things in order; we like to regulate, organize, enumerate (men love to talk about numbers and statistics), and fit things into rules and patterns. Remember the example of the male guide at Williamsburg? It's not unusual for men to take the time to put their CDs and videos in alphabetical order, to figure out how long it takes to walk two miles or drive eighty-five miles to their favorite fishing hole.

We have a cabin ninety miles from our home and I've broken the trip down into segments. I can tell you how long it takes to go from point A to B, B to C, C to D, D to E. I enjoy it. When stress hits, men get organized. When they experience a devastating loss, they use structure to gain security. It protects, screens, and acts as a barrier. Men use this to filter out painful feelings and keep them at bay. Being able to box in and control emotions is a big relief. Unfortunately it can deaden the positive and pleasurable feelings as well. Men relate to other men with structure; it's a common language for them.

Ever wonder why some men have a set routine on Saturday? Maybe it's wash the car, mow the lawn, trim the roses, and take a nap. And it's always done at the same time in the same order.[7] It provides structure and conserves energy. Keep the word *energy* in mind, for it's the source of contention between men and women.

The way in which men use their brains is an exclusive mode. (Some women refer to it as tunnel vision!) It can exclude everything except what he is focusing on. It shuts out other possibilities. And men exert an abundance of energy to stay in this position. Most men like to know exactly where they are and what they are doing at a given point in time. It's a way to stay in control.

Life seems to revolve around them. They like the sameness of their environment. It gives them security and is less of an energy drain when things stay the same. If a man walks into his living room and the furniture has been rearranged, his wife may be delighted but he is bothered because he has to reorient himself. If he wasn't notified of the change in advance, he feels even more out of control. And he works to get back in control.

So when a husband is at home and his attention is locked onto the TV, the newspaper, or fixing the car, he's in his exclusive mind set. If his wife talks to him, he feels an interference or intrusion. And for him it's an energy leak. He hopes it will leave! When he does exert energy to shift from whatever he was doing to concentrate on his wife, he's upset because of the energy expenditure. He has to change his focus and shift it elsewhere because he can't handle both at once. She feels he's inconsiderate for not listening and he feels she's inconsiderate because of the intrusion. Actually, neither is. They just don't understand the gender difference. If they did, they could each learn to respond differently.

Women are inclusive and can jump in and out of different topics. There's no energy drain for them. A woman actually picks up energy by entering into new experiences or changes. She is able to see the situation and beyond. She sees and responds to life like a camera with a wide-angle lens, whereas his camera has a highly focused microscope lens. He sees the tree in great detail; she sees the tree, but she also sees the grove and its potential. A woman's expectation of a man's perceptual ability should be tempered with this knowledge.[8]

Because of this brain difference a woman may recover some of her functions following a stroke whereas a man is limited. Her ability to use both sides means that the undamaged side can step in and begin to fill the void left by the other.

This difference is evident in other ways as well. Women are more empathetic than men. This fact was verified in sixteen different studies. And in seventy-five studies women are shown to be more adept than men at picking up and reading nonverbal cues.[9]

Both men and women have a tendency to prefer one side of the brain or the other, and this does affect our approach to life and work. We do not change our preference or dominance throughout our lifetime, but we can develop the skills of the less-preferred side of our brains. And remember, our culture tends to reinforce these bents and inclinations.[10] An excellent resource on developing the skill of using the least-dominant side of the brain is the book *Whole Brain Thinking* by Jacquelyn Wonder and Priscilla Donovan.

Listen to what three people said about the result of genetic brain differences:

"I'd like her to accept me the way I am. She thinks I'm this endless source of energy. I'm not. I get tired but she thinks I'm lazy."

"I can handle one task in an afternoon but not this endless list. But she just can't seem to understand that."

"He's lazy. Or he doesn't care about the home projects. He has energy for his puttering around. I'd like a nap Sunday afternoon too, but there's always work to do."

Complaints! I've heard them and so have you. Many complaints are tied into not understanding a gender difference called energy. Women do have more energy than men, even though men have more start-up energy. Many women are like the Energizer ad on TV that shows the batteries continuing to run and run and run. Men use up their allotment of energy and then need to stop to be recharged. A man goes on a personal retreat by taking a nap, resting, reading, or watching TV. He needs aloneness to recover his energy whereas women are capable of rebuilding energy while carrying on their normal activities.

The problem of energy or lack of it arises when a man doesn't know in advance the details of a project his wife wants him to work on. Even though it may be limiting to a woman, a man needs to know what the task is and how long he's expected to work. Why? He wants to know in advance so he doesn't run out of energy. No, it's not an idea concocted by men to get out of work. A man's metabolism and fat system is different from a woman's. Women have a fat reserve that gives them energy; men do not. A woman's muscles use energy in a much more efficient manner than a man's do.

Men do not want what energy they have to be misused.

A woman may feel restricted by her husband when he says, "Here's the job we need to do. We'll start here, go to this, stick to this plan, and be done in two hours." She asks, "Why?" Being boxed in is an energy drain for her. That's why many couples have difficulty working together. She may want to take some side excursions and detours and he wants to stay on the main highway. He needs to stay focused to conserve energy and she needs variation for the same reason.

Women don't have to be as careful as men in planning the use of energy. A common response from husbands is, "Why didn't you tell me ahead of time?" A wife may want to talk with her husband while he is relaxing. That's energy boosting to her but draining to him.

Since a man focuses on one thing at a time and a woman can handle several things, if she's doing two or three things while talking to him, he feels she's not paying attention to him. If she were interested, she would look at him with 100 percent attention.[11] Here's a choice example I've heard so many times:

> Men also can't understand how women can leave the theater or the living room during the most important part of a movie and go to the bathroom. A man will hold it! He has his priorities. He also has a larger bladder! On the other hand, the woman's "inclusive" mode gives her a sense of what's going on in the film, and she can still "watch" the film while she's in the bathroom. If the man is not physically watching the movie, he misses out. Even though she may not have caught all the details, she doesn't have a sense of missing anything.[12]

If Joyce and I are going to rearrange a room, I would rather figure out in advance where everything goes than shift furniture around several times. Most husbands do not want their wives to carry on a conversation with them while they're doing a task. It's distracting, throws them off-balance, and uses up extra energy. But get several women together to decorate and they enjoy moving something here and there and back and forth. (Once again, there will be exceptions to the pattern I'm describing.)

It's helped me to understand that part of my own reluctance to change has to do with energy drain. And if I initiate the change, I've figured out the time and energy needed. But if someone else wants it done and is too general about the details and amount of time needed, I don't know how much energy to set aside and I may be a bit resistant at first. I guess I'm somewhat normal.

It doesn't get any better the older we are. Research shows that at age sixty, men have only 60 percent of the physical strength and flexibility they had at age twenty. But women have 90 percent of the physical strength and flexibility they had at age twenty.[13]

All it takes for a couple to be able to work well together is to recognize and acknowledge these differences, discuss them, and talk about how they affect their work together. This recognition will help them understand if what they want their partner to change is reasonable and attainable. If not, expectations and desires can be adjusted and a greater level of acceptance attained.

HOW'D THEY DO IT?

"I can remember two things I wanted to change: The way my husband dressed (very casually) and the level of care he gave to our house and property.

"I'm not sure I'm at all responsible for his change in this or any area, but I threw out a very old shirt he loved. It upset him, but he got over it when I pointed out how very worn it was. Then I bought him a few comfortable but nice-looking things to wear, which he approved. (I should say, he bought them but I took him shopping!) Over the years he has become more careful about what he wears when we go somewhere or when guests come over.

"I grew up in a home where my father took a lot of pride in landscaping and was efficient with home repairs, too. When I got married, it was hard to see the lawn deteriorate or the repairs not getting done. It took a long time for my husband to show interest in the yard, but when he saw me working on a garden of flowers, he became more interested in keeping it nice, too. Now he does a lot of work on the yard that he didn't do when we were first married.

"He was easily discouraged when home repairs went wrong and he still procrastinates sometimes. I did (and do) complain when a repair needs to be done and doesn't get taken care of... but I recall attempting to fix a few things myself, sometimes with success. He seemed pleased that I pitched in and that not everything fell on his shoulders. He's been much better about taking care of things since then. We both take pride in our home.

"I feel most changes (maybe all good changes) come in marriage when we want to please one another. It's God who really works within us. My husband and I discussed this and he agrees."

TAKE ACTION

1. List five ways you and your spouse are different and five ways you are similar.

2. Go back to the early portion of the chapter and indicate which of the statements about men and women you've heard or said before.

3. How will the information in this chapter change the way you respond to your spouse?

4. Describe an experience in your marriage in which the issue of being intuitive, focused, or having different levels of energy has been a concern.

CHAPTER FIVE

We Are Different, Aren't We?

(Part Two)

H. Norman Wright

"For the first time in nine years of marriage we're getting along," Tom told me. "The first few years were terrible: fight—argue—resist. We just seemed to clash and compete constantly. Then one day we ended up at a marriage seminar and all the speaker talked about was how to be compatible. I was amazed at how he described us and probably everyone else there. We learned about male-female differences and personality differences. That was the beginning. We now know how to approach each other differently, especially when we'd like the other person to do something differently. And we can now accept our differences."

Tom is like many men and women who are learning to be compatible with their partners.

Let's consider more gender differences and how men and women can use this knowledge to approach each other in a more accepting and supportive way.

DIFFERENT WORLDS

Women view themselves in relation to other people around them. They're not at the center of their world. This feeling of being connected to others has a meaning to it that most men don't understand. I hear it expressed by men when they ask, "Why is she so involved in other people's lives? Why can't she pay more attention to her own life?"

She is. Women look outward and are concerned for others and their needs. They are caregivers in the good sense of the word. A woman defines her sense of self through her relationships. Some are more involved than others. It's a matter of degree. Not only are women more involved with others, they are adept at doing so. Unfortunately, some women become overly involved with others and neglect their marriages.

Men are concerned with themselves first and others next. A man's world view has himself at the center. His tendency is to think, act, and feel in a way that reflects his sense of self as the most important thing. He develops this sense and his identity from the challenge of vying with others. The more he does this the greater his self-confidence. The down side of this is if he becomes too concerned with himself and neglects to cultivate the ability to relate to and care for others.

Men need to see the value of relationships that are more give than take. If a husband can become more outwardly directed and concerned with meeting his wife's needs, he will soon discover how well his own needs are met without the use of demands or withdrawal.

Can either gender change this tendency in the other? No, but perhaps both men and women need to work toward a balance within their own lives. Hopefully, becoming aware and understanding the meaning behind why each responds in this manner will lessen the pressure we place on our partners to be different.[1]

The difference is that women talk their way through things and men think their way through things. Talking is something you do with somebody. Thinking isn't. It stands to reason that women are going to spend more time with others when they have something important to deal with. Men, thinking alone, never really get at what is troubling them because they're not talking, not explaining, not asking questions, not using someone else to figure out their own feelings. Of course, they can't do that unless they are going to fully share all of what they are thinking. Men just don't do that with their friends.

Women lighten their load by sharing the weight. We men tend to think it's the manly thing to do to carry all the weight ourselves. That's why men get what I call "emotional hernias." We need to learn from women to share the load.[2]

Our son Matthew was born profoundly mentally handicapped.

After we learned the severity of his retardation, I didn't cry over it for months. I still had a sense of disbelief. One evening, about ten months later, we were watching a television show called "Then Came Bronson" in which the main character traveled around the country on a motorcycle. In this particular episode, Bronson worked at a ranch for autistic children. He worked with one child day after day and week after week. At the end of the program, the child spoke one word.

When I saw that, it was as if a key had unlocked the vault door holding back my grief. As I felt the flood coming, I quickly left the room (the old message was intact—don't cry in front of anyone), went to the kitchen, and wept by myself. Fortunately, Joyce came in and held me so we could grieve together. We men need our turn to grieve, no matter what the loss.[3]

THE NEED FOR CLOSENESS AND INTIMACY

For years I've heard women express their need for more closeness with their husbands and the men complain about being smothered. As we've seen, women are drawn more to people than are men. They want more intimacy, closeness, and the sense of being connected. And women are more comfortable expressing their emotions than men are.

For many men, self-disclosure means you're giving your partner influence and control over you. The information you give can be used either for your welfare or against you. That's too risky!

Venturing into their feelings is as risky as walking into a dark cave without a flashlight. You can get hurt. The world of feelings or emotions is unknown territory. Telling a husband that he isn't sensitive not only creates more distance, it isn't true. Men are sensitive but they lack a vehicle for their feelings. Even though a man may be an extrovert or highly verbal, he may not be able to express any of his feelings.

Many men would rather not open up. By staying closed they can retain their sense of power and perhaps attain power over others. As one husband told me, "I'm afraid that if I'm no longer a mystery I'll lose my control over others. And that in itself is scary!"

Every couple needs to discuss what closeness and intimacy means to each of them and then adapt their level of intimacy to a comfort zone each is satisfied with. Major problems occur when you have an "intimacy pursuer" or "clinger" married to a "distancer." The more a spouse intensifies his or her pattern of relating, the more the other spouse expresses the opposite style.

You can't demand intimacy; demandingness only breeds withdrawal. Too many wives become emotional interpreters for their husbands. When a wife supplies a husband's emotional responses for him, she protects him from the discomfort he needs to feel to grow. Here's the experience of one husband:

> I think that whenever you're learning something new, you naturally want to know how you're doing. The more unsure you are, the more you want some indication that you're on the right track. As far as expressing feelings went, the hardest thing for me to get used to was that there was no way I should feel. There is just the way I do feel. I used to wait until somebody else, like my wife, said how she felt. If I didn't feel the same thing, I didn't share my feelings because I thought they were wrong. It was as if I wanted to know how I should feel before I checked to see how I did feel. Now that I'm not concerned with how I should feel, I find it a lot easier to know how I do feel.[4]

Michael McGill, who has written extensively about men and intimacy, makes a helpful suggestion. He talks about disconfirmation, which is the realization that the way we behave now is not producing the results we want. This discovery of new information helps us decide to change our behavior. This is what he says:

> Disconfirmation has powerful potential as a motivator of more intimate behavior in men. The reason for this is that disconfirmation requires no goal change. For example, men generally desire to be seen as manly by others. If men were suddenly to perceive that the way to be manly was to be open, self-disclosing, and loving, they would behave in those ways. They don't need to set aside the goal; it remains important to them. They have only to change their behavior. If, on the other hand, men were asked to give up the goal of being manly, we can predict that there would be very little in the way of change.
>
> To use disconfirmation as a means to motivate men to be more loving requires starting with what men value, what their goals are. Men value control, and they avoid the disclosures required for intimacy because they are seen as a threat to control. If men can be made to see that intimacy increases their self-awareness and

therefore their control, they will be motivated to behave in more intimate ways. Some women have come upon this strategy almost by accident.

One woman said, "I pointed out to my husband that the reason he always gave in to me was that he couldn't deal with my emotions. When we fight, he's always so detached and rational, while I'm yelling, crying, laughing. He can't match my emotional level, so he gives in. When he realized that's what was happening, he started to try to be more expressive of what he was feeling. He's not as far as I am yet, but he's moved a long way from where he was. Now he's more comfortable with my emotionality because he's showing his emotions, too. Now he even wins sometimes."[5]

The common complaint I've heard from men is usually, "Why is she so emotional?" and from women, "Why isn't he in touch with his emotions?" A man seems to need a reason why his wife is emotional. But she may not know why or be able to ever give an answer. Men expect women to have not just a reason but a "good" reason for their emotions. When he doesn't get an answer, he uses up more energy trying to find out why.

For a woman emotional expression is positive and healthy, but a man views his emotions with alarm. And again we need to understand that there are some physiological bases for the differences. The portion of the brain associated with emotions is larger in women than men. This, as well as the societal encouragement to express emotions gives women an advantage. Most men, on the other hand, have to first of all access their emotions through their thoughts. A man thinks about what he's feeling first, whereas a woman just experiences it. Men think about what they feel and then do something about it. Women just experience the feeling and go with it. An emotional response comes into a man and he intercepts and interprets it with his thoughts.[6]

DIFFERENT EMOTIONAL MAKEUPS

One of the requested changes men want from their wives is to be less emotional. Wives would like their husbands to be more emotional. Each is frustrated by the other. Unfortunately, this difference is intensified by the negative labels we slap on the differences. She says, "He's so cold and unfeeling." He says, "She's so hysterical and out of control."

There are several reasons why men have difficulty when their wives talk with them in an emotional way. First of all, a man's orientation is to fix things when there's a problem. This applies to every aspect of life. When men hear strong or emotional responses, they also hear, "Help me! Fix this problem for me." Sometimes we men think we are showing love by sharing solutions because we tend to be solution-oriented. Unfortunately, comments like the following abound:

"Don't worry about that; it's no big deal."

"Look, just make up your mind and do something. You'll feel better."

"Why would you feel that way? It's not worth it."

"Well, here's what I would do… "

"Well, are you going to just talk about it, or do you want a solution?"

"Why gripe? Just call them and tell them."

"Why tell me? You don't do what I say."

As helpful as a man may think these words are, they all have one thing in common: They discount the woman's feelings. Men fail to remember that just listening and reflecting the woman's feelings is a solution to her. But men try to fit women into their culture.

Another reason for trying to fix the problem is to keep it from going on and on. I've heard men say, "My wife sometimes carries on for an hour. I can handle ten minutes, but when it goes on it doesn't reduce the problem. It gets worse. There's no end in sight. So I want to fix it as soon as I can."

All these attempts at solutions end in failure, which is even more upsetting. If a husband would remember just two things, this wouldn't have to be a problem. The first is to ask his wife what she would like—to be listened to, to be held, to be given advice. The second thing to remember is that what a wife wants one time may not be what she wants the next. A man might set a routine but he can't expect a woman to follow suit.

It helps to keep in mind that men don't have the emotional resiliency women have. Whereas a man has difficulty shifting from one emotional state to another, women often can switch from crying to anger to forgiveness. Of course this varies because of personality type and other factors. But if men can allow for emotional shifts in women and not assume it's going to be never-ending, it will help their communication.

Wives can assist in the process as well. A wife can simply let her husband know what she wants. And if her upset is directed at someone else, she should be sure to clarify this since he tends to take the upset literally. This way the husband can be relieved of the responsibility when appropriate as well as feel successful in helping.

It helps if a woman can be specific and not exaggerate or embellish, since men tend to take what a woman says literally. If a woman says she's going crazy, going to quit her job, send her kids to a boarding school, never going back to that church, will never visit her mother again, he might take it at face value (especially if he's an introvert and she's an extrovert, which is the topic of the next chapter).

Sometimes the statements women make to their husbands contain advice or hidden criticism or both. A man ends up feeling controlled. One author listed a sampling of these statements:

1. "How can you think of buying that? You already have one."

2. "Those dishes are still wet. They'll dry with spots."

3. "Your hair is getting kind of long, isn't it?"

4. "There's a parking spot over there, turn (the car) around."

5. "You want to spend time with your friends, what about me?"

6. "You shouldn't work so hard. Take a day off."

7. "Don't put that there. It will get lost."

8. "You should call a plumber. He'll know what to do."

9. "Why are we waiting for a table? Didn't you make reservations?"

10. "You should spend more time with the kids. They miss you."

11. "Your office is still a mess. How can you think in here? When are you going to clean it up?"

12. "You forgot to bring it home again. Maybe you could put it in a special place where you can remember it."

13. "You're driving too fast. Slow down or you'll get a ticket."

14. "Next time we should read the movie reviews."

15. "I didn't know where you were." (You should have called.)

16. "Somebody drank from the juice bottle."

17. "Don't eat with your fingers. You're setting a bad example."

18. "Those potato chips are too greasy. They're not good for your heart."

19. "You're not leaving yourself enough time."

20. "You should give me more (advance) notice. I can't just drop everything and go to lunch with you."

21. "Your shirt doesn't match your pants."

22. "Bill called for the third time. When are you going to call him back?"[7]

Emotions motivate us. They drive us to go ahead, push us backward, stop us completely, determine what we do, how we feel, what we want, and whether we get what we want. Our hates, loves, fears, and what to do about them are determined by our emotional structure. There's nothing in our lives that doesn't have the emotional factor as its mainspring. It gives us power or makes us weak, operates for our benefit or to our detriment, for our happiness or confusion.[8]

Most men are at a loss when it comes to knowing what to do with their emotions. Most men haven't learned how to understand or maneuver in this realm. And they see emotion as a woman's world, a territory to be sidestepped. A man wants to feel competent, but in the world of feelings, he feels inadequate. If a man is forced to face his feelings he often feels inept. This is unacceptable to him. To be seen as competent, he must be in control. So he eliminates anything from his life that makes him feel incompetent. How? One way is to invalidate the importance of feelings and leave it to women.[9]

It's easy to understand why men resist change. Many feel they're being pressured unfairly by their wives to be something they've been trained not to be. Men have been trained from generation to generation to be a certain way and that, coupled with their physiological uniqueness, develops an aversion to being intimate and emotionally expressive. When women tell them they shouldn't be that way, they're confused and resistant. What women are asking for is what men have worked so hard to keep from becoming.

EMOTIONS ARE FOR EVERYONE

Everyone, including men, experiences emotions. Not only are all emotions created by God, but everyone has them. It doesn't matter if you are male or female, young or old, black or white, rich or poor—we all experience and, in one way or another, express emotions. Not only do all of us have emotions, but each of us has the capacity to experience a range of emotions.

But keep this in mind: Men have a more difficult time expressing emotions. One reason is because we were raised emotionally handicapped. We were not taught to express our emotions nor were we taught a feeling vocabulary. And society reinforces this problem.

Few people ever asked how I was doing when they learned our son was mentally retarded. Fortunately, when Matthew died people asked me as much as Joyce about my feelings. But too often the messages a man receives verbally and nonverbally reinforce the expectation that "You're not going to get all emotional on me now, are you? You're not going to be vulnerable or afraid or cry or show me weakness, are you?" But why not? Why should we struggle to respond differently from the way God created us?

Perhaps the struggle is best depicted by this statement reflecting the pattern of our culture: "In our society men are taken seriously because they don't open up, because they don't talk about their feelings. Women aren't taken seriously because they do talk about their feelings."[10]

Learning what emotions are and sharing them are essential ingredients in healthy marital relationships. Sometimes, inadvertently, wives hinder their husbands from intimacy. Here is what several husbands have said:

"I was at a party with my wife at church and she shared something it took me weeks to tell her. She was angry with me that night and she shared this as a joke and I was embarrassed. I was hurt and ticked off at her. If she shared this, what would happen if I really opened up? I don't want it used against me. No sir!"

"My wife is an expert on what is a 'feeling' and what isn't a 'feeling.' I've tried to tell her what's going on inside of me and she tells me, 'But that's not a feeling.' Where is this book she uses to tell her what's a feeling and what isn't? I feel like giving up if I'm never going to get it right."

"Yeah, I shared my feelings. And you know what happened? I'll tell you. I opened up about work and my frustrations and she said I just wanted sympathy and attention. I tried to show her some love and attention and she said, 'You must want something, like sex. You've got some other motive in mind.' I try to be what she wants and I get criticized because my motives are suspect."

"My wife tells me what I ought to be feeling. If she feels a certain way, I should feel the same way. If we watch a gripping movie, she wants me to feel what she feels. When she cries at church, she says, 'But didn't you feel the same way? How could you not feel that way about what was shared?' Women's feelings are not the only right feelings, and if I have to feel the same way, it will never work. Can't two people in the same situation feel differently and with a different intensity—and even express it differently?"

A man expects to be in control, not to lose control. He's expected to be confident and assertive, not afraid, hesitant, anxious, insecure, or sad. He's supposed to be sufficient and know what he's doing; rational and analytical, not passive, dependent, bewildered, or in need of support or comfort. Men are well aware of these expectations and try to live up to them. They guard against what they must not be in the eyes of society.

What's the best way for a wife to respond when she expresses her emotions? If possible (by planning ahead and practicing), don't dump them all at once. If emotions are expressed piecemeal, a husband can handle them better. Think of it as speaking your language to someone from a non-English-speaking culture. I've learned to do this with my Asian students and they appreciate it. Overloading another person tends to short-circuit their response. Two wives shared with me what they told their husbands to pave the way for better communication.

One said, "Honey, when I share my feelings with you it's difficult for me to edit, and I'll probably talk too much and dump a load of emotions all over you. I just wanted you to know this in advance. You don't have to catch them all, just listen."

Another wife told her husband, "I appreciate you sitting and listening to all this stuff. I'm not sure of all I said right now. You probably feel the same way. Let's not talk now but think about it and then sort out everything. What do you think?" Both of these wives made it easier for their husbands.

When a husband expresses his feelings (which most women count as a gift) there are several things to keep in mind. Never, but never, interrupt. I remember the first time I shared with my wife, Joyce, the times in my life I had been depressed. I sat at the table in the dining area and Joyce was thirty feet away with her back to me doing the dishes. When I started sharing, she soon stopped what she was doing and came over, sat down, and listened. Never once did she interrupt or make a value judgment on what I was sharing.

Interruptions cause a man to retreat into his castle and be very hesitant to venture out. Remember, it takes more effort, energy, and concentration for a man to share his emotions than it does for a woman. And because we need to stay focused on one thing at a time, interruptions throw us off course. Since men are goal-conscious, they like to stay on course and complete the process.

Men take more time to sort through what's going on inside and distractions make it difficult to do that. Most men are not emotionally articulate because they lack language skills in this area. When our wives are patient and accept this lack, it helps us to talk more.[11]

A wife shared with me a commitment note she gave her husband. She said it brought about the change in her husband she'd wanted for years. The note read, "Since sharing of your emotions with me is such a cherished experience as well as vital to a wonderful sexual relationship, I commit myself to you to respond in the following manner. When you share, you can count on me to listen, not expect you to describe your feelings exactly as I do, not interrupt, nor make value judgments. And finally, if we do enter into a discussion, I will limit my participation to fifteen minutes."

Two days later she received a dozen roses and a note that said, "Thank you." And then, "My commitment when you share is 'ditto' and I will not try to solve the problem unless you ask me to!"

It is possible for men to become more open. Two husbands had this to say:

> "I simply would not be the way I am today if my wife hadn't stood by me every step of the way. It was still hard to set aside years of socialization and actually become a new, loving man, but knowing that I had someone by my side to help me get over the rough spots made all the difference in the world. There were a lot of rough spots, too; anybody who thinks there won't be is fooling himself. To my way of thinking, anybody who tries to go it alone is just as much of a fool. It simply can't be done. As much as any man likes to think he can do things on his own, when it comes to being more loving, a man has to have help. There are just too many things that can go wrong.

> "One of the first things I had to learn was to shut off thinking. There's such a difference between feeling and thinking. Thinking

is what we men are good at; the rational, logical approach is how we go at things. When a problem comes up, my first response used to be, 'What makes sense here?' Now I'm trying to hold off on what makes sense and ask instead, 'What do I sense here?' There's a big difference."[12]

A man can change. But discovery and recognition are necessary for a man to change. If he sees the problem existing outside of himself, it's easier for him to change. But if he sees himself as the problem, it's much more difficult.

Men don't usually change by choosing to be different. They change by deciding to behave differently. They need some objective awareness, not a feeling, for the change to occur. And that point is crucial for wives to remember. When a man can think, "There's a problem out there. I can do something different to fix it," change is on the horizon. When a man thinks, "I'm the problem; I'm at fault," change is nowhere in sight. Men do change. Let me repeat that. We do change! Yes, it's possible, but we are only interested in changing, as Dr. John Gray suggests, when we feel appreciated, accepted, and also realize that we are not creating the desired result and are responsible for it! Then we feel motivated to change.[13]

I would also add that if my wife approaches me by using my language style and respecting my personality uniqueness, I am better able to consider her requests. If we men are given time to mull over the situation and figure it out without hearing critical, corrective statements, there's a strong possibility for change.

Women are different. They tend to change when they can share their feelings, thoughts, and wishes without fear of being invalidated. They need to feel the freedom to talk; they want safety, acceptance, and respect for their needs, as well as time to bring their feelings back into balance. Then change is possible for them. Giving a woman advice or telling her how to do something and what to do won't work.[14]

I think there's another basic principle involved in change. Years ago I had the privilege of studying under Dr. William Glasser, a psychiatrist who wrote *Reality Therapy*. One of his main beliefs was that before people will change, they must make a value judgment on what they are doing. He didn't say others were to make the judgment. Individuals must decide for themselves if what they are doing is right or wrong, good or bad, positive or negative. When they make that decision, they will decide to change.

Often in my counseling, I use a different phrasing, which could probably be used in the husband-wife context as well. I ask, "What you're doing seems to be working for you and you're comfortable with it. I wonder if you would like to consider another way that might work even better than what you're doing now? It's up to you."

Sometimes when you don't push your spouse to give up what they are doing but simply encourage them to add to their repertoire of responses, they're more open to considering your request. It's something to think about. This leads us to another general gender difference.

ENGULFMENT AND ABANDONMENT

One of a man's fears is to be engulfed, whereas a woman is concerned about being abandoned.

Even when a husband isn't being engulfed by his wife, he may feel as though he is because of his need for distance. It only adds to the problem when a husband doesn't know how to share with his wife in a loving, tactful manner that he feels invaded, smothered, and needs some space. Most men either express this need in anger or they withdraw into the paper, TV, work, or with their male friends. This is a man's way of getting relief.

But this behavior creates feelings of abandonment in wives because it neglects their need for intimacy. When a wife experiences stress, she moves toward her husband to seek comfort. She feels threatened by his withdrawal and then begins to blame herself, "What am I doing wrong? Why doesn't he love me? Why is he avoiding me?"[15]

I've heard some wives refer to this withdrawal tendency as "the trance." It's like a self-hypnotic oblivion that shields a man from the world. As one wife put it, "We could be at a family dinner or I could be talking to him about my women's group and I see his eyes glaze over. I know that he's just retreated into his own inner world. Sometimes I wonder if I've given him a self-hypnotic suggestion!"

For many wives the dictionary definition of the word trance seems to fit: "a state of partly suspended animation or inability to function; a somnolent state or a state of profound absorption." It's true that certain situations or comments can send a man into his trance if he cannot leave physically. It's his way of screening out some of the female stimuli, and it helps him to control his emotions. In a trance a man is aware that someone is talking to him and he may even respond. But he doesn't hear. It doesn't register. Many men have used this method of withdrawal all their lives. They learned it in their interactions with their mothers. They continue to use the trance because it's a habit and it provides safety.[16]

What can husbands and wives do about these differences? A husband can accept that his wife's need for closeness may be greater than his. At the same time, he can verbalize his need for space. "I need some time alone for a while either working on my car or watching TV. I'll spend time with you tonight after 8:00." When a wife expresses a need for closeness and intimacy and a husband wants space, they need to discuss (briefly) then and there which need will be met immediately and which will be met later. It helps if a husband gives more frequent affirmations such as "I care about you when we're together and when we're apart."

A wife can accept that her husband has different intimacy needs. Notice the symptoms of his desire to withdraw such as anger, tenseness, or terse comments that terminate conversations. Encourage him to spend time alone. When you give him space, he will have more desire to move closer. Wives, be careful that your style of communication and response isn't triggering a trance. If you know his mind is elsewhere, don't say anything important at that time. Don't interpret his withdrawal personally, but view it as a normal part of his behavior.[17]

I DON'T NEED NO HELP!

Another apparent difference between the sexes involves decision-making and asking for help. Although there are many individual differences within each gender as well as personality differences, *generally speaking, men tend to be more immediately decisive than women.* Some wives feel frustrated when their husbands announce a decision without telling them how they arrived at it. When a wife asks her husband why he made that decision (because she's interested in the step-by-step process, not because she's challenging the decision), the husband is often defensive. He interprets the questioning as a challenge.

Part of the reason is that men look at the facts and usually ignore the element women focus on—the human dimension. Women like to figure out how their decisions will affect not only themselves but those around them. They enjoy evaluating numerous possibilities as well as reflecting upon their feelings. They enjoy asking questions, gathering information, and searching for solutions. Because of their concern for others, after they make a decision they may agonize, "Was it the right decision or not?" "What if it hurts others or someone doesn't approve?" Usually when a man makes a decision, it's been cast in cement.

Women seek the opinions of others more than men do. They enjoy including others in the decision-making process. They invite others to share in the process, whereas a man deals with a situation within the privacy of his mind and then consults others. If he receives favorable feedback, he moves ahead. If not, he'll reconsider. He rarely asks for help—in any arena—because he wants to feel self-sufficient.

A classic example of this is the man who drives somewhere and gets lost. You know what I'm talking about. A woman will suggest stopping at the nearest gas station or making a phone call to get directions. To the man this means admitting he's out of control and can't solve his own problem. To him this feels like failure. If he does stop for help, who usually goes in and asks for assistance? You guessed it, the woman.

Feeling out of control is one of the main causes of stress in a man's life. Consider some of the other sources of stress based in feeling out of control:

- Men are stressed when they're forced to ride in the passenger seat rather than have control of the automobile.

- Men are stressed when they must wait for a table at a restaurant or in line for a movie; they frequently choose to forego the meal or movie to regain their sense of choice.

- Men become infuriated by road construction and exasperated at "stupid" drivers who distract or detain them.

- Men dread funerals and psychotherapy, and sometimes equate the two as depressing reminders of life's uncertainties.

- Men postpone dental appointments and other procedures that require them to put themselves in others' hands.

- Men are terrified of illness or injury that may interfere with their ability to be in charge of their daily lives.

- Men prefer requests to demands, and free choice to requests—

and they will demonstrate this by saying no to demands for things they might actually have enjoyed.

• Men prefer dogs as pets over cats since dogs are more responsive and can be controlled. Cats are independent and get into power struggles with their owners.[18]

On the other end of the scale, a woman views getting lost as an adventure: "We discover how to get there and when I ask for help and get it, I'm thrilled. I've found what I needed and I enjoyed talking to that helpful person."

For a man to admit that he's lost is not just an admission of being out of control, it's an admission of being wrong. Most men dislike being wrong, being told they are wrong, even considering they might be wrong, or the worst scenario of all, discovering their wife knew they were wrong before they did! For most men, it's the ultimate in feeling helpless and humiliated. (I've seen exceptions to this based on the security a man finds through a personal relationship with Jesus Christ, allowing Him to refine the man's attitudes and beliefs.)

To sum it all up, men fear being wrong. Fear makes us expect the worst, misinterpret what others say, and act overly defensive. When a wife offers unsolicited advice or suggestions, often it's not perceived as helpful. If a wife says, "Oh, not that way honey, try it this way instead," many men hear it as, "That's the wrong way. Can't you figure it out?" When she suggests stopping and asking for directions, he hears, "Dummy! How could you get lost? You can't even figure this out."

Because of our defensive filters, husbands and wives often hear something different from what was actually said. It's not so much a matter of being right or wrong as it is a lack of understanding. Marriage provides the opportunity for education, clarification, and refinement.

One husband volunteered: "During the first five years of marriage, I was quite defensive when Mary made suggestions or gave me any feedback. One evening when we were out to dinner, she asked me, 'What do you hear me say when I give you a suggestion or some advice?' I thought a minute and said, 'I guess I resist it a bit and get defensive... and I think you're saying I'm wrong and I'm not doing it right.' Mary said, 'Do I use the words, "You're wrong" or "inept" or "incompetent" when I offer my suggestions?' And I said, 'No, but I guess I hear that; I guess I'm afraid of being wrong.'

"Mary went on to say, 'Could I say it in a different way that would make it easier to accept?' At first I was going to say that might be the answer but then I realized the problem was not with Mary but with me, and I told her so. I suggested that I try not to assume she was saying or implying I was wrong. She smiled at me and said, 'That would be great. I don't like to feel I'm wrong either, so I have an idea of how you might feel. Perhaps we could both see one another's suggestions as an opportunity to grow and become even more proficient than we are now.' That was a great and enlightening evening for us!"

How can this information about decision-making and asking for help be used to learn how to respond to one another? Talk over your decision-making styles. Encourage your spouse to use his or her style and affirm the positive features of it. Be willing to try your partner's style in order to understand his or her perspective, as well as to expand your own repertoire of choices. Don't interpret your spouse's questions as a challenge or a stall. Be open to another perspective.

It helps when a wife understands and accepts that her husband may not ask for help immediately. Encourage him to figure it out for himself, but let him know that if he can't, it's all right. It's a sign of strength and wisdom rather than a weakness to seek help and guidance. The book of Proverbs states:

... making your ear attentive to skillful and godly Wisdom, and inclining and directing your heart and mind to understanding—applying all your powers to the quest for it. **Proverbs 2:2,** AMPLIFIED

Lean on, trust and be confident in the Lord with all your heart and mind, and do not rely on your own insight or understanding.

In all your ways know, recognize and acknowledge Him, and He will direct and make straight and plain your paths.

Be not wise in your own eyes; reverently fear and worship the Lord, and turn entirely away from evil. **Proverbs 3:5-7,** AMPLIFIED

The way of a fool is right in his own eyes, but he who listens to counsel is wise. **Proverbs 12:15,** AMPLIFIED

He who refuses and ignores instruction and correction despises himself, but he who heeds reproof gets understanding.
Proverbs 15:32, AMPLIFIED

It goes a long way when a husband affirms his wife and her ability to get other opinions. I heard a husband tell his wife, "I admire your ability to dig up all the facts from other people. I wish I could do it that easily, but I can't. So, I'll just depend on you." That was a wise husband.[19]

SHE'LL SHOP TILL SHE DROPS

We joke a lot about another apparent gender difference—shopping styles. I admit that Joyce and I fit the pattern. In fact, I'm sure that whenever we drive by a shopping mall Joyce's head begins to turn automatically and her eyes glaze over. And we don't call it shopping any more, we call it grazing.

When Joyce shops, I tend to walk through a store, scanning to see if what I'm looking for is there. If not, I move on. Why stay? We accept our different styles and enjoy them, but we're also willing to flex and follow the other person's lead. I'm willing to go shopping (and even browsing with no game plan in mind) if it's not going to be for several hours. And Joyce is willing to shorten the excursion and go with a list of what we need.

Sometimes Joyce leaves me in a book store or pet store and I'm happy. She also goes out and scouts around to find items I might like so I can go directly to the two stores she's found. Or sometimes she brings home several shirts or ties and I can make my selection right at home. That saves me time when I'm busy and she enjoys the selecting process and helping me.

I depend on her knowledge of color and style. When I go to pick out a suit or sport coat I wouldn't dream of leaving Joyce at home. We've discovered you can work together even when you're different. But many people haven't learned that yet. As I watch men shopping with their wives, many have an expression of resignation, agony, and exhaustion.

Like many women, Joyce sees shopping as a time of discovery and enjoyment. Men see it as a task. When we men don't find what we want, we say, "What's wrong with this dumb store, anyway?!" I've heard strong, virile men say, "The very thought of going shopping makes me tired. My wife seems to come alive when she shops. It's like a shot of energy. And she enjoys it when she doesn't buy anything! I see it as a trip into purgatory."

This brings up a major factor in husband-wife conflicts we talked about earlier: energy. While shopping a man tends to expend more energy than a woman. Why? Because he has to reorient himself each time he moves from one section of the store to another or from one shopping mall to another. His focus is narrower and it takes more energy to adjust. But a woman is energized by the variation of new sights, sounds, and aromas. Her energy increases while his decreases.[20] Marketing techniques take these differences into account. Have you ever noticed that when you enter a department store, the men's section is one foot inside one of the main entrances? That's so a man can come through the door and say, "Great. It's right here. I don't have to walk far. I can get this over with quickly and get out of here." I think it's also placed there so wives will look through it on the way to their department. I've heard some men say they would like to see a drive-through lane put in the men's section!

Can you change your partner's shopping style? Perhaps not. But you can make it more palatable by adapting to one another and coming up with creative lines like: "Jean, why don't you take several hours and go shopping. I'll give you a list of things to scout out for me and I'll watch the kids."

"Tony, let's go shopping at the mall. I have two items I want to look for and I need your opinion. I'd like to be out of there in forty-seven minutes and you can keep me on track."

MEN, WOMEN, AND FRIENDS

Another difference between men and women is perhaps best typified by the title of a book, *The Friendless American Male*. Women are interested in building friendships and are better able to do it than men. This would be in keeping with the pattern we've already described concerning gender differences. Women's friendships are more intense, close, and demonstrative. Women are three times more likely to have a close confidante than a man.[21]

Many men say they don't need friends. That's why they don't have close personal relationships. They say:

"I don't see what women find to talk about so much. Maybe they need to talk and share that much, but not me. I can handle it myself."

"I don't have what you would call close friends. I don't belong to any groups as such. I go to church and to the classes, but I don't belong. I don't see any real need for more involvement."

"I know a lot of guys, and we can shoot the breeze. I like them, but I don't need to get any closer. I don't want to spend any time with them."

"Friendships can be a pain in the neck at times. It takes time and I don't know if I'd be any better off with them than I am now."

"If I need the friendship of another man, that means I can't make it on my own. I don't like that. If I relate to another guy, it's because I want to, not because I need to."

A woman asks another woman to lunch and she says, "Oh, great. I'd love to." A man asks another man to lunch and he says, "All right. What's up?" Men see time spent with other men as a task-oriented purpose. What do we have to accomplish? Developing the relationship is not high on his list of objectives.

Friendship means something very different to men than it does to women. Even if there's a close, intimate relationship between one man and another, it rarely approaches the depth of openness that occurs between women. Few men reveal much of their personal and private selves to other men.

A typical male friendship pattern is to have "many friends," each of whom knows something about the person but no one individual knows too much. No other man has all the information about him. If he has ten "friends," it would take all ten of them coming together sharing the fragments of information they have about him to try and construct who this man is. He relates differently to everyone. Most male friendships originate in the context of common occupational or recreational interests.

Many men play it safe by erecting walls between themselves and other men. *Competition* is one wall. Two men meet for the first time and introduce themselves. What is each one thinking? "How much better a man am I than he? How much less a man am I than he?" Men who use the wall of competition constantly compare themselves to other men. This wall contains bricks labeled job, title, money, and status symbols (such as the label on the suit the other man is wearing or whether he drives a BMW, Jaguar, or Honda).

These value comparisons keep a man from appreciating the uniqueness and quality in the other person. The wall of competition is a reflection of low self-esteem. To overcome this, he uses comparisons to establish his self-worth.

Fear is another wall. No man wants rejection, judgment, or criticism by other men. All men are sensitive to what other men think but these insecurities are kept hidden, because if other people knew they might use it against them.

Many men struggle with a sense of discomfort in their man-to-man relationships. They fear being intimate but experience isolation and loneliness when they are not. Few are comfortable sharing their down times, including worries, disappointments, or failures. Why? They're afraid of being rated as weak and unmasculine. They are also reluctant to share their successes or times of delight over an achievement because of the fear of appearing boastful or, worse, inciting competitive jealousy.

Men are told they have to choose between manly strength and being expressive with others, which can lead to deep relationships. Most men do not open up unless driven to the wall or to despair—and even then it's not easy. This reinforces the tendency men have to see sharing their deepest feelings as weakness, and it leads to shallow relationships between men.

Some men can share on the deepest levels without fearing what others will think. I've seen it and I've experienced it. Once a man overcomes his initial fear or embarrassment, he finds the results overcome the risk. Men who know Jesus Christ as their personal Lord have an entirely new world available to them. But it still takes time, effort, and risk to overcome our societal conditioning.[22]

If your wife spends too much time with her friends, or your husband doesn't have close friends and you're concerned, what can you do? You can encourage change, but in either case they need to see the benefits of changing. They need to see why their lives would be better than they are now.

Yes, differences abound. Learning about them, learning to accept them, learning to work with them will help you discover what can be changed, what can be modified a bit, and what can't.

HOW'D THEY DO IT?

"I'm a stickler for being on time. Always have been. Bev's family doesn't know the meaning of being on time. Her parents were late for our wedding. I try to be patient and understanding and I've loosened up on some things, but being on time is a necessity. I really get uptight and then snap at everyone. When we go to church or when we have to meet someone, I want to leave early. That's not important to Bev. Talking to her didn't work, so I decided to try something wild. I gave Bev a short letter stating why being on time was important to me. I listed the situations and activities in which being on time wasn't important and the two that were essential to me. Then I suggested several options and asked her to consider which one she wanted. They were:

1. I could be the timekeeper and gently remind you every fifteen minutes.

2. You could be the timekeeper and gently remind yourself every fifteen minutes. (We'd need a plan for this.)

3. We could have the kids be the timekeepers.

4. We could postpone some of our cleanup before we leave until we get back.

5. I could leave at the appointed time without you and you could come in your car.

6. None of the above if you have a better suggestion.

7. I will pay more attention to the times you are on time and affirm you and say less about when you're late.

"Did it work? Yes. I wasn't looking for 100 percent improvement but I did get 75 percent. And we both feel better. But the payoff came several weeks ago when Bev came in fifteen minutes early and said, 'I'm ready. How come you're not? Let's go!'"

TAKE ACTION

1. What examples can you think of in your own life and your spouse's that fit the descriptions in this chapter?

2. In your marriage who is most emotionally expressive? If your partner isn't emotionally expressive, what steps could you take to assist him or her to grow?

3. What three characteristics of your spouse can you work on becoming more tolerant of?

4. Go back to the list of twenty-two statements at the beginning of this chapter. Indicate which of these you've either heard or said and what could be said to replace them.

5. What steps will you take to complement one another in the area of your gender differences?

6. The following books may be helpful:

   The Friendless American Male by Dave Smith (Thomas Nelson, 1990.)

   Real Men Have Feelings Too by Gary Oliver (Moody, 1993.)

   The Friendships of Women by Dee Brestin (Victor Books, 1988.)

CHAPTER SIX

It Takes
All Types

Gary J. Oliver

Is your partner ever frustrated with you because "you're just too nit-picky"? Have you ever been frustrated with your spouse because he or she always seems preoccupied with "heaven only knows" what?

Do you start the day with great intentions to get a few specific things done but get distracted?

Have you ever been excited about going to a church fellowship so that you can spend time with a lot of your friends, while your partner complains about having to endure another evening of shallow conversation?

Does it ever surprise you that people view you as insensitive and uncaring when deep down inside you are very sensitive and care deeply for people?

Have you ever left a social gathering confident that you've made a good impression only to find as you drive home with your spouse that there were at least ten things you could have said much better or shouldn't have said at all?

Do you have friends who seem to be calm and relaxed with ample time to play, while you feel like a hamster on a treadmill?

Nowhere is the breadth of God's creativity more evident than in humankind. No two of us are exactly alike. Even identical twins can have opposite personalities. Each of us has a combination of gifts, talents, attitudes, beliefs, needs, and wants that are different from anyone else's. That's part of what makes life so exciting. It's all right to be different! But is it all right for your partner to be different?

If you've ever observed families with more than one child, you've probably been amazed that children from the same gene pool, raised by the same parents, in the same neighborhood, eating the same diet, going to the same school and church, can be totally different. What accounts for these differences?

Why do some people love to be alone for hours on end and others go crazy if other people aren't around? Why is one person always coming up with new ideas and inventing things while another is content to use things the way they are "supposed to" be used? Why do some people like to talk things out while others prefer to work it out for themselves and then talk about it? Why does one person welcome a new employee and another act as if it's the end of the world? How can some people read a book for an hour without being bored or distracted while others start climbing the wall after only ten minutes? Why do some people take pride in having a clean and neat office while other offices appear as if they've been used for nuclear testing?

In Psalm 139:14 we read, "I will give thanks to Thee, for I am fearfully and wonderfully made; Wonderful are Thy works" (NASB). The Bible clearly teaches that every person is made in the image of God and is of infinite worth and value. We all acknowledge the fact that every person is unique. Yet most of us find it much easier to value the qualities in our spouses that are similar to ours. We rarely argue with our spouses when they *agree* with us. Yet we frequently argue with them when they *disagree* with us.

What's the first thing that comes to mind when you hear the word *different*? What kinds of meanings do you associate with different? Are they primarily positive or negative associations? If I were to walk up to you on the street and say "You sure look different today," how would you take it? Would you think I was giving you a compliment and reply "Well, thank you very much"? Or would you think I was being critical?

Different suggests a deviation from some kind of standard or norm. It suggests that something is not quite the way it usually is or the way it should be. Many people interpret *different* to mean "unusual, inappropriate, inferior, or wrong." Now if I were to say to you "You sure look like a deviate," you would know I was being negative and critical.

How about a different word association? Ready? What do you think of when you hear the words *unique* or *special*? Do you tend to have a more positive response to those terms? Every person is different. Yet often those differences are neither understood nor valued.

In an earlier chapter I talked about the importance of understanding God's unique design for each one us. In Proverbs 22:6 we are encouraged to discover the unique aspects of each one of our children's personalities and to raise them according to the unique design God has given them. We're exhorted to approach each child differently because God has chosen to make them different. What is a key principle in understanding our children is also a key principle in understanding our spouse.

THE LAW OF DIFFERENCES

After many years of working with people I've discovered that while few people will dare to fight the law of gravity, many attempt to fight the law of differences. Even when the differences are recognized, they are rarely appreciated or understood. Think about it. When was the last time your spouse complimented you on some aspect of your personality, your opinion, or your way of doing something that is different from the way that he or she would have done it? When was the last time you complimented your spouse for these differences? Is there some way we can understand and make sense of these differences?

First of all, we need to acknowledge that personality differences exist. Often during the courtship phase couples find it difficult to focus on anything but what they have in common. It's fun to discover that you like the same kind of music, you both enjoy one scoop of chocolate chip and one scoop of mint chip ice cream on a sugar cone, you agree that having three kids would be just right. In a marriage it's important to have some shared beliefs and values, to have some "common ground" on which to build the relationship.

It's also important to acknowledge how you differ. Those differences helped attract you to each other. But the same differences can become a tremendous source of irritation and frustration in your first few years of marriage. The differences that add depth and breadth also contain potential for irritation. Here's an example of a few differences that started out positive but ended up negative:

She married him because he was such a "powerful and dominating man"; (now she's frustrated with him because he's such a "domineering male").

He married her because she was so "delicate and petite"; (now he's frustrated with her because she's so "weak and helpless").

She married him because he knows how to "provide a good living"; (now she's frustrated with him because "all he ever thinks about is his business").

He married her because she was so "steady and sensible"; (now he's frustrated with her because she's "boring and dull").

She married him because he was the "strong silent type"; (now she's frustrated with him because he "never has anything to say").

He married her because she was "such a beauty"; (now he's frustrated with her because "all she thinks about are her looks").

She married him because he was so "muscular and athletic"; (now she's frustrated with him because "all he thinks about is sports").

He married her because she was "so crazy about me"; (now he's frustrated with her because "she's so insanely jealous").[1]

Second, it's important to appreciate the value of individual personality differences. In 1 Corinthians 12-14, the apostle Paul compares the Church to the human body and tells us that every part of the body is important. Even those parts we may see absolutely no use for are important. Paul teaches us that diversity or differences do not necessitate division. Part of what it means to "grow up" and become a "mature" Christian involves learning how to accept and appreciate the value of our differences.

If I do not want what you want, please try not to tell me that my want is wrong.

If I believe something different from your beliefs, at least pause before you correct my view.

If my emotion is less than yours, or more, given the same circumstances, try not to ask me to feel more strongly or weakly.

If I act, or fail to act, in the manner of your design for action, let me be.

I do not, for the moment at least, ask you to understand me. That will come only when you are willing to give up changing me into a copy of you.

I may be your spouse, your parent, your offspring, your friend, or your colleague. If you will allow me any of my own wants, or emotions, or beliefs, or actions, then you open yourself, so that some day these ways of mine might not seem so wrong, and might finally appear to you as right—for me.

To put up with me is the first step to understanding me. Not that you embrace my ways as right for you, but that you are no longer irritated or disappointed with me for my seeming waywardness.

And in understanding me you might come to prize my differences from you, and, far from seeking to change me, preserve and even nurture those differences.[2]

While the first two steps—acknowledging personality differences and valuing those differences—are important, the third step is critical. We need to find a way to *understand* or make sense of those differences. Just as there are different routes one can take to get to the same destination, there are different ways to understand personality and individual differences.

In his book *Standing Out,* Chuck Swindoll beautifully illustrates the importance of understanding and valuing individual differences. He quotes the following article, printed in the Springfield, Oregon, Public Schools Newsletter:

Once upon a time, the animals decided they should do something meaningful to meet the problems of the new world. So they organized a school.

They adopted an activity curriculum of running, climbing, swimming and flying. To make it easier to administer the curriculum, all the animals took all the subjects.

The duck was excellent in swimming; in fact, better than his instructor. But he made only passing grades in flying, and was very poor in running. Since he was slow in running, he had to drop swimming and stay after school to practice running. This caused his web feet to be badly worn, so that he was only average in swimming. But average was quite acceptable, so nobody worried about that—except the duck.

The rabbit started at the top of his class in running, but developed a nervous twitch in his leg muscles because of so much make-up work in swimming.

The squirrel was excellent in climbing, but he encountered constant frustration in flying class because his teacher made him start from the ground up instead of from the treetop down. He developed "charlie horses" from overexertion, and so only got a C in climbing and a D in running.

The eagle was a problem child and was severely disciplined for being a non-conformist. In climbing classes he beat all the others to the top of the tree, but insisted on using his own way to get there....

Swindoll comments on this story by observing that:

The obvious moral of that story is that each creature has its own set of capabilities in which it will naturally excel—unless it is expected or forced to fill a mold that doesn't fit. When that happens, frustration, discouragement, and even guilt bring overall mediocrity or complete defeat. A duck is a duck—and only a duck. It is built to swim, not to run or fly and certainly not to climb. A squirrel is a squirrel—and only that. To move it out of its forte, climbing, and then expect it to swim or fly will drive a squirrel nuts. Eagles are beautiful creatures in the air but not in a foot race. The rabbit will win every time unless, of course, the eagle gets hungry.[3]

MEET DICK AND JUDY

Differences are one of the great joys of relationships. They bring a richness and diversity to our lives. Sometimes it's the differences between two people that attract them to each other. That was the case with Dick and Judy. Dick grew up on a farm in central Nebraska. Judy was raised in southern California. When they met during their freshman year at a Christian college they were immediately attracted to each other.

Judy's dad was a fine man but had experienced difficulty holding down jobs. By the time she started her freshman year in high school they had already moved nine times. She had grown tired of the insecurity and instability. Dick had spent his entire life in the same state, in the same county, and on the same square mile of irrigated farm land. All of his life Dick knew exactly what he wanted to do. This strength, confidence, and security attracted Judy.

Because Dick's dad raised both corn and livestock there was always a lot of work to do on the farm, twelve months out of the year. Both Dick's father and grandfather were quiet men. Dick was too. He assumed it was genetic. The men in his family just didn't talk a lot. Dick liked people but was uncomfortable in large groups and didn't feel secure in social situations. Judy was just the opposite. She could walk into a group of strangers and feel at home. Within five minutes she knew the entire life history of at least three people and counted them as good friends.

After dating two years they were married, and after a couple more years they moved back to the farm. This was a decision they had both looked forward to. Dick was excited to move "back home," and Judy was looking forward to getting her "own" home established and starting a family.

On the outside it looked as if they had the perfect marriage. After five years they had two lovely children, a boy and a girl, a nice home, a nice church, but they also had a marriage that was falling apart. The differences that had brought them together had become bricks in an ever-growing wall between them.

Since Judy had never spent much time in a rural community she didn't realize how much she would miss all of her friends and the many activities in their large church. She also had no idea how much work was involved in planting, cultivating, and harvesting corn while at the same time raising livestock. In their college years she and Dick had spent a lot of time together. Suddenly it seemed as if he was never around. When he was around he was exhausted, preoccupied, or both. With a sigh of deep frustration Judy said, "At times it seems as if we are roommates and the only thing we share is where we live."

Dick was confused. He didn't see any problem. He didn't need to talk about everything all of the time. He was working hard and doing the best he could. "I don't understand what her problem is" Dick blurted out. "This is just the way life is. It's not always easy, it's not always fun, and it takes a lot of hard work. If things are going to work out between us she's going to have to make some changes."

There it was. That response that so many of us have to the differences we don't understand. If the other person isn't happy they must have a problem and they need to change. Notice the motivation for change doesn't come out of an understanding of who the partner is and how God has designed them to function. It doesn't come out of understanding, compassion, and sensitivity. It comes out of frustration, discomfort, anger, and, yes, fear.

Rather than being appreciated and understood, differences are often attributed to gender, stubbornness, selfishness, pride, ignorance, laziness, stupidity, or sin.

Now I'm not suggesting that at times sin can't be a significant factor in relationship problems. It most definitely can. However, in over twenty years of marriage and family counseling I've seen far too many times when sin became the categorical garbage can for legitimate differences that weren't acknowledged or understood, and thus couldn't be appreciated.

Dick and Judy loved each other. They wanted their marriage to work. But they were stuck in hurt, pain, and misunderstanding. They believed the other person was the one who had the problem and needed to change.

Toward the end of my first session with Dick and Judy I shared a story about Michelangelo, the great Renaissance sculptor, painter, architect, and poet. "One day Michelangelo was looking at a freestanding mass of rough Carrara marble and exclaimed, 'There's an angel in that stone and I'm going to liberate him!'"

That's one of the ways we might look at one another, as someone to encourage, influence, and help become "liberated" to be and become all God has gifted them to be. But first we need to recognize that God has already given them a certain design. It's true that the level of maturity and effects of sin in their life may obscure the design, but it's there!

The problem occurs when we get confused about our role in the process. Some people believe they are the Michelangelos whose job it is to determine what needs to be "liberated," what the person is to be and become. (Those are the same people who are patiently waiting for a vacancy in the Trinity.)

God has already started a work of art in a life. He has already determined what He wants it to be. He is the Master Craftsman whose job it is to select the marble, create the design, and determine where to start and how to progress.

God may want to use us as one of many tools to help "release" or change that person. He may need us to help chip off some of the rough edges, or to help polish the person to give them added life, luster, and beauty. Our job is to be available as tools in God's hands to understand His will and design for them and then to be available to be His assistant in completing the final work.

I went on to tell Dick and Judy that before they could be at the place to work on changing they needed to spend more time learning how to understand each other. Not just understanding who they were, but also understanding their God-given uniqueness.

When some people think of changing their spouse they overlook the fact that they are only, at best, a tool in the Creator's hands. One of the first and most important steps in helping someone to change is to discover his or her unique "design." This takes time and patience. You can't do it overnight. In this process you will not only gain a new sense of appreciation for them, you will become better equipped to meet their real needs.

A GUIDE TO PERSONALITY DIFFERENCES

One of the most helpful tools to understand and appreciate some of the natural personality differences in people was developed by Swiss psychiatrist Carl Jung. In 1921 he introduced the concept of psychological type to help explain some of the natural differences in personality. He suggested that much of what appeared to be random variations in human behavior actually involved characteristics that were quite orderly and consistent.

After years of watching people, he discovered that some of the most important ways in which people differ could be grouped into three basic patterns. He suggested that people could be more easily understood when we knew how they perceive or take in information and the kinds of information that are important to them, how they use that information to make decisions, and whether they are energized by focusing their attention on their inner world or by being actively involved with other individuals in their outer world.

Psychological or personality type provides a kind of map to help us understand some of the most important parts of a person's personality. Keep in mind that while a map doesn't give us all of the information we need, it does point us in the right direction. It provides markers along the way to let us know if we're going in the right direction. Some of the most important things we need to know about people to better understand them can be discovered by identifying their personality type.

What is personality type? Where did it come from? How does it work? Personality type consists of several inborn preferences or tendencies that have a strong impact on how we develop as individuals. Everyone begins life with a small number of inherited personality traits that makes each person a little different from everyone else. Do you know what some of yours are? What was it about you that made you a little bit (or a lot) different from your mom and dad, brother or sister? Each trait is a fundamental building block of personality. These basic inborn traits determine many individual differences in personality.

While core traits are present at birth, they are influenced and modified by our environment and how we are raised. There is an interaction between how God has designed each child and the way in which he or she interacts with the world. Every child is an *initiator* who in part creates his own environment. He is a *reinforcer* who selectively rewards or punishes people in his environment for the way they treat him. He is also a *responder* who interacts with the effects of the environment on his personality.[4]

Several years after Jung's basic work was published, a mother and daughter team here in the United States significantly expanded his foundational work. Based on years of their own careful research and observation Isabel Briggs Myers and her mother Katherine Briggs added a fourth category of personality traits and began to develop a useful tool to help identify a person's preferences on all four dimensions. The end result of their many years of research resulted in the Myers-Briggs Type Indicator (MBTI).

We've used the MBTI for many years as one way to help couples see each other through different eyes. We have found that the MBTI "provides a practical way to identify, translate, and understand core differences in personality." The MBTI identifies four sets of contrasting personality traits or preferences: extrovert and introvert, sensor and intuitive, thinker and feeler, judger and perceiver. Each trait can be identified by its complete name or by the single letter assigned to it. A "preference" is the conscious or unconscious choice a person makes in a certain designated realm.

Extroversion (**E**)_____(**I**) Introversion

Sensing (**S**)_____(**N**) Intuition

Thinking (**T**)_____(**F**) Feeling

Judging (**J**)_____(**P**) Perceiving

According to type theory, everyone uses all eight of the traits but one out of each of the four pairs is preferred and more fully developed. It's similar to the fact that while we have two hands and use both of them, we tend to prefer one hand over the other. Most people are either right-handed or left-handed. When using your most preferred hand, tasks are usually easier, take less time, are less frustrating, and the end result is usually better.

Here's a simple way to experience what I mean. Take a pen or pencil and put it in your less-preferred hand. On line #1 write your full name as quickly as you would if you were using your preferred hand. What did it feel like to write with your other hand? Now place your pen or pencil in your preferred hand and write your full name on line #2.

#1 _____

#2 _____

Did you notice any difference? Of course you did! When most people do this simple exercise they say that using their less-preferred hand is more awkward, frustrating, takes more time and concentration, and has an inferior result.

That's the way it is with personality type. When we're forced to face certain tasks in life with one of our less-preferred and less-developed traits, the activity often feels more awkward, frustrating, takes more time and concentration, and often produces an inferior result.

Dick was an introvert and Judy was an extrovert. Dick liked to solve problems by going off by himself and thinking about them. Judy liked to solve problems by getting them out in the open and talking about them. For Dick to problem-solve by immediately talking about it or for Judy to problem-solve by going off by herself to think about it was at best difficult and at worst impossible.

Having a mature, healthy relationship not only involves being able to see things from our own perspective, but also being able to see through the eyes of others. Someone once said that, "If the only tool you have in your tool chest is a hammer, you will tend to see every problem as a nail." If the only language you speak is your own, if you're only able to see things from your point of view, if your way almost always seems like the "right" way, then you're in for some difficult times.

As you can see from the diagram above, each of the eight traits has a letter associated with it. Your preference on each one of the four categories is indicated by a letter and your four letters are considered your personality type.

The first letter will always be an E or an I. The second letter will always be either an S or an N. The third letter will always be either a T or an F. The last letter will always be either a J or a P. If you count up the various combinations you will find that there are sixteen different personality types, made up of an individual's preferences on each of the four major categories.

ISTJ	ISFJ	INFJ	INTJ
ISTP	ISFP	INFP	INTP
ESTP	ESFP	ENFP	ENTP
ESTJ	ESFJ	ENFJ	ENTJ

Our personality can be better understood as we consider how all four preferences work together, how they modify each other, and how they interact to create the unique person that is you.

When I first came across the concept of personality type I thought it was simplistic. But as I've used these insights for the past fifteen years I've been amazed at how helpful they can be. Personality type can be an invaluable aid in navigating the minefield of the differences between you and your mate.

In the next two chapters we're going to get better acquainted with Dick and Judy through the eyes of personality type. You'll discover how understanding their personality preferences helped them to change and be used by God to change each other. You will probably be surprised at how practical these insights are, and how easily they can be applied to your own marriage relationship.

The purpose of the next two chapters is to help you understand and appreciate some of the differences between you and your mate. As you understand your partner's unique design it will be easier for you to know what can be changed, accept what can't or shouldn't be changed, and be available to God to be used in your partner's life to help develop his or her potential.

As you continue to read, you will discover some differences that influence your relationship every day. You will find there are important differences in how people perceive or take in information, how they make decisions, whether they are energized by being with people or being alone, and how they choose to organize their outer world.

These chapters will help you see how the very differences that discourage and divide can be used of God to complete you as a couple and work for you to help you see and live and experience life in a richer way. It can not only help you clarify who you are, but you can find creative ways to fit together, understand each other, and live in harmony.

HOW'D THEY DO IT?

"I'll admit I'm not the most open person to change. But I guess I've changed quite a bit. I'd like to think it was all my decision and my choice to change, but in reality, Bill was the instigator. And part of it was that he believed I could change and he created a safe atmosphere to do some things differently. It was OK if I failed.

"I had some frustrations in both business and social gatherings. I tended to be too accommodating with others and often I would end up regretting my decisions. When I talked them over in advance with Bill, he asked me a question I've now learned to ask myself. 'Is what I want at this time what I *really* want or what I think I should want to make others happy?' Since he worked with me on that, I've changed my responses to others.

"When we went out socially, I always felt pressure to talk with everyone and make sure they were having a good time. It was really draining and I'd come back from parties or dinners at church second-guessing myself and wishing I hadn't gone. Bill started asking me the question, 'Are you having a good time? If not, why not?' during such an event and it really got me thinking. He also asked me, 'Are these people really expecting you to do all you do or are these your own expectations?'

"Sometimes those questions irritated me, but in his gentle way Bill forced me to challenge my beliefs and then evaluate them. I've learned that I was making a lot of unfounded assumptions as well. Yes, I've changed, but I have to give Bill a lot of credit."

TAKE ACTION

Before you jump into the next chapter you may find it helpful to take a short quiz to help you identify what your own preferences are.[5]

Word Choice Quiz[6]

Here are thirty-six word pairs. In most cases, one word of each pair will seem more like your style than the other one.

Number a sheet of paper from 1 to 36. (It will be easier to find your score if you make two columns, just as the word pairs are given.) Write down the letter of the word you prefer in each pair.

| 1. a. people | 2. a. structure | 3. a. forest | 4. a. mercy |
| b. places | b. freedom | b. trees | b. justice |

| 5. a. reflect | 6. a. organized | 7. a. broad | 8. a. curious |
| b. act | b. flexible | b. deep | b. decisive |

| 9. a. facts | 10. a. head | 11. a. observant | 12. a. enthusiastic |
| b. possibilities | b. heart | b. imaginative | b. consistent |

| 13. a. party | 14. a. plan | 15. a. theoretical | 16. a. question |
| b. library | b. improvise | b. practical | b. answer |

| 17. a. private | 18. a. work | 19. a. write | 20. a. cool |
| b. public | b. play | b. speak | b. warm |

| 21. a. city | 22. a. manager | 23. a. contented | 24. a. truth |
| b. forest | b. entrepreneur | b. restless | b. tact |

| 25. a. production | 26. a. order | 27. a. look | 28. a. values |
| b. design | b. harmony | b. leap | b. logic |

| 29. a. insightful | 30. a. fair | 31. a. change | 32. a. start |
| b. sensible | b. kind | b. conserve | b. finish |

| 33. a. tortoise | 34. a. relational | 35. a. discuss | 36. a. process |
| b. hare | b. analytical | b. consider | b. outcome |

Key

1. After each number, circle the letter of the answer you chose.
2. For each vertical column (E, I, S, etc.), count the number of circled letters and write the total in the space provided below.
3. Notice that the vertical columns are arranged in four groups of two: E/I, S/N, T/F, and J/P. Take the letter with the highest total in each group and write it at the bottom of the chart ("My Personality Type Code"). For example, if you circled 3 E-answers and 6 I-answers, write an I in the first space.

4. To understand what your four-letter code means, read the next two chapters!

	E	I	S	N			T	F	J	P
1.	a	b				2.			a	b
3.			b	a		4.	b	a		
5.	b	a				6.			a	b
7.	a	b				8.			b	a
9.			a	b		10.	a	b		
11.			a	b		12.	b	a		
13.	a	b				14.			a	b
15.			b	a		16.			b	a
17.	b	a				18.			a	b
19.	b	a				20.	a	b		
21.	a	b				22.			a	b
23.			a	b		24.	a	b		
25.			a	b		26.	a	b		
27.	b	a				28.	b	a		
29.			b	a		30.	a	b		
31.			b	a		32.			b	a
33.			a	b		34.	b	a		
35.	a	b				36.			b	a

TOTALS

(E: ___ I: ___)   (S: ___ N: ___).   (T: ___ F: ___)   (J: ___ P: ___)

My Probable Personality Type Code: __   __   __   __

(E/I)   (S/N)   (T/F)   (J/P)

CHAPTER SEVEN

How'd You Reach *That* Conclusion?

Gary J. Oliver

In the next two chapters we'll be following the story of Dick and Judy, the couple I introduced in chapter 6. As we discuss each of the four basic personality functions—sensing, intuiting, thinking, and feeling—we'll be looking at these preferences through the eyes of one couple. However, you won't have to read very far before you will start to see yourself, your mate, and probably a lot of other people you know.

As you read through the various preferences we encourage you to not only look at the distinctives of each preference, but also at the ways in which the opposites can actually complement and balance each other.

DID WE MAKE A MISTAKE?

"We hadn't been married for more than twenty-four hours when I knew we were going to have problems," Judy said. I had asked Dick and Judy when some of their differences first came to the surface. Before I finished the question Judy jumped in with her response.

"We had spent our first night together as husband and wife and were on our way to Canada for our honeymoon. I was so excited. This was my first full day as Dick's wife. It was my dream come true.

I was overwhelmed and excited about our ten-day honeymoon together. And I wanted to talk about it."

Judy went on to explain that as she became more enthused, Dick got quieter and quieter. "After about an hour I asked if something was wrong," Judy said. Dick replied that "No, nothing is wrong. I just feel a bit overwhelmed right now." Judy became concerned and asked, "Is there something wrong?" After what seemed to Judy to be an uncomfortably long pause Dick replied, "No, nothing's wrong. I think I just need some space, some time to think."

Judy immediately became alarmed. Why didn't he want to talk about their wonderful wedding and all the things they were going to do on their honeymoon? Was Dick afraid he had made a mistake? Was he not excited about spending time with Judy? Why did this man who had so eagerly made conversation during their courtship suddenly seem like he was withdrawing? This was the first of many differences that began to make their appearance.

Many couples have had similar experiences on their honeymoon. During the dating period and even during courtship, it seems like we have so much in common. We spend hours and hours doing things together, talking on the phone, writing to one another. Then we get married and it doesn't take long to realize we also have a lot of differences.

When Dick and Judy took the Myers-Briggs Type Indicator they came out as exact opposites on all four of the categories. "Well, that sure explains it," Dick said with dejected resignation. "I guess there's not much hope."

After a brief pause I replied, "On the contrary. There's a lot of hope. You and Judy have great potential to complement each other, to balance each other out. God can use the differences that seem so contradictory to complement each other. It's just a matter of both of you taking the time to understand your differences and to learn how to speak each other's language."

HOW WE TAKE IN INFORMATION— SENSING OR INTUITION

"Dick and I can go to the same social event and talk to the same people. But when we discuss those conversations on the way home you'd think we had been at two different places," Judy said. Dick jumped in with, "The first year of our marriage was extremely frustrating for me. I wanted to discuss the details of a conversation we had both been a part of and Judy acted as if it was new information to her."

As Dick began to understand some of their basic personality differences he realized that since he prefers the sensing function, when he hears a conversation he automatically listens for the facts—the details. In fact, he thrives on them.

Judy, however, is an intuitive. When she's involved in a discussion, she automatically listens for the big picture. "I may not remember all the specifics, but I can tell you where the person is coming from, what some of their values are, and if they can be trusted."

At any given time we are either taking in information or making decisions based on the way we receive information. Sensing and Intuition are two different ways of perceiving or gathering information.

Detail people (sensers) are influenced more by what they actually see, hear, touch, taste, and smell than by the possibilities of what might be. They are not necessarily more sensible or sensitive. Dick is a senser. While he uses his intuitive function, he prefers or is better at sensing. He has a here-and-now orientation. He is very observant and pays attention to detail. He stays focused on the task at hand and prefers to deal with things that are practical. He is the kind of person who, as a child, always colored within the lines and was proud of it!

The possibility people (intuitives) process information by way of a sixth sense or hunch. They rely strongly on their intuition. Judy is a possibility person. While she uses her sensing function, she prefers or is better at intuition. She has more of a future orientation. When she was in school, there were times she found it hard to concentrate on what the teacher was saying because she was thinking about the possibilities and options of a previous statement. She can get bored with details or mundane tasks. She loves to create. As a child, when she would color, she wasn't too concerned about staying within the lines. She looks at what is and imagines what might be.

The difference between sensing and intuition is critical to relationships because the way in which we gather information and the kind of information we pick up provides the raw material for how we look at life, the issues we need to address, and how we address those issues. The way we receive information is the starting point for almost everything else we do.

Failure to understand and appreciate the differences between sensing and intuition can negatively affect a relationship. Why? Because couples who don't understand and value this difference have a difficult time developing much intimacy. Poor communication is one of the most basic barriers to closeness.

How do sensers and intuitives differ in their communication? When Dick is asked a question he usually gives a specific answer. When Judy is asked a question she usually gives a more general answer and tends to answer several other questions at the same time. Consider the following sensing-intuitive (S/N) conversation based on a relatively simple request:

S: "What time is it?"

N: "It's late!"

S: (somewhat surprised): "What time is it?"

N: (insistent): "It's time to go!"

S: (getting impatient): "Hey, read my lips! I asked what time it is!"

N: (equally impatient): "It's past three."

S: (exasperated): "Close, but no cigar! I shouldn't have to ask a simple question four times to get a close answer."

N: (perturbed, because he believes he answered correctly the first time): "You shouldn't be so picky."[1]

Dave and Jan Stoop have made the helpful observation that many intuitives have a difficult time finishing their sentences. "Ideas run through their minds so quickly that, before they can finish a sentence, they're on to a new thought. Sometimes two intuitive people who have known each other well for a number of years can talk together, and an outsider who is listening may think that neither of them ever completes a thought. Yet they understand each other perfectly. It's as if they speak a private code."[2]

Several years ago I was leading a workshop for pastors and church counselors on the Myers-Briggs Type Indicator (MBTI) in Denver. A carload of six people drove down from a small town in Wyoming. As I was finishing my discussion on the differences between sensers and intuitives one of them started laughing. In fact, she was laughing so loud everyone turned around to look at her.

"Now I know why I thought I was going crazy," she blurted out. "I prefer sensing but I've just spent four hours riding in a car with five intuitives. They jumped from topic to topic, didn't complete their sentences, brought in information that seemed to me to be totally irrelevant to the topic, whatever it was, that was being discussed." The rest of the grouped cracked up and the others who preferred sensing began to nod their heads.

"What was the most frustrating part of it?" I asked her. "Well," she paused, "it seemed like it all made sense to them, like the pieces fit. It seemed as if they all thought this was the normal way to communicate." Like the good intuitive I am, I paused, looked her straight in the eyes, smiled and said, "Well, isn't it?" The answer from the intuitive is yes. The equally valid answer from the senser is a resounding no. Before I could move on to the next part of the workshop she added, "Well, now that I understand this the trip home won't be nearly as frustrating or painful as the trip down here."

Frustrating. Painful. Those are apt descriptions (I've heard even more colorful ones) of what it can be like to try to communicate with someone with an opposite preference. Especially if you don't understand the differences. I hope it's becoming clearer to you that if you want to be effective in helping your partner change and grow, you've got to understand how to speak the appropriate language. What are some other distinctives of the senser and the intuitive?

Those who prefer sensing tend to be much more literal in their communication. They stick with the topic. They answer what they've been asked. It's not too difficult to stay on track in a conversation between two sensers. The Stoops have observed that while sensers end their sentences with a period, intuitives are more likely to end their sentences with a dash—there's always room for more.[3]

One of the easiest ways to determine if a person prefers sensing or intuition is to ask directions. The senser will give you specific details. "Go four miles north, make a right turn on Hampden Avenue, go seven blocks east and make a right on University (it's the second stop light), and it's the fourth house on your right."

If you ask someone who has a strong preference for intuition, they first have to stop and try to remember where they are. Once they get their bearings they'll give you their version of how to get there: "Go north toward the mall, and then after you pass Wendy's you'll want to make a right; I think it's the fourth or fifth street. Anyway, after you make a right you'll go past an elementary school, or maybe it's a junior high school... anyway, you'll go over two speed bumps, and watch out for the second one, I scraped the bottom of my car on it the last time I drove over it. Let's see, where are we? OK, after you've gone past the second speed bump look on the righthand side of the street for a kind of Cape Cod-looking house, make a right on the street after the one with the Cape Cod on the corner and their home is in the middle of that block. I'm pretty sure it's on the righthand side. They have a huge oak tree in the middle of their front yard so you can't miss it."

What a difference between those two descriptions! If a senser gives another senser directions, the second senser will usually get there. If an intuitive gives a senser directions and doesn't take into account their need for the specifics, the senser may end up lost for hours.

Another important difference between a senser and an intuitive is that when intuitives describe something, they often experience what they are describing. Many intuitives enjoy planning a trip as much as actually going on the trip. I worked with one couple where the husband, Tom, preferred intuition and his wife Bridget preferred sensing. Early in their marriage Tom described to her a fantasy he had held for many years. As you read this conversation remember that Bridget had never been out of the United States but Tom had traveled and studied in Europe and the Middle East on several different occasions.

Tom described to her his dream of getting together with two or three other couples, flying to Amsterdam, buying two used camper vans, and driving around the world. He described what it would be like to drive along the Rhine river, to visit Paris, to see the beauty of northern Italy, to lie on the beaches of the Greek islands, to visit Israel, and on and on. The more he talked the more excited he got as he described the beauty of the places they could visit. "As I was talking I could visualize Bridget and me actually walking along the beaches together, or standing by the garden tomb in Jerusalem."

When he finished he turned to his wife, eager to see her equally enthusiastic response, and said, "Well honey, isn't that exciting? What do you think?" Later he told me that as soon as those words came out of his mouth he knew he had asked the wrong question. His wife's face was pale and she looked panicked. "Well, that's interesting," Bridget responded. "But we'll never be able to afford it. And how will we communicate in all of those different languages? And what if someone gets sick? And what if one of the vans breaks down; you don't know how to fix anything."

Her husband turned to me and said, "With her response she didn't just rain on my parade. A sink-hole opened up and sucked my entire parade into it. I couldn't believe it. She had missed the entire point."

Do you see what happened here? Tom shared his dream in a typical intuitive fashion. If Bridget had understood Tom's language she would have known she didn't need to take what he was saying too seriously, and that all he wanted to do was to share his dream with her.

At the end of the conversation Tom felt frustrated and discouraged. Bridget felt overwhelmed. Why? Simply because they didn't understand each other's language and didn't know how to communicate and listen in ways consistent with their spouse's preferences.

To help you better understand the differences between these two different yet equally valuable ways of taking in information, I've prepared two different lists. As you read through the lists, you can note some of the important differences. Which of these describe you? Which describe your spouse?

SENSING	INTUITION
Looks at specific parts and pieces.	Looks at the broad overall patterns and all of the possible and probable relationships between the specific parts and pieces.
Focuses on the immediate, enjoying what's there.	Focuses on the future, enjoys the anticipation of all the exciting and important things that might be.
Prefers handling practical matters.	Prefers imagining all of the potential possibilities for themselves, their family, friends, their world, and even other worlds.
Asks "Will it work?"	Asks "Is it possible? If so, what do we need to do? If not, why not? And who says why not?"

Likes things that are definite and measurable.	Likes opportunities for being inventive and if not given the opportunity will go ahead and do it anyway.
Starts at the beginning and takes one step at a time.	Isn't sure where the beginning is, doesn't think it's important, jumps in anywhere, leaps over steps, and doesn't usually know that they've skipped anything.
Enjoys reading instructions and notices details.	Skips instructions and follows hunches, until they've tried two or three times and can't figure it out. Then they either call an "S" friend for help or, as a last-gasp effort, look at the instructions, if they can find them.
Can't see the forest for the trees.	Can't see the trees for the forest, in fact, they may not even be looking at the forest that is in front of them because no matter where they are their mind may be somewhere else.
Likes set procedures, established routine.	Likes frequent change and variety. They may have come up with three or four different ways to come home from work because it's too boring to come home the same way every day.
Looks for the evidence.	Looks for the potential, the possibilities, the options, the way to take what isn't and bring it to pass, the way to find new solutions to old problems.
They may seem too practical, boring and literal-minded to N's.	They may seem like fickle and impractical dreamers to S's.

Did you notice anything different about these two lists? An S would love the list on the left. It is precise, concise, and specific. An N would appreciate the list on the right. It was written by an intuitive for intuitives. It is much more creative and expansive. It may wander a bit but that makes it even better.

Go back over each of these two lists and imagine what it would be like to have one preference but to be raised in a home where you were expected to be the total opposite. Imagine what it would be like to be an intuitive child who was talked to and expected to act like a senser. What would the message be? Would there tend to be more miscommunication and conflict? Would you tend to feel misunderstood and out of place? Would you be more likely to think something was wrong with you? Would you wonder if God had made a mistake?

HOW TO INFLUENCE A SENSER

Start with the details, then move to the big picture. Intuitives start with the forest and then maybe get to talking about the trees. Sensers work best when they have the specifics, then it's much easier for them to make sense of the big picture. Start with what they can see, then move to what they can't see.

Be factual and specific. Don't ramble. Show an appreciation for their love of detail but don't overwhelm them with too much information. Remember that intuitives tend to communicate with a dash rather than a period. If you want to increase the probability that the senser will both hear you and understand what you want to say, learn how to end your sentences with a period. If you want something done, tell them the why, when, where, who, and the how of the task. And be sure to let them know when you are changing subjects.

Let them know how you want them to listen. Do you remember the frustration Tom and Bridget experienced when he shared his dream of driving around the world with her? He would have been much more successful, and she would have been much less frustrated, if he had started by saying something like, "Bridget, I've had this dream for a long time. I know it may not be very practical and I don't know if or when we would ever be able to do it, but I'd love to share it with you."

Do you see how helpful that would be? Now, Bridget knows how to listen. She doesn't need to be concerned about all of the details and specifics. She doesn't need to wonder if Tom wants to leave on this trip within the next month. She knows that to a great degree he is simply thinking out loud with her. And because she loves him, she wants him to share his dreams with her. Even outrageous ones like this.

Use concrete examples. Sometimes intuitives can paint a picture with such a broad stroke that the senser isn't sure what they mean. By giving concrete examples you are able to make sure that the message you intended to send is the same message your partner receives.

One day Judy came back from a home show and said to Dick, "With all the entertaining we do I think we need to expand our living room and possibly add an extra bedroom onto the back of the house." His initial response was negative. He said, "Oh no! Here she goes again." Judy immediately picked up his negative response, "You never like any of my ideas. If you had your way everything would stay the same." What had started as an innocent conversation turned into a major disagreement with Judy feeling hurt and Dick feeling frustrated.

After teaching them some of the insights of personality type I asked Judy to replay that conversation. "How might you communicate the same message to Dick using his 'native tongue'?" After a few moments of thought she turned to her husband and said, "Dick, I just came back from the home show. I saw a home with a living room the same shape as ours only a bit wider. It is shaped something like Jim and Donna's and it has a window seat. I also got the idea that it would be nice if someday we could add an extra bedroom downstairs on the back of the house. Nothing too big, maybe the size of Tim's room. That way when my folks or some of our friends came to visit they wouldn't have to be upstairs with the family."

When Judy replayed that conversation, Dick responded, "That's much better." "What was 'better' about it?" Judy asked. "Well, you didn't sound so intense, like this was something you really wanted to do and had to do immediately." He continued, "I got the sense that this is something you would like but it sounded like you were thinking out loud with me rather than expressing an immediate expectation."

Show a senser in specific ways that what you are talking about is realistic and workable. One of the most frustrating differences between a senser and intuitive is that it's easy for the intuitive to forget that the senser doesn't get excited about possibilities. In fact they can feel overwhelmed by them. What energizes an intuitive can overwhelm a senser. They are more interested in and more secure with what is practical. If you want to communicate your dream, do it in such a way that the senser can understand how it might work.

Now that those of you who prefer the intuitive function have some hints on how to influence a senser, here's a list for those of you who prefer sensing.

HOW TO INFLUENCE AN INTUITIVE

Start with the big picture. Remember that the intuitive language is enthusiastic and imaginative. Feed their imaginations. Remember, they like to see the forest and not just the trees. Try to show how the specifics relate to the big picture. If the intuitive forgets some of the facts it's not necessarily intentional. Intuitives are more likely to remember the facts if they are tied to the big picture.

If you want to get their attention, point out an interesting possibility or ask some questions. Asking questions taps into their possibility banks. When they're into their possibility mode don't constantly correct them with the exact details unless that information is critical for the discussion.

When they ask you to do something make sure they clarify exactly what they want. Don't assume that what they really want to communicate is contained in the exact words they've used. It's common for intuitives to think they've given more specifics than they really have. If you need more specific information (and many times you will), just ask for it. Don't criticize or shame intuitives because they don't think like you do.

Don't overwhelm them with details. When intuitives ask, "What did you do today?" they're not asking for a breakdown of everything you did in fifteen-minute intervals. They're more likely to want a general sense of what you did.

Don't be afraid to let them jump into the future. In fact, one of the ways you can love intuitives is to dream with them. Once Dick understood that Judy didn't want to attempt major reconstruction on the house he no longer had to "put the brakes on" her ideas. He was free to encourage her imagination. It's OK for a senser to want to have a string on the kite of the intuitive's imagination. However, if you understand how God has made intuitives and how their minds work, you will be able to give them a lot of string.

IT'S TIME TO MAKE A DECISION!—THINKING OR FEELING

Dick and Judy experienced the effects of their differences in decision-making when Judy suggested to Dick they go off on a weekend retreat to get away from the home-life pressures and focus on their relationship. Dick didn't hear the "why" behind Judy's suggestion; he didn't hear her concern for him and for their relationship.

The first thing Dick did was consult his budget and checkbook balance. Based on what he saw there he made a unilateral decision that they couldn't really afford it and so the retreat was out of the question.

What started out as a simple request for some special time together suddenly became another stand-off between two frustrated and misunderstood people. They were divided by two different ways of making a decision. Each wanted the other to understand unspoken thoughts, but they weren't trying to understand each other.

When it comes to making decisions, people prefer either the thinking function or the feeling function. Whenever we make decisions we utilize both the thinking and feeling functions but we prefer or are better at one or the other. Those who prefer the thinking function tend to decide on the basis of linear logic and objective considerations. Those who prefer the feeling function decide more on the basis of personal, subjective values.

To a great degree, it is a person's preference on the thinking-feeling dimension, not whether they are male or female, that determines whether they will be seen as tough-minded or tenderhearted. These are the only preferences where there is a difference between male and female. Approximately 60 percent of males prefer thinking with 40 percent preferring feeling; about 60 percent of women prefer feeling with 40 percent preferring thinking.

Dick prefers the thinking function. When he is asked to do something he's likely to ask why. It's not that he's being rebellious. He is not cold and unemotional. He simply prefers to make decisions based on reasons. He wants to know why; "just because" is not an acceptable answer for him.

At times Dick wonders why Judy gets "so emotional." If someone disagrees with Dick he's likely to want to know what the reasons are. Sometimes he can be so matter-of-fact that he comes across as cold and uncaring. But that's not true. Underneath that seemingly cold and logical exterior is a tender and sensitive man. However, honesty and fairness are very important to him. He tends to see things as black or white, right or wrong. There aren't a lot of gray areas.

Judy's preferred decision-making function is feeling. Feeling refers to a person- or value-centered decision-making process. It doesn't necessarily mean she is more emotional or illogical. While Dick tends to approach problems in an objective manner Judy's preferred approach is more subjective. Judy "thinks" as well as Dick does, but as a person who prefers feeling she simply incorporates different values into the decision-making process. If someone disagrees with Judy she will often let it go because of her desire to maintain harmony.

When it comes to making a decision Judy will weigh heavily the feelings of others. It's easy for her to put herself in someone else's shoes. She's concerned about how what she does will affect others. At times she's so concerned about others that she forgets to take care of her own needs.

When Judy is asked to do something in a situation she doesn't understand, she's more likely to do what is asked out of her desire to please. Spouses who prefer the feeling process can be especially sensitive to the emotional climate in the home. Constant conflict can lead to emotional and even physical problems.

Dr. David Stoop describes the difference this way:

> The thinking person uses pro-and-con lists in order to arrive at the best decision. The feeling person will probably make a bad decision if he or she relies only on factual information. The feeling person needs to look at the values and emotions involved in order to make a good decision. The way we handle our emotions is related to our preference on this trait, even though the trait has nothing directly to do with emotions. Those who score on the thinking side are often uncomfortable talking about the area of feelings. They may also not be as comfortable in the area of aesthetics and the cultivation of relationships. To others, they appear cool and aloof; sometimes they are accused of having ice in their veins, even though they are very sensitive.
>
> Feeling persons, on the other hand, can be quite comfortable in the area of emotions. They are usually aware of what they're

feeling and can tune in to what others around them are feeling as well. When they make a decision, they're concerned about how it will affect the others involved.[4]

Let's look at how these important differences might affect a thinker and feeler as they try to make a decision about letting their teenager use the family car. Early in the week they had promised their daughter she could take the car to a party on Friday night. However, an unexpected snowstorm developed and the roads had become dangerous. This new "data" meant that their earlier decision had to be reevaluated. Otto Kroeger and Janet M. Thuesen illustrate how the thinking dad and feeling mom arrive at the same conclusion using their different decision-making preferences.

Arguments for Letting Her Use the Car:

Thinker: "We can each learn a lesson from this. Parenting involves learning how to take risks and growing up requires learning how to take responsibility. Parenting involves training yourself to let go and this will be good practice for letting go when she is no longer under this roof. According to my calculations, the risks here are outweighed by the benefits of the learning experience."

Feeler: "How would I feel if the car was indiscriminately snatched out from under me without any regard for my personal feelings? She will feel embarrassed if she has to call her friends and ask for a ride when she was going to be one of the drivers. If I were she I would be crushed and understandably so. There's no way I could be so insensitive."

Arguments Against Letting Her Use the Car:

Thinker: "Parenting is a tough role and difficult decisions must be made. They are not always decisions everyone likes, and sometimes they lead to temporary unhappiness. However, I am not called upon as a parent to be liked or to make others happy. As a parent I must make responsible decisions that reflect a competent role model and that are in the best interests of everyone."

Feeler: "I remember when I was a teenager, one of the ways my parents told me they loved me was not to always give me what I wanted. Even though I felt crushed and wounded at the time, when I got over it I really felt as though they cared about me enough to look out for my best interests. The only loving thing to do is not let her use the car."[5]

Let's take a look at two lists that summarize some of the more significant differences between two important and equally valuable ways of making decisions. As you read through each list you will probably see some statements in both lists that describe you. However you will also find that one list feels much more like "home base" for you.

THINKERS	FEELERS
Decide with the head.	Decide with the heart.
Decide by linear logic.	Decide by personal convictions.
Concerned for truth and justice.	Concerned with relationships and harmony.
Need to understand emotions before they experience them.	Need to experience emotions before they understand them.
More firm-minded.	More gentle-hearted.
Experience life as on-looker from outside a situation.	Experience life as a participant, from inside a situation.
Take a long view.	Take an immediate and personal view.
Spontaneously find flaws and criticize.	Spontaneously appreciate and praise.
Can speak the truth but but not always in love.	Can have difficulty speaking the truth if it might hurt someone's feelings.
Want to understand intimacy.	Want to experience intimacy.

Can be a "romantic" yet not be romantic.	Love courtship and romance.
Naturals at analyzing plans.	Naturals at understanding people.
May have the gift of justice.	May have the gift of mercy.
See things in black and white.	See a lot of gray areas.
May seem cold and condescending to F's.	May seem fuzzy-minded and emotional to T's.

What are some of the benefits of understanding your partner's decision-making preferences and your own? What are some possible consequences of not understanding your partner's preferences or your own?

Go back over each of these word lists and imagine what it would be like to have one preference but live in a home where you were expected to be the total opposite. Imagine what it would be like to be a feeling person who was talked to and expected to act like a thinker. What would the message be? Would there tend to be more miscommunication and conflict? Would you tend to feel misunderstood and out of place? Would you be more likely to think something was wrong with you? Would you wonder if God had made a mistake?

HOW TO INFLUENCE A THINKER

Explain yourself clearly, logically, and concisely. Thinkers often want to know the "why." Give them the reasons before they ask for them. As Judy began to understand Dick's preference for the thinking function, Dick helped her to change the way she asked for things.

Rather than asking for "some extra money for this afternoon" she learned it was more helpful to Dick if she would list two or three of the items she wanted to purchase or why she needed them. Dick said, "I really appreciated it when Judy told me, 'Tim's soccer practice is this afternoon and he's grown out of the shoes he used the last two years. I'm going to buy some new shoes and socks and will probably order his new uniform.'" He continued, "She doesn't need to get my permission to spend the money or to justify her purchases. I just appreciate the specific information." Most T's would say the same thing.

Another important part of this first point is to define your terms. For an F, the statement "I love you" doesn't need any definition. It speaks for itself. For a T, the same simple statement can mean any number of things. "Exactly what do you mean when you say 'I love you'?" Many F's would need to ask that question. Most T's can't help but ask it.

Listen for what T's say before attempting to interpret how they said it. I've led workshops on the MBTI for over ten years. When I ask T's to list some of the things that frustrate them about communicating with F's, there is one that's always in the top two or three. One man summarized his frustration by saying: "If we are in the middle of an intense discussion, my wife will frequently ignore *what* I was talking about and take a detour to discuss *how* I said it. Most of the time we get sidetracked and never finish dealing with the initial issue."

Dick expressed the same frustration in one of our sessions. He was starting to "open up" and share some of his concerns. After a few minutes Judy jumped in and criticized him for how he had worded a certain statement. "I don't know how you can talk about something so sensitive in such a callous way." As soon as the words came out of her mouth I knew Dick would respond.

"Can we ever have a discussion without you commenting on 'how' I said something?" Dick said with a great deal of intensity. He looked directly at Judy and continued, "For once I'd like you to try to understand 'what' I'm saying before you jump in trying to interpret what I might have meant by 'how' I said it!"

Don't personalize what a T says or how they say it. Because they make decisions based on reason and logic they may not always think of how it may affect people. That doesn't mean they don't care about people. It's just that the care and compassion may get expressed in other ways.

Be especially careful not to automatically personalize their criticism. T's are the most critical of all the types. Many T's express affection by caring enough to make a critical observation that will help the other person be more accurate or more effective.

Encourage their feeling side. Help them find labels for what they are feeling. Most T's value precision and if you help them become more accurate in "what" they say they will be grateful. Remember that, in many ways, T's and F's have a different vocabulary. It's not a matter of eliminating your vocabulary, it's more a matter of expanding your vocabulary and helping your partner's to expand, too.

Try to be calm and objective. As we were discussing some of the differences between those who prefer feeling and those who prefer thinking Dick said, "Judy complains that I don't share very much. I'm afraid to talk with Judy about things because I'm afraid she'll become so emotional about it I'll have to deal with the emotional response as well as the original problem. Sometimes I don't have the energy to deal with my own emotions let alone somebody else's."

I understand that if a subject is emotionally intense it may be hard to keep your cool, but if the conversation becomes too emotionally charged, or if you start using overgeneralizations like "you always" or "you never," most T's will "check out" of the conversation. They'll be looking at you but you'll know they're not really there with you.

By this time it's easy to see how helpful these practical suggestions can be. Now let's turn to some ways in which those who prefer the thinking function can influence those whose decision-making process favors the feeling function.

HOW TO INFLUENCE THE FEELER

Provide plenty of verbal affirmation. Most F's thrive on praise and encouragement. Take the time to notice and comment on little things that tell them they're important and valuable to you. Be sure to compliment them on who they are and not just on what they do.

Remember that the language of an F is in some ways different from the language of a T. Attempt to be more animated, warm, real. Put a bit more of yourself into the conversation. Begin some sentences with the words, "I feel," or "I was really excited when." One couple described it this way. "As a T, I usually communicate in black and white. My F spouse is more likely to communicate in color." What is the color? It's the passion, the intensity, the emotion, the personal, the sharing of self, the moving beyond abstract ideas to how they might affect the people involved.

Also be sensitive about your use of criticism. What may be nothing more than an intellectually aerobic debate to a T may be wounding and discouraging to an F. Most T's view criticism as an important step in finding the best solution. They often subject their plans to an uncompromising examination that uncovers all flaws in their data or logic. What may work great with data and logic may lay an egg with relationships. Many T's are good at sarcasm and put-downs. In fact I know many male T's who express affection by saving their best put-downs for those they care about the most. Trust me! This is not the love language of feelers.

Don't underestimate the value of "small talk." To most F's there is no such thing as small talk. When they share their day with you they aren't just down-loading a list of data. They are giving you a part of themselves. If you appear bored with what they're saying you may unconsciously translate it to mean you are bored with them.

When Dick and Judy were dating they shared all kinds of details about their days. "After we were married Dick suddenly became the master of the one-word or one-sentence response."

Dick replied, as if a light had gone on, "That's just the way I think. I guess I thought I didn't want to bore you with the mundane details of my day."

Judy turned to Dick and said, "When you take the time to share some of the things of your day that may seem boring and insignificant to you, it tells me I'm important to you. It helps me understand what you're going through and how I can better pray for and support you. It's not as much what you did that's important. It's that you did them and how it affected you."

Don't listen to how logical their reasons are for what they are saying but for what they are feeling. Ask questions that draw them out. Ask open questions that require more than a one-word response. Then listen. When you think you've understood, ask one more question... then respond.

Listen for the message behind the message. Learn to listen for what they mean and not just what they said. For feelers a conversation is more than an exchange of information. It is sharing lives and hearts. It is giving a part of the self. I've worked with countless couples who are stuck in the rut of being separated by the same language. If one prefers thinking and the other prefers feeling it's common for the F to express the frustration that, "They just don't listen to what I'm saying."

I'm sure you won't be surprised to know that Dick and Judy experienced this common problem. When Judy talked to Dick he worked hard to listen and pay attention to her. If she misused a word or got one fact wrong he would jump in and correct her. At times Judy would respond by saying something a bit different from what she had originally said. Dick would respond, "But honey, that's not what you said." Judy would immediately reply, "Well, it's what I meant."

LOOKING AT THE COMBINATIONS

As Dick and Judy went through the descriptions of each preference category I could see lights coming on, illuminating their understanding of themselves and each other. While understanding the individual traits is important, it is also valuable to understand how they interact with each other when combined. What happens when your preference for sensing or intuition and thinking or feeling are combined?

In chapter 6 we talked about the value of understanding how our various preferences work together to influence who we are, what we do, and how we interact with each other. Before going on to look at the final two personality preference categories, it will be helpful to look at the ways in which our preferences in the perceiving functions and the deciding functions combine to affect who we are and how we come across.

So far we've discussed the two perceiving functions, sensing and intuition, and the two deciding functions, thinking and feeling. That means that at this point we have the possibility for four different personality patterns:

1. sensing and thinking (ST)
2. sensing and feeling (SF)
3. intuition and thinking (NT)
4. intuition and feeling (NF)

Dr. Gary Harbaugh has written a practical book that many couples have found helpful in understanding and appreciating these four combinations. In *God's Gifted People* he observes that each of the four types have a special "gift" to give to others.[6]

The ST is a person who prefers sensing and thinking. Dr.

Harbaugh says that these folks have the gift of practicality. They are well equipped to live in the here and now, to make decisions based on specific facts, to handle technical tasks. They are often the ones who will stand firm for traditional values. In a marriage relationship the ST has the skills to keep the marriage on track.

SF people prefer sensing and feeling. They have the gift of personal helpfulness. They have great potential for being able to notice the details and specifics of everyday life and apply them to build and encourage people. I've worked with some SF's who can intellectualize their emotions.

The NT is a person who prefers intuition and thinking. This person has the gift of looking ahead. NTs are inquisitive, ask a lot of questions, are open to new ideas, help others see the possibilities and the big picture, and can face changes logically. They have an insatiable quest for competence and can be the most critical of the four combinations. Some NT's may spend more time thinking about how much they love someone and too little time actually showing them.

The NF prefers intuition and feeling. These folks have the gift of possibilities for people. They often have the gift of encouragement. These are the teddy bears of life. They are always good for an individual or a group hug. They are insightful, thoughtful, look for the possibilities in people and relationships, value harmony and work hard to create it, and have an intense desire to grow. At times their need for harmony can keep them from making the tough decisions.

Now remember that nothing is wrong with any one of these combinations. Not one of them is better or more valuable than the others. Each one has some unique strengths or gifts. But when that uniqueness is not understood or appreciated, what has the potential to provide balance and harmony can also produce frustrating dissonance.

Can you imagine what it would be like for an ST to marry an NF? That's what happened with Dick and Judy. Before they understood these important differences, Dick's sensing kept bumping into Judy's intuition, and Judy's feeling kept getting stomped on by Dick's thinking. Not until we began discussing personality was Dick really able to acknowledge Judy's gift of possibilities for people and Judy saw Dick's gift of practicality.

In the next chapter we're going to look at the four attitudes, extroversion and introversion, judging and perceiving. If you think you've gained some insights in this chapter, you'll find that even more "lights come on" in the next.

HOW'D THEY DO IT?

"I was kind of puzzled about how to get my wife to even consider doing a few things differently that tended to bother me. But one day I read about an idea in a book on marriage and decided to try it. I probably changed it some, but it gave me some direction. We were having a cup of coffee one morning and I guess I floored her with what I said. I told Jill I needed her assistance on something. I told her I'd identified several things about myself that I thought were weaknesses or deficiencies and would like her feelings about them. I asked her if she could point out some others that I had missed. And right away she said I was overly picky and controlling. She was surprised when I agreed with her.

"I then asked what I should do and how I should express it when I had one of my picky concerns. Jill said it would help if I could make it more tentative or a request and then tell her why it's so important to me. I asked if it would help if I shared the degree of importance. She said no, just telling her what was important would help her be more open to considering the request. Also, she wanted the option to try it but also to return to the original way if she felt it didn't work. I figured this was better than not doing it at all. So I said yes. Jill also said it would help her if I complimented her efforts to try something new. I agreed and then said I would make it a point to be more positive overall. I guess we both made some changes and it's working."

TAKE ACTION

1. Before you start the next chapter I think you'll find it helpful to turn to Appendix B and complete The Marriage Type Identifier and The Marriage Type Verifier.[7] These two helpful tools were developed by David L. Luecke, author of *Marriage Types and Prescription for Marriage*.[8] He has graciously given us permission to include them as a resource in this book. They will not only help you confirm your preferences on the four functions but also better understand each one of the four combinations of type. Take a couple of minutes to complete them now.

CHAPTER EIGHT

You're Either an "In-y" or an "Out-y"

Gary J. Oliver

Do you remember Judy's story about the disappointment and frustration she experienced on the first full day of her honeymoon? If she had understood Dick's preference for introversion she wouldn't have been nearly as disappointed. And if Dick had understood Judy's preference for extroversion he wouldn't have felt "pressured" to talk.

I think that the terms *extroversion* and *introversion* may well be two of the most misunderstood words in our vocabulary. What do you think of when you hear the word *introvert*? Is your first response positive or negative? For most people (including introverts) their first response is more negative than positive. Introverts have been described as loners, wallflowers. On the other hand, extroverts have been described as loud, overbearing, obnoxious.

Extroversion and introversion are two different ways of relating to the world around us. The preference for one or the other identifies where we are most comfortable focusing our attention and where we are energized. Everyone uses extroversion and introversion, but each person prefers or is more comfortable with one over the other.

If you are an extrovert you are energized by people, action, and the things going on around you. You don't only focus on the outer world, you are energized by your contact with it. You don't necessarily talk more than introverts, and not all extroverts are party ani-mals. You simply draw energy and inspiration from the outer world of people and things.

If you are an introvert you are more likely to be drawn to the inner world of reflection. You like people and may have great com-munication skills, but you recharge when you are away from large groups of people. It's not that you like people any less than extro-verts. And it's not even that you talk less than extroverts. You simply feel uncomfortable spending a disproportionate amount of time "socializing" in the outer world. Extroverts can view introverts as unfriendly or cold, but this isn't necessarily true. An introvert's nat-ural, God-given design leads them to be energized by time alone. Thus, when they have to deal with people who may not be close or familiar to them, they may well feel like a fish out of water.

In the popular children's story, *The Little Prince,* Antoine de Saint-Exupéry describes how to tame a fox. This process was also illustrated in the recent movie *Dances with Wolves.* If an extrovert was the first to see the fox he would say to himself, "Oh boy, a fox! Wouldn't he make a great pet. I'd love to be his friend," and run right up to the fox. The fox, being wily yet cautious, would immedi-ately disappear into his hole. After all, he's never seen this boy before. How does he know what his intentions are?

Saint-Exupéry explains that the way to tame a fox is to go to a place a good way off from the fox and just sit there and wait. This gives the fox time to size you up from a safe distance. The next day go back and move a little closer. Sit there quietly and let the fox study you some more. If you patiently continue the process, each day sit-ting a bit closer, the fox will eventually have studied you enough to know and trust you. Over time you will have tamed the fox.

Mark A. Pearson writes that "Introverts need to be 'tamed' in the same way."[1] This dimension isn't a measure of how *much* a person talks, but much more *what* they talk about. While a hard-core extro-vert may self-disclose every one of his indiscretions in the first five minutes of a conversation, most introverts will need to know some-one for years before they will share what is most important to them.

Clearly, Judy prefers extroversion. She has an outgoing and bub-bly personality. She has a lot of friends at church and in her neigh-borhood and would much prefer being with several friends than being alone. She is stimulated by being with and doing things with people. She will approach strangers and immediately share her name, the names of her family members, and ask a personal question about the stranger. She is comfortable in the outer world. When she processes information she likes to talk about it. When Judy comes home after a busy day she will immediately want to have some friends over. If she can't do that she'll find someone to talk with on the phone. For an extreme extrovert it can be painful not to talk.

While Judy has a difficult time being alone, Dick loves to spend time by himself reading, thinking, or working on his computer. He is energized by being alone. Dick is friendly, likes people, and is a good communicator. But he doesn't seek people out in large groups. He has a couple of "best" friends and that is enough for him.

At the end of his workday, Dick will often go to his study to read or to his garden to work on a project. During these private times he doesn't like to be interrupted. He tends to not say very much until he has known a person for a while. Even then he doesn't share much personal information until he knows the person quite well. When you ask Judy a question she will respond immediately. In fact she may start to respond before you have even finished the question. When you ask Dick a question he prefers to take some time to think about it.

Judy was surprised at what a strong introvert Dick was. She said, "When we were dating we talked all of the time. He would call on the phone, initiate conversations in the car, even talk during movies." She turned to Dick and asked, "Do you remember that?" He replied, as only a strong introvert could, "Yep." Judy continued, "As soon as we were married it seems as though somebody turned off his talk switch." After a pause she concluded, "I can't figure out what happened."

I told Dick and Judy that many spouses have made similar comments. Why? Because the process of dating is more of an extroverted process. It involves getting to know one another, sharing each other's likes, dislikes, ideas, and dreams. It's quite common for an introvert to act like an extrovert during the dating process. Once they know enough of the person to have made a commitment, there isn't the need for as much conversation.

On their honeymoon Judy was doing what extroverts do best, processing things externally, thinking out loud. She was thrilled by their wedding, the friends, the flowers, the beautiful church, the musicians, and of course, the ceremony. She was overwhelmed by God's goodness to her and Dick. Although physically exhausted she was emotionally charged up, and like every other extrovert she wanted to talk about it.

Dick was also grateful to God for His goodness to them. The wedding was much more of an emotional experience than he had anticipated. But of course he hadn't spent a great deal of his life dreaming about his wedding day. Many relatives had come from all over the country and the entire week before the wedding was spent making last-minute arrangements, meeting family and friends, answering questions. He enjoyed checking things off his list and taking care of all the details. But by the time they left the reception he was both physically and emotionally exhausted. However, like every other healthy introvert before him, the way he recharged his battery wasn't to talk, but to go inside, to ponder, pray, reflect or, in Judy's terms, "to vegetate."

As we talked about the natural "bent" of introverts and extroverts Judy said, "I wish I had understood it years ago. I can see that for much of our marriage I have viewed extroversion as normal and Dick as abnormal. I thought I was trying to change him for his own good when really I was trying to make an extrovert out of an introvert. I was trying to change him into someone God had not designed him to be." I complimented Judy on her profound insight.

In later sessions we talked about the fact that, while God had made Dick an introvert and Judy an extrovert, they both had things they could learn from each other. I told them, "It's important to remember that whatever your preference, you need some of the skills of the opposite preference for balance."

For example, extroverts tend to think while speaking or after speaking. During one of our sessions Judy made a statement and then, after hearing what she had said commented, "You know, I don't really agree with that." Dick laughed. Yet Judy's ability to think out loud allowed Dick to understand her train of thought, how she reasoned through problems, and the kinds of information that were important to her when she made a decision. This is a skill that introverts need to add to their relational tool chest.

Most introverts think before speaking, therefore whenever they say something they've probably spent some time processing it. This is a skill that would be helpful for many extroverts to put in their relational tool chest. I've heard countless stories from extroverts who've regretted times when they "put their foot in their mouth" or, as one person described it, "opened my mouth only to change feet."

Introverts need some extroversion skills for balance. Extroverts need some introversion skills for balance. Dick and Judy were starting to see that the differences that had divided them were a gift from God and a source of potential blessing and balance.

Here is a list of some of the differences between introverts and extroverts. If you're like most people you will find some things in both descriptions that sound like you. However, you'll also have a pretty clear sense that you prefer, or are better at, one or the other. The first time you read through the list look for yourself. Then read through the list again and see which one best describes your spouse.

EXTROVERTS	INTROVERTS
Feel drawn outward by external requests and opportunities.	Feel pushed inward by external requests and intrusions.
Energized by other people and external experiences.	Energized by inner resources and internal experiences.
An interruption is an opportunity.	An interruption is an intrusion.
Enjoy people.	Enjoy pondering.
The unlived life is not worth examining.	The unexamined life is not worth living.
Act and then (maybe) reflect.	Reflect and then (maybe) act.
Seek activity.	Seek solitude.
Are often friendly, talkative, easy to know.	Are often reserved, quiet hard to know.
Express emotions.	Keep emotions to themselves.
Solves problems externally.	Solves problems internally.

Value relationships.	Value privacy.
Give breadth to life.	Give depth to life.
They may seem shallow to I's.	They may seem withdrawn to E's.[2]

What are some of the benefits of understanding your mate's preference for extroversion or introversion? What are some possible consequences for not understanding his or her preference?

Go back over each of these word lists and imagine what it would be like to have one preference but be in a relationship where you were expected to be the total opposite. Imagine what it would be like to be an introverted spouse who was talked to and expected to act like a extrovert. What would the message be? Would there be miscommunication and conflict? Would you tend to feel somewhat misunderstood and out of place? Would you be more likely to think something was wrong with you? Would you wonder if God had made a mistake?

HOW TO INFLUENCE AN EXTROVERT

Let your extrovert be an extrovert. Let them know that you appreciate their social skills. Be patient with what may, at times, appears to be rambling. Remember that extroverts think while speaking or after speaking. Don't interpret their chatty nature as being shallow or superficial.

When an extrovert says something don't assume he or she has thought about it. Remember that extroverts prefer to process information externally. Find out if they are merely thinking out loud or if they've given the idea or suggestion some thought and it's something they want to do. It's common for introverts to take seriously what an extrovert is merely tossing around as an idea. It's equally common for an extrovert to take as a casual idea something the introvert has spent days or weeks thinking about.

Be a ready listener. Extroverts love to talk. Sometimes it's good to encourage them to think out loud and to do some of your thinking out loud with them. When you talk to an extrovert make sure your pauses aren't too long. A hard-core extrovert may mistake your taking a breath as a sign that you have completed your thoughts and are ready for him or her to jump in.

If something is important to you, let them know. Since extroverts think out loud they tend not to assume something is as important as it may be to you. Dick and Judy shared numerous examples of times when they experienced major (and frustrating) miscommunication because they either under or overestimated the importance of what one of them had communicated.

Encourage their time with friends. I've read that men and women differ in the frequency with which they contact friends during a week. In my experience it's not as much a male-female issue as it is an extroversion-introversion issue. I heard a speaker talk about a survey he did of six hundred people. In it he found that the frequency of contacting friends was more a function of people's preference for introversion or extroversion than it was being male or female. The extroverted-feeling women were only slightly ahead of the extroverted-feeling men in their frequency of talking with friends. The introverted-thinking men and women were at the bottom of the list. Extroverts recharge their emotional batteries by being with people. Introverts recharge their emotional batteries by getting away and being alone. One is not better or healthier than the other. Both are equally valid and valuable.

HOW TO INFLUENCE AN INTROVERT

Let your introvert be an introvert. Don't assume that something is wrong with him or her that needs to be changed. Remember, introverts can be as lonely in a crowd as you can be when you are alone. I heard one speaker say that "Introversion isn't a disease that needs to be surgically removed." He was right. In the United States approximately 75 percent of the population prefers extroversion and only 25 percent prefers introversion. However in Japan the percentages are just reversed. The majority of the population there prefers introversion.

For most of their marriage Judy tried to turn Dick into an extrovert. She thought she was doing him a favor. She looked Dick straight in the eyes and said, "I'm sorry, honey." He reached over and took her hand. Judy continued, "While there are times when I wish you would share more of yourself with me and the kids, I want to learn how to understand and honor your need for solitude and reflection." Now that was a healthy response.

Be patient with introverts. Their initial response to new ideas can appear to be more negative and they tend to be slower to change. Don't jump to conclusions (something introverts are rarely accused of doing) and assume they are stubborn, unwilling to bend, or uninvolved. Because of their preferred way of processing information they may take longer to come to a conclusion, but when they do make a decision it's likely to have been well thought out.

Give them time and space. Remember it often takes many introverts a little longer to "warm up." Researchers have done time studies on how long it takes extroverts and introverts to respond to a question. The results indicate that the average response time for an extrovert is under two seconds. That's no surprise! Keep in mind that their initial response may not be very profound. However they do start talking.

The same research showed that introverts wait an average of over seven seconds—a lifetime to an extrovert—before they say anything at all. Many extroverts jump to the erroneous conclusion that if introverts aren't saying something, it must mean they are bored, confused, asleep, want the extrovert to say more, or are playing passive-aggressive power games.[3]

Ask for their opinion, and then when they give it listen, ask a few more questions, and look into their eyes. An introvert may take more time to communicate a thought than you do. Don't assume that when they stop speaking to take a breath they are finished. For an introvert a three-minute pause is a short period of time, for an extrovert the same three minutes can seem like an eternity. I don't know of anyone who likes to be interrupted. Introverts are no exception.

Don't assume they don't have an opinion or don't want to talk. Encourage them to think out loud. Invite them to share where they are in the process of thinking about an issue. Remind them that they don't have to have everything thought out before they share it with you.

After reading the last few pages you may have a new perspective on introverts and extroverts, especially if your spouse's preference is different from yours. Now we'll move on to consider the different ways people organize the world around them.

HOW WE DEAL WITH THE WORLD AROUND US— JUDGING OR PERCEIVING

"When Judy and I first met, one of the things that drew me to her, that made her stand out from all the rest was her creativity and spontaneity." I had asked Dick and Judy to share what had initially attracted them to each other and neither one of them had any problem remembering.

After basking for a moment in Dick's compliment and the memory of their first contact Judy responded, "I was attracted by his strength, stability, and organization." She continued, "He always knew what he was doing, where he was supposed to be, and when something was supposed to be done. If Dick said he would do something by a certain date I could always count on him to have it done. He felt like such a rock."

Of course over the years, and without understanding personality type, what Judy had first perceived as strength was now being experienced as stubbornness. And it didn't take long for what Dick had at first experienced as "creativity and spontaneity" to feel like "irresponsibility and disorganization."

Judging and perceiving are known as lifestyle attitudes. These are the two opposites that were added by Isabel Briggs Myers and Katherine Briggs. They reflect different lifestyle orientations and different ways people relate to the outside world.

Dick has a clear preference for the judging lifestyle that is decisive, planned, and orderly. This doesn't necessarily mean he is a judgmental person. It means that he relates to the external world in a structured and organized way.

Even as a little baby Dick loved to line up his toys in a straight line. He had a certain place for everything and he would get upset if things weren't where they should be. While he can be spontaneous, he prefers order and structure. He loves to plan ahead and see things come to a conclusion. He doesn't like to be late for Sunday school or church. And he doesn't especially appreciate surprises. Too much change throws him off.

As Dick and Judy discussed his preference for structure and organization I shared a story about a "hard-core" structured person. The story took place in a small, Midwest town close to the Mississippi that from time to time experienced floods. It had been raining for several days and the river was flooding over its banks. One family had moved their valuables up to the second floor of their home. The daughter was looking out the window at the rising water flowing down the street when she shouted, "Mom, come here!" Her mother sensed the urgency in her voice and ran over to the window. "Mom, I think there must be a whirlpool around our house. Most of the water is running down the street but there's a brown hat that keeps coming around our house." Her mother didn't understand but she decided to stay at the window to see what her daughter was talking about.

Sure enough, in less than a minute her mom saw a brown hat that appeared to be floating around the house. As soon as the mother saw the hat she turned to her concerned daughter and said, "Oh, don't worry about that, honey. That's just your dad. Don't you remember? Yesterday he said he was going to mow the lawn tomorrow come hell or high water!"

"That's my kind of guy," Dick volunteered.

The person who prefers structure doesn't just *like* to plan, they *need* to plan. Their motto is "Plan your work and then work your plan." Not only does Dick have a Day-Timer, he enjoys knowing what the schedule is and keeping to it. One of his favorite parts of the Day-Timer is the six-year planner. He feels more secure when he can look ahead and know what's going on.

As I listened to Dick talk I was reminded of another hard-core organizer I had met. Several years ago when I was visiting Hearst Castle in Cambria, California, I met a couple on vacation. As we talked they shared that he had recently retired from the Army and they were on a three-month vacation. I said, "That sounds great. You must be having a wonderful time."

"Actually," the wife said, "we're exhausted." She went on to say they had planned this vacation for years. In fact, her husband had planned *all* ninety days of the vacation. He had mapped out the trip, determined how many miles they would drive each day, and where they would stop. In fact, he had even made reservations for all ninety nights. They were just starting the fourth week of their dream vacation and "we're so exhausted that he's decided to cancel all of the remaining reservations and just take one day at a time," she said. Not only do structured people like calendars, they also like lists. In fact I know some people who make up lists and put things on the list they have already done just because it feels good to cross them off. When I shared that insight Judy turned to Dick and laughed. Dick broke out in this huge smile and said, "Well, it does feel good to look at one of my lists and see some things already crossed off."

Judy clearly prefers a perceiving (P) lifestyle and tends to be more unstructured, adaptable, and spontaneous. Once again it's important to understand how these words are used. Those who prefer perception aren't necessarily more perceptive than J's. However, they are more curious and flexible and they handle change well. They are the free spirits of life.

Judy relates to the outer world in a much more casual and laid-back manner. She couldn't care less if things are in a straight line or if they are scattered all over the floor. She enjoys surprises and responds well to the unexpected. Judy is easily distracted. In fact one time Dick made the humorous observation that "she got lost between the front door and the car." She starts a lot of projects but often has difficulty completing them because something else has caught her attention. She's a lot of fun and brings fun and laughter to those around her. Change is no problem for Judy. In fact change helps relieve the monotony of life.

If you aren't sure if someone you know prefers judging or perceiving, one simple way to find out is to walk into their office. The office of the structured person is neat and orderly. Books are organized by topics and are a half-inch from the edge of the shelf. The desk is uncluttered and the files are neatly organized in the file cabinet.

If the person prefers perception, after you walk in the door you may have to shout to see if anyone is there. Why? Because you can't see behind the piles of books and papers stacked on the desk. An important distinction between the structured person and the free spirit is that the structured person files things horizontally and the free spirit files things vertically. A pile of papers to the structured person is nothing more than a mess to be cleaned up. A pile of papers to a free spirit is like compost. If you leave it there long enough, something good will happen.

However, those who are structured need to be careful not to assume that the "piles" of the free spirit are unorganized. They may appear to be unorganized, but if you ask them for a certain report they'll go to the third pile, down about a foot-and-a-half from the top, reach in, and pull out the report you were looking for. You see, many of them organize things differently than their more obviously structured counterparts.

Another difference on this dimension that frustrates many couples is the ways in which they handle deadlines. This is one of the differences that became evident to Dick and Judy while they were still in college. When Dick got an assignment he would go to the library and head directly for the card catalog. He even knew where it was. He would research the topic, go to the *Reader's Guide to Periodical Literature* for additional information, do a rough draft outline, show it to his professor for his approval, and then do the paper.

When Judy got the assignment she would talk about it with her friends, think about some of the possibilities for it, and then move on to something else. A couple of days before the project was due she would remember the deadline and suddenly become intensely focused on getting the paper done. "I discovered that if I tried to do everything as far in advance as Dick liked to do it, I would get sidetracked or just plain stuck." Dick jumped in, "Up until now I never could figure out how Judy could wait until the last minute to do a paper, and then get as good a grade on it as I did."

What Dick was starting to understand is that Judy was "wired" differently than he was. His natural way of doing things, what came easily for him, was not necessarily the best way and certainly not the only way. Judy was also starting to understand that what she had at times interpreted as Dick trying to "control" her was more accurately a reflection of his need for order and structure.

The following list provides a brief summary of some of the differences between those who prefer a judging lifestyle and those who prefer a perceiving lifestyle. If you're like most people, you will find some things that describe you in both lists. However, you will probably be able to identify one of the two as your favorite or more preferred way of functioning.

JUDGERS	PERCEIVERS
Prefer an organized lifestyle.	Prefer a flexible lifestyle.
Need definite order and structure.	Like going with the flow.

Their motto is work now, play later.	Their motto is play now, work later, or (even better) play while you work.
Like to have life under control.	Prefer to experience life as it happens.
Enjoy making decisions.	Enjoy getting more information.
Like clear limits and categories.	Like freedom to explore without limits.
Feel comfortable establishing closure.	Feel comfortable maintaining openness.
Can't relax until the task is completed.	Can easily interrupt a task if something more interesting comes along.
Enjoy deadlines and like to plan in advance.	Meet deadlines by last-minute rush.
The product is more important than the process.	The process is more important than the product.
The most important part of a trip is arriving at the destination.	The most important part of the trip is traveling to the destination.
They may seem demanding, rigid, and uptight to P's.	They may seem disorganized, messy, and irresponsible to J's.[4]

What are some of the benefits of understanding your spouse's J or P preference? What are some possible consequences of not understanding your partner's preference?

Go back over each of these word lists and imagine what it would be like to have one preference but to live in a home where you were expected to be the opposite. Imagine what it would be like to be a judging spouse who was talked to and expected to act like a perceiving spouse. What would the message be? Would there tend to be more miscommunication and conflict? Would you tend to feel misunderstood and out of place? Would you be more likely to think that something was wrong with you? Would you wonder if God had made a mistake?

HOW TO INFLUENCE THE
STRUCTURED PERSON (JUDGER)

Be sensitive to his or her time clock. Time is very important to a J. If you say you'll be somewhere at a certain time, be there. "One of the greatest sources of frustration in our marriage has been that Judy is always late," Dick said with more than a hint of irritation.

"Well, I'm not always late," Judy retorted. "Besides that," Judy continued, "Dick not only wants to be somewhere on time, he would like to be there fifteen minutes early. That seems like a waste of time to me."

As you'll see later on, Dick and Judy learned how to change each other in this regard in a way that respected each other's needs, yet reflected a sensitive accommodation to each other's preferences.

Follow through on your commitments. If a J asks for something to be done by a certain date, and if the request is reasonable, make sure it's done by that date. Be prompt and follow through on your commitments. Don't make promises that you aren't willing to keep. Most J's would rather have people not commit themselves than have them say yes with great intentions but then not do it.

Don't mess up their space. J's love organization and structure. With most things in their lives there is a place for everything and everything goes in its place. They not only love organization, they need it. When you use something belonging to a J, put it back where you got it. This shows respect and will make it more likely for the person to respect you.

Let the person know when something is going to be different than it usually is. Most J's don't like surprises and spur-of-the-moment changes. They can view change as disruptive. In fact it's much more difficult for most J's to change than it is for P's. And don't assume that a J is angry. Most J's are so goal-driven that when something moves them off their task or when they are slowed down they can become even more intensely focused and respond in ways that may seem angry.

Dick expressed the problem well. "It really bugs me when I'm intensely focused on something, I'm on a roll, and Judy interrupts me. If I don't respond in a certain way her feelings get hurt and she wants to know why I'm so angry. Then I not only have to respond to her interruption but decide whether I want to enter into what is usually a dead-end discussion trying to convince her that I'm not angry. It's just the way I respond when interrupted... by anybody."

I turned to Judy and asked her, "What did you just hear Dick say?" She replied, "Well, first of all, he doesn't like to be interrupted and it frustrates him." I turned to Dick and waited for his response. "Judy, that's partially right. I don't enjoy interruptions but it's not so much the interruption that's the problem. I know that sometimes you need to interrupt what I'm doing. What I really don't like is your automatic interpretation that if I don't respond with a certain tone of voice something is wrong or that I'm mad at you."

Dick was communicating this issue with more clarity than he ever had before, and this was helping Judy understand him better, to look at the situation through the eyes of his personality type preference. "So are you saying that, while you don't enjoy interruptions, you wouldn't mind it as much if I interrupted, got the information, took it at face value, and went on my way?" Judy asked. "Bingo!" Dick replied.

Encourage their flexibility. J's can become too rigid, inflexible, and dogmatic and thus restrict not only their lives but the lives of those around them. They have a tremendous need for closure and sometimes this can come across as a need to control. Judy made this insightful observation: "When we were first married I thought Dick had this tremendous need to control everything. I'm beginning to see that what felt to me like Dick's need to control was more his need to wrap things up so that he could move onto the next item on his list."

Along with encouraging their flexibility it's also important to encourage their attempts at play. Many J's have a hard time playing. They don't play golf, they work at lowering their handicap. They don't play tennis, they work on improving their backhand stroke. When J's structure their days they rarely include time for play.

Somehow it just doesn't get on the list. And if they don't put it on the calendar it probably won't happen. You might want to share with a J this quote from a delightful little book, *Meditations for Parents Who Do Too Much.*

Parents who do too much are overbooked, our weekdays jammed full of errands and activities, with no room left for spontaneity or surprise. If something comes up—some "irresistible distraction"—some unexpected fork in the road, we can't take advantage of it, because we fear that if we veer off our route even slightly we may never find our way back.

Living by the calendar is a necessary evil, especially in these fast-paced times. But we should not be so overscheduled that we can't be lured away when something just happens to turn up. Our kids are as overcommitted as we force them to be, and with no time left to follow a whim or chase a shadow, their lives, too, may feel orchestrated and unspontaneous.[5]

HOW TO INFLUENCE THE FREE SPIRIT (PERCEIVER)

Be sensitive to the perceiver's need for flexibility. Practice going with the flow. Remember that there's more than one way of doing things.

Honor the perceiver's way of organizing the things that are important to him or her. Remember, you aren't doing anyone a favor when you ignore a person's natural bent and try to squeeze that personality into your mold. I had one P tell me, "My wife is an organizer. Her motto is 'I love you and have a wonderful plan for your life.'" He continued, "I know that she has the best of intentions, but it bugs the dickens out of me." Well, it "bugs the dickens" out of a lot of people to experience someone trying to control who they are and how they do what they do.

Be open to the perceiver's requests for more information. While J's have a great need for closure, P's have a need for openness. One of the weaknesses of some J's is to bring closure to a situation, to draw a discussion to a conclusion before enough information has been gathered. Dick said, "One of Judy's many strengths as a mom is that she doesn't jump to conclusions. When the kids are fighting I'm more likely to walk in, assess what's going on, and divvy up the consequences. Sometimes I'm right and sometimes I'm wrong." He went on to say that Judy is much more likely to take the time to ask a few more questions and then decide what the appropriate consequences might be. He concluded "I've learned a lot from this part of Judy's personality."

Enjoy the spontaneity. Allow for last-minute changes. Understand that some P's have a shorter attention span than J's do and may be more easily distracted. What can appear to a J to be a distraction or interruption can also be an opportunity for a new insight, a new experience, a new opportunity to grow.

Learn to communicate your concerns using shorter sentences. Judy expressed frustration at the way Dick could, at times, go on and on. "Sometimes I wish he would just get it out and get on with it. I hate lectures." Of course Dick's immediate response was usually a frustrated or insulted, "I'm not lecturing!" Well, what may not seem like a lecture to a J can feel like one to a P.

And remember that when P's, especially NP's, change the subject, it's not because they are bored or don't care about the topic. It's consistent with how God has made them. They tend to have a shorter attention span, are more easily distracted, and don't like to be pinned down. They think better by casting a wider conversation net while many J's feel more secure in what can become a too narrowly focused rut.

SEEING EACH OTHER WITH NEW EYES

A very normal part of being married is dealing with each other's differences. Some degree of frustration resulting in conflict is inevitable in any relationship. Clashes between different personality types is to be expected. But when we understand personality type, when we understand the different relational languages God has given each one of us, we can significantly decrease the unnecessary conflicts and misunderstandings that plague us.

With the insights of personality type you are less likely to spend time trying to squeeze your partner into your own mold. You are less likely to attempt to change things that really shouldn't be changed. However when there is something that can and should be changed, you're much more likely to be able to communicate that need for change in ways your partner will be able to hear and understand. You are more likely to be in a place where God can use you to help them become the unique person God designed them to be.

When Dick and Judy understood that many of their differences were simply the way God had made them, they didn't look at them so negatively. They began the process of learning how to benefit from each other's gifts. Dick realized that while he was an introvert and his father and grandfather had been introverts, he could benefit from developing some extroversion skills. He found it wasn't too difficult to talk to Judy more than he did, especially about their relationship. He began to understand that what was "small" talk to him was "valuable" talk to Judy. He learned that by thinking out loud with Judy, rather than doing it all in his head and announcing his conclusion, she began to better understand what was important to him and the kinds of information he needed when making a decision.

Judy realized that Dick's quietness and withdrawal wasn't a passive-aggressive way to punish her, it was in part how God had made him. She realized that while she was a full-blown extrovert, she could benefit from developing some introversion skills. She began to be more comfortable with, even to value, silence and time alone. She learned that while it was OK to think out loud, there were times when it was much better to think before speaking, to weigh the consequences of a statement before verbalizing it.

Dick realized that when Judy asked him to change by dreaming with her she wasn't requesting major personality reconstruction involving genetic reconstitution. Instead she was requesting a relatively small and realistic change on his part that would make their relationship better for the both of them. Judy realized that she could talk facts without becoming a "boring, factual person."

Judy discovered that Dick was more likely to hear her and be open to change when she gave him reasons that were logical. Her emotional pleas tended to fall on insensitive ears. It was like a foreign language to him. Dick learned that Judy was more receptive to suggestions when he made a sensitive case for change. When he showed how his requests were based on what was in the best interest of the individuals involved, and not just his need for control or structure, Judy was not only more open but at times even enthusiastic about them.

One of the biggest areas of change for both of them dealt with their differences on the judging and perceiving attitudes. Dick began to see that he would have become a much more predictable and boring person if Judy was just like him. He became a bit more flexible. He didn't take his Day-Timer everywhere and he began to develop more spontaneity. The kids were the first to notice, and celebrate, this change in their dad.

Judy was able to admit that Dick's structure helped her untangle her life when she had taken on too much. As she added more structure to her life she was able to set clearer boundaries, decrease her tendency to be used by people (the rumor was that if you needed a job done, ask Judy; she'd say yes to anything), and complete the things that were really important to her. She bought a calendar. Not only did she buy it, she used it. She wrote everyone's activities on it and, like the good P that she was, scheduled times to "be spontaneous."

The insights of their personalities also had a tremendous influence on how Dick and Judy solved problems. They learned how to utilize each other's strengths to compensate for their individual weaknesses. When it came to the first step of problem-solving—defining the problem—Dick's preference for sensing gave him the ability to thoroughly define problems, to gather all of the facts and determine exactly what was needed.

However, when it came to the second step of problem-solving—brainstorming or generating options—Dick didn't do very well. He tended to see only one or two options. Judy on the other hand loved to brainstorm. Her preference for intuition gave her the ability to generate all kinds of possibilities and options. At times she would see things Dick hadn't even thought of. However, she wasn't too good at defining the problem. In fact, there were times she would be trying to solve problems she hadn't even defined.

The third step of effective problem-solving is a critical analysis of all of the options. What's the most time-effective, cost-effective, and resource-effective option? This step involves a rigorous and impersonal analysis. Dick's preference for the thinking function prepared him well for this task. He not only did it well but he said, "I thoroughly enjoy tearing each idea apart piece by piece, looking for the fatal flaw, coming up with the best solution." This wasn't Judy's strong suit but because of her personality type she was able to understand that it was an essential and valuable part of the decision-making process.

The fourth step of effective problem-solving was one that Judy was especially good at. After they had narrowed down their options to one or two, the last task was to determine which decision was more consistent with their beliefs and values, and how it would effect the people involved. There are times when a decision might be more cost-effective but it may compromise a deeply held value or it might have an unnecessarily painful effect on someone you love. Judy's preference for the feeling function uniquely equipped her to weigh the consequences of a decision through her personal and relational eyes.

While they shared the decision-making process, Judy learned to rely on Dick's ability to define problems and weigh the options. Dick learned how much he needed Judy's ability to generate possible solutions and weigh their final decision in light of their beliefs, values, and important relationships. It took time, work, patience, some agreeing to disagree, and a lot of prayer. But Dick and Judy learned more than merely how to put up with or endure their differences. They learned how to value, even celebrate, each other's God-given uniqueness, how to see each other through new eyes. They also learned how to utilize each other's strengths and add new tools to their relational tool chests.

In this chapter we've only been able to scratch the surface of the important insights of personality type as identified by the Myers-Briggs Type Indicator. I'm not even coming close to suggesting that the MBTI insights will transform every marriage. They won't. However, even with this brief overview I'm sure you can see how invaluable these insights can be, not only in understanding your partner, but in communicating in ways that are meaningful to him or her.

As married couples we have the greatest influence on how our spouses learn, how they understand themselves and others, and how well they grow according to the God-designed "bent" in each one of them. The differences in personality type appear to profoundly affect a person's learning style and developmental pattern.

You can become aware of how your own personality preferences and expectations either blend or clash with those of your spouse. You can learn how to speak your partner's language and thus increase the probability of clear communication. If you understand some of the most important personality differences between you and your beloved, you are likely to be more successful in nurturing the other one's growth, encouraging his or her spirit, and bringing about change in your "better half."

WHAT'S YOUR PREFERENCE?

I would strongly encourage you to do some additional reading on personality type. At the end of the chapter I've listed some of the most helpful resources available. They are packed with practical illustrations of how to apply the insights you've just read about in your marriage and family.

Before moving on to the next chapter I'd like you to take a couple of minutes to complete the following exercise. I've included a very brief summary of the MBTI categories. On each of the four lines I'd like you to think about what your preference is and what the preference of your spouse is. Then write each one of your names where you see yourselves. If you have a strong preference for introversion, you would write your name next to the I. If you think you're an introvert but it's not a strong preference, you might write your name closer to the middle. Go ahead and do this with all four of the preferences.

E_____I

Direction of focus and interest: Does it flow mainly to the outer world of actions, objects, and people, or to the inner world of concepts and ideas?

Extroverted types are regarded as primarily focused on the outer world of people, objects, and actions, tending to become caught up with whatever is happening around them.

Introverted types have more of an inward focus and they tend to detach from the external world in favor of focusing on concepts, ideas, thoughts, and internal images.

S_____N

Information-gathering: Is the focus more on the immediate realities of direct and personal experience, or to the inferred meanings, relationships, and possibilities of experiences in the future?

Sensing types focus on perceptions received directly through the sense organs, noticing concrete details and practical aspects of a situation in the here and now.

Intuitive types rely on a more impressionistic approach in order to maximize their spontaneous hunches. They prefer to deal with abstract, inferred meanings, and the hidden possibilities in a situation as they look toward the future.

TF

Decision-making: In making decisions is the reliance more likely to be on logical order and cause-and-effect or on priorities based on personal importance, values and relationships?

Thinking types rely on logical structures to clarify and order particular situations; they are skilled at objectively organizing material, weighing the facts, and impersonally judging whether something is true or false.

Feeling types are adept at understanding others' feelings and analyzing subjective impressions, based on their judgments of personal values.

J_____P

Lifestyle: Is there a preference for living systematically, well-organized, attempting to control events or with flexibility and spontaneity, curiously awaiting events and adapting to them?

Judging types are structured, organized and systematic, living in a planned, orderly way, seeking to regulate their environment and control it.

Perceptive types are more flexible, curious, and open-minded, going through life in a spontaneous way, aiming to understand life and adapt to it.[6]

HOW'D THEY DO IT?

"My husband Mike is an attorney and is very proficient and successful... at the office that is. At home it's sometimes a different matter. And that's what bothers me; he can be one way in his profession and another way at home. And our discussions didn't bring about much change either. One evening Mike was talking about contracts and how much he enjoyed creating them for the various companies that retain him. I learned a lot about their structure and how they worked so I figured if they work at work, they could work at home.

"I knew what I wanted Mike to do differently and I knew what he wanted from me even though he wasn't demanding. One Sunday when we were having a relaxed time I said that I could see the value of a contract and I would like his opinion concerning this contract. Mike was surprised and asked who the contract was going to be with. When I said 'You,' I really got his attention. I went on to tell him that both of us had some concerns and requests for the other that weren't yet being fulfilled. They weren't major but each of us would be more fulfilled if these requests were met. I began by showing him my part of the contract. It went like this:

The following contract will be in effect from the date of signing by both partners and will be open to review and a re-signing of the commitment on the first day of each month. Each person will be responsible for the self-motivation necessary to follow through with his or her own commitment although the partner will be allowed one reminder per week if necessary.

I, Denise, agree to the following in this contractual agreement with my husband Mike:

1. I agree to cook Mike one of his favorite dishes with a home-made dessert one night of the week and the night will be mutually agreed upon.

2. I agree to accompany Mike to one of his conferences every six months.

3. I agree to having sex with Mike a minimum of twice a week.

4. I will give Mike several days warning if there is a major task I need his help with on the weekend.

I, Mike, agree to the following in this contractual agreement with my wife, Denise:

1. I agree to call Denise if I am going to be late for dinner or if I can't make it. The call will be made no later than 4:30.

2. I agree to give the boys their bath and put them to bed two nights a week and we will select the nights in advance.

3. I agree to take Denise out to dinner (just the two of us) at least once a month at a romantic, cozy restaurant (not McDonald's, Wendy's, or Taco Bell). During the dinner we will not discuss work, dinner, or my mother.

"Mike was delighted with the contract and made a big deal out of it. He had it retyped on special paper (fortunately he typed it and not his secretary!) and we had a special signing. It's working! There wasn't anything I wanted that was new. I just repackaged it."

TAKE ACTION

Now, starting with the extroversion-introversion attitudes, go through each one of the four preferences and ask yourself these simple questions:

1. What is one way that God might want to use our differences to strengthen me and our relationship?

2. What is one thing about the opposite preference that I could incorporate into my own life for greater balance and effectiveness?

3. What is one of my beloved's strengths that God might have me incorporate into my own relational tool chest?

CHAPTER NINE

Learning to Speak Your Partner's Language

H. Norman Wright

L et's eavesdrop on two couples:

Jean: How was your day?

Alan: All right.

Jean: What happened today?

Alan: The usual.

Jean: What do you want to do this Saturday?

Alan: I don't care.

Jean: Do you want to get together with our friends?

Alan: I don't know … where's the TV section of the paper?

Jean: Alan, why don't you talk to me? I'm trying to find out what you want to do!

Alan: (Surprised at her outburst and silent)

Jean: Alan, do you care about us?

Alan: Well, of course I do! Why ask a weird question like that?

Jean: Well, you don't act like you care. We don't talk anymore or I should say I talk and you act like I'm imposing on you. How can you not have an opinion? What do you care about?

What's wrong here? Alan and Jean are communicating but not very well. Or is this what we should expect out of marriage after a few years? Let's look in on another couple:

Herb: I just don't see why we have to go to that meeting!

Amy: I've told you several times why. How many more times do I need to tell you?

Herb: I just can't picture why it's so vital that I go.

Amy: But I've told you again and again. Don't you listen to me?

Herb: I just think it's kind of shortsighted of you to give me only two days' notice. I was looking forward to doing something else that day.

Amy: Now what are you saying, Herb?

Herb: Don't you understand? Can't you see that I'm already tied up?

THE LIFEBLOOD OF RELATIONSHIPS

Herb and Amy are talking but they're arguing and talking past one another. It's as though neither of them hears the other or else doesn't understand. Why? How could they learn to connect with one another?

Communication is the lifeblood of a relationship. When it disappears the relationship dies. A relationship can't exist without it. We've been talking about communication throughout the entire book. But since we're considering the process of changing one another, let's look specifically at the elements of communicating to bring about change. There will be no communication between a husband and wife unless someone listens.

Years ago I read a statement that went like this: "Listen to all the conversations that occur between married couples as well as the nations of the world. They are for the most part dialogues of the deaf." We all like to talk but few like to listen. As far back as the Roman Empire communication was a problem. Seneca cried out with the words, "Listen to me for a day... an hour!... a moment! lest I expire in my terrible wilderness, my lonely silence! O God, is there no one to listen?"[1]

One of the greatest gifts one person can give to another is the gift of listening. It can be an act of love and caring. If a husband listens to his wife, she feels, "I must be worth hearing." If a wife ignores her husband, he thinks, "I must be dull and boring."

Look at these verses from the Word of God that talk about how God listens to us:

> The eyes of the Lord are toward the righteous, and His ears are open to their cry. The face of the Lord is against evildoers, to cut off the memory of them from the earth. The righteous cry and the Lord hears, and delivers them out of all their troubles. The Lord is near to the brokenhearted, and saves those who are crushed in spirit. Psalm 34:15-18, NASB

> I love the Lord, because He hears my voice and my supplications. Because He has inclined His ear to me, therefore I shall call upon Him as long as I live. Psalm 116:1-2, NASB

> Call to Me, and I will answer you, and I will tell you great and mighty things, which you do not know. Jeremiah 33:3, NASB

The Word of God also gives us directives concerning how we are to listen:

> He who gives an answer before he hears, it is folly and shame to him. Proverbs 18:13, NASB

> Any story sounds true until someone tells the other side and sets the record straight. Proverbs 18:17, TLB

> The wise man learns by listening; the simpleton can learn only by seeing scorners punished. Proverbs 21:11, TLB

> Let every man be quick to hear (a ready listener).
> James 1:19, AMPLIFIED

Listening does not come naturally nor does it come easily to most of us. Most of us prefer to be the one speaking. We like to express our ideas. We feel more comfortable identifying our position, asserting our opinions and feelings. Actually, most of us do not want to hear as much as we want to speak and be heard. Because of this we concentrate more on getting our word into the conversation, rather than focusing on what our partner is saying. And all too often we filter the other person's remarks through our own opinions and our needs.

For example, a wife mentions that she's tired of housework. Her husband hears what she says, but the message he receives is that she's unhappy because he isn't providing her with household help like her mother has. That's not what she said, but it's what the husband heard. Ever since they were married it has bothered him that he cannot provide help for the home like his wife's father does. It's easy to see how the message came through differently from what the wife intended. Filtered messages are seldom accurate. They cause misunderstanding and exaggerate problems.

When both husband and wife recognize the importance of listening objectively and giving each other full attention, they are taking big steps toward building strong lines of communication.

WHY CAN'T WE HEAR CORRECTLY?

It's important to identify some of the attitudes that prevent a husband or wife from listening. Reading these statements may be uncomfortable, but that may indicate a problem attitude.

"I'm right and you're wrong." When this is the attitude, you become preoccupied with proving this to your partner and you embark on a crusade to convince him or her, which usually backfires. You don't hear your partner.

"You're at fault." When blame is the name of the game, you see yourself as 100 percent innocent and your spouse as 100 percent guilty. You're convinced he or she "should" be blamed. You don't listen to your partner.

"I'm the victim." If you have a need to feel you've been victimized and your partner is insensitive as well as selfish, you won't hear the explanations or the apologies. Your partner can express it a dozen different ways but you won't really listen.

"Self-blindness." There is no way that you see yourself contributing to a problem. You complain about your partner and fail to see how you both cooperate and participate in the issue. The barriers are up against hearing your spouse's perspective.

"Domination Phobia." You're afraid if you listen to your partner you'll end up being controlled, having to do it in his or her way. You hit the "listen off" switch when your spouse makes any suggestions to you.

"Defensiveness." You live with the fear of being criticized because it hurts so much. You don't listen to evaluate what is said but reject all statements. Sometimes you expect to be criticized so you hear it when it's not even there.

"Mistrust." You don't trust your partner. You believe your husband or wife is lying before he or she says anything. You feel that if you show any indication that you're listening, your partner will take advantage of you.

"Self-centeredness." This can also be called selfishness or narcissism. There is no understanding directed toward the other person's needs or concerns. Your partner is hardly even thought of except to deny his or her right to feel, behave, or say anything to contradict you.

Well, these attitudes are not too pleasant, are they? But they do exist in many marriages and they keep growth and change from taking place.[2]

Let's take a look at what real listening entails.

Is there a difference between listening and hearing? Yes, there is. Hearing is gaining content or information for your own purposes. Listening is caring for and being empathic toward the person who is talking. Hearing means that you are concerned about what is going on inside yourself during the conversation. Listening means you are trying to understand the feelings of your spouse and are listening for the sake of the other person.

Let me give you a threefold definition of listening. Listening means that when your spouse is talking to you . . .

You are not thinking about what you are going to say when he or she stops talking. You are not busy formulating your response. You are concentrating on what is being said and are putting it into practice (Proverbs 18:13). It also means you are looking at the person and listening with your eyes as well as with your ears.

You are accepting what is being said without judging what he or she is saying or how it is being said. You may fail to hear the message if you're thinking that you don't like your spouse's tone of voice or words. You may react to the tone and content and miss the meaning. Perhaps your spouse hasn't said it in the best way, but why not listen and come back later when both of you are calm and discuss the proper wording and tone of voice? Acceptance does not mean you have to agree with the content of what is said. Rather, it means that you understand that what your spouse is saying is something he or she feels is important.

You should be able to repeat what your spouse has said and what you think he or she was feeling while speaking to you.

Real listening implies an obvious interest in your spouse's feelings and opinions and an attempt to understand them from their perspective. It means you let your partner know, "I hear what you're saying, I understand what you're saying, and I want to respond."

When you listen to another person, you can actually disarm him or her, especially when you are being criticized. Arguing with a critic rarely works but agreeing builds a closer relationship. When you listen you don't defend yourself, but neither do you have to agree with all that is said. If you can find some small element of truth to agree with, your spouse will be less on the offensive and more open to listening to you and considering your request. As a result, your desire for him or her to change may receive consideration.

REFLECTIVE LISTENING ENHANCES CONVERSATION

It's a technique we use constantly in counseling that helps the listener gain greater understanding and clarification. It involves a sense of empathy as well.

Empathy focuses on the thoughts and feelings of the other person. It tells your partner, "I really want to understand. Help me know if I'm connecting with you." Empathy is the ability to involve yourself in the life of your partner. Reflective listening uses the following phrases:

"You're feeling…"

"As I get it, you felt that…"

"I'm picking up that you…"

"If I'm hearing you correctly…"

"To me it's almost like you are saying, 'I…,"

"I sort of hear you saying that maybe you…"

"So, you feel…"

"So, as you see it…"

"You appear to be feeling…"

"Your message seems to be, 'I…,"

"I gather…"

These serve to give you the information you need in order to stay in a conversation with your partner. And when true communication occurs, change is possible.

When you listen you are showing love, concern, and respect. When you avoid interrupting it prevents sending a negative message such as, "I don't care what you feel or think," or, "You're not worth listening to." When you listen you step down from being an expert on what your partner really thinks, feels, and believes.

A BASIC DIFFERENCE BETWEEN MEN AND WOMEN

When communicating, women tend to focus more on others and men focus more on themselves. This helps to explain why women tend to expand topics whereas men like to shrink-wrap their presentation. Men like to keep it short and to the point.

Often a man has had his topic on the back burner and it has simmered for a while, so when he's ready to communicate it's cooked and ready to serve. This is especially true if he's an introvert. He speaks when he's ready. Discussing it privately with himself inside his head helps him get ready to communicate. But too often his spouse may interpret this as not being interested or attentive or as withdrawing from her. This may not be the case at all. I've seen problems in a marriage clear up when the husband explains this tendency to his wife.

One husband told his wife, "Honey, I am interested but I've got to have time to mull it over first and then I can give you my solution. And, get this! I've finally realized that you want to hear about the process of how I reached my conclusion, so as best as I can I'll explain that to you as well." Now he had a happy wife.

One wife left her husband a note on a funny card which said, "Have I got a deal for you! Try and turn this one down. I like your conclusions and I'd like them even more if you'd take a couple of minutes and tell me the process of how you arrived there. You know me. I'm just interested in how anything works. And you can count on me working on being more bottom line when I'm talking with you. How about it?" It worked.

Most women enjoy sharing and expanding their topic out loud. When a man starts talking, he usually knows where he's going unless he's an extrovert and just thinks out loud. But when many women begin talking, it's a discovery process. They're not always sure where it's heading and where it may end up. But thinking out loud helps them decide.

Bob told me, "I always thought when Marge did this she wanted my advice or interaction and this used to cause major conflicts. One day, she told me what she was doing and why. You know what I said? I told her, 'We're just the opposite. I do it entirely differently than you do. Now it's beginning to make sense.'"

A wife shared, "I asked my husband whether he wanted me to do my out-loud thinking in front of him or outside in the garage. He looked at me kind of strange and said, 'Of course, I don't want you to go outside. I'll work at getting used to it. That stuff we heard on gender differences has helped me make sense of it too.'"[3]

A common complaint I hear in counseling is the concern over the noncommunicative husband. Most wives either engage in a direct frontal attack, which doesn't work, or withdraw into resentment, which does little to encourage a husband to open up.

Sometimes an introvert husband is not always ready to give more than a yes or no response. So some women "rescue" the uncomfortable silence by filling it in with their own words. It's better to say, "I'm interested in what you have to say, but you may need to think about it for awhile. That's fine with me; take your time. When you're ready to talk about it, let me know." Giving permission for silence will take the pressure off both of you.

Another way to invite your husband to interact is to address his silence directly. You could say, "Honey, I'm looking for a response from you and you appear to be thinking about something. I'm curious what your silence means at this time." Then wait.

Or, "The look on your face tells me that you have something on your mind. I'd like to hear what it is." Or, "You may be concerned about how I will respond if you share what's on your mind. I think I'm ready to listen." Or, "It appears that you're having difficulty speaking right now. Can you tell me why?" Or, "Perhaps your silence reflects a concern about saying something correctly. You can say it any way you'd like."

One wife said, "Sometimes when I want to talk with you, you seem preoccupied or hesitant. I wonder if it's the topic or if there is something I do that makes it difficult for you to respond. Maybe you could think about it and let me know later." Then she stood up and began to leave the room. But her quiet husband said, "Let's talk now. I'm ready to comment on your last statement."

Because men tend to be more focused and women have this intuitive awareness of the needs of others, many couples experience conflict over this difference. A wife sees unawareness on the part of her husband as not caring or thinking that everything is fine in the relationship even when she feels it isn't. This may cause her to resent his not caring, or feel she has to carry the burden of the relationship, or even question her own perception. By understanding that he is focused and can be distracted from family issues by work, she will realize there is one solution to this problem—help him become aware of the needs of the relationship by communicating them to him. A wife cannot expect her husband to know automatically what she knows.[4]

Women must be willing to ask for support—and continue to ask. Most women don't want to ask. They expect men to anticipate female needs and to feel obliged to fulfill them. Women commonly fall prey to the negative myth, "If he loves me, then he will know what I want." This expectation hurts a relationship.

Women in general already take on too much responsibility for the feelings and needs of others. Just as a man becomes resistant to fulfilling the needs of others, she feels compelled to fulfill them at the expense of not fulfilling her own needs.[5]

I am not implying that the needs of the relationship are a woman's responsibility. I am saying, however, that she carries a responsibility to herself to persist in communicating those needs, striving to do it in new ways that don't make him feel he is in the wrong.

For example, a woman needs to remind a man how important time shared with him is to her. This is hard to do, as we have said, because she believes that if he really loves her as much as she loves him, then she wouldn't have to ask. The truth is, if he were a woman, then she wouldn't have to ask him for more participation in the relationship. As she learns to ask for his participation without secretly resenting him, he can more readily remember that both of them need to relate. He can recall how much better he feels when he's receiving her love and giving his.

Keep in mind that it's best not to judge another by your own communication style. What is typical and comfortable for you may not be for your partner. An example would be that most women show concern by following up a person's statement with a question about it. Women are used to this and comfortable with it. But if a man changes the subject, she may view this as indifference. "After all, if he was sensitive, he would follow up with some questions about what I said," she thinks. But that's not the typical response for many men. Not asking additional questions could be his way of showing respect for her privacy or independence. For a man, asking questions could be viewed as pushy, intrusive, or unnecessary.[6]

Most men tend to feel more comfortable speaking in public than in private, intimate conversations. With most women it's just the opposite. Women enjoy private, one-on-one conversations because they are more personal, intimate, and they build relationships. For most men, conversation is used to gain status, to negotiate and solve problems, to get attention, and even keep their independence.[7]

Communicating for change involves requests. But too often requests sound like demands. Listen to your tone of voice. When a husband or wife makes a request, timing is essential. If a husband asks for something when his wife is in the midst of some project, he can't expect an immediate response. And perhaps he doesn't, but his wife may interpret that he wants one now. I've learned to say, "I'm not asking for it or needing it right now, I just want to know if…" or "Could you get this by tomorrow?" If a wife sees her husband just about to do a task, it's best not to ask him to do what it's obvious he was going to do. If he's focused on some project, wait or leave him a note.

Be clear and specific with your request. If your personality style is that of an intuitive and you ask your senser spouse to stop at the store and pick up an item you need, be sure it's just one item, or enumerate how many, because you will be taken literally.

Recently, I came across an interesting concept in which the author (a man) made a very precise suggestion for women when they ask their husbands to do something. When asking a man to do something it's important to use the words, "Would you," rather than, "Could you." When the word *could* is used, it's like asking are you able to? The phrase, "Would you?" is asking for a decision as well as a commitment.

This was illustrated for me when I used to go fishing with one of my former students. We'd be at opposite ends of the boat and at times I'd ask him, "Do you have the bait over there?" and he would reply with a yes and then do nothing! I knew that he knew I was asking him to pass me the bait. But since he had listened to my class presentations on being precise and direct on communication, he would wait until I stated my request clearly instead of interpreting what I wanted. "Will you please pass the bait?" would bring the bait my direction.

Here are some examples of direct and indirect requests:

INDIRECT REQUEST	DIRECT REQUEST
The kids need to be picked up and I can't do it.	Would you pick up the kids?
The groceries are in the car.	Would you bring in the groceries?
I can't fit anything else in the trash can.	Would you empty the trash?
The backyard is really a mess.	Would you clean up the backyard?
We haven't gone out in weeks.	Would you take me out this week?[8]

SPEAK ENGLISH, PLEASE

Perhaps next to listening, the most fundamental concept in communication is learning to speak your partner's language. The best way to illustrate how to communicate in a person's language is an example from a counseling session. I've discovered this is the best way for people to understand these principles. As you read, notice the different words used. This is key to relating to another person. In every book I write I emphasize this concept. Perhaps you've read it before, but it bears repeating. When you can adapt your communication style to connect with your partner, what a difference it can make! Read on.

"Bob, you've said that your family seem to focus in well together as you talk, and Jean, you feel good about your communication with your mom. But what about the two of you together? What will it take for you two to communicate so that you understand each other? You've shared with me that it's difficult."

Jean and Bob looked at each other and then back at me. I waited and then said, "It's something to think about." I turned to Bob and asked, "Bob, are you and I communicating? Do you think we see eye to eye? Do we *understand* each other?"

He replied, "Oh, yes. You seem to *see* what I'm talking about, and I'm getting the *picture* of this whole discussion of how Jean and I differ."

"Jean, how do you *feel* about our communication? Does it make *sense* to you?"

She said, "Very much so. You seem to have a handle on what I'm *feeling,* and what you say registers. We seem to be on the *same wavelength.*"

I replied, "It's important that we learn not only to speak the same language but also to make sure we mean the same thing with our words. I've run into so many couples who get irritated and upset in their marriages because of such a simple matter as having different definitions for their words. You know, two people can speak Spanish and not mean the same thing. Two people can speak German and not mean the same thing. We're sitting here speaking English and using some of the same words, but we might have different meanings for them. Your experiences in life, your mind-set, what you intend can give meaning to your words. My wife might ask, 'Could we stop at the store for a minute on our way home, Norm? I'll just be a minute.' I might take the word 'minute' literally, but I had better not, because years of experience have taught me we're talking about fifteen to twenty minutes."

"Bob, has Jean ever said to you, 'Could I talk to you for a minute about something?' and you said yes assuming she meant a minute, but you're still discussing the issue thirty minutes later?" They both looked amazed, and Bob said, "Thursday night. That very thing happened. Jean wondered why I was getting uptight."

Jean broke in with, "Well, it was important. Did it matter how long it went on? You agreed we needed to talk about it, and I had felt that way for some time."

Bob responded, "Oh, no, it was all right. I just figured it'd be short, since you said a minute. And sometimes I need more time to just mull over what you've brought up."

Jean replied with a bit more feeling, "But many times I feel you've set a time limit on our conversations. I almost sense that you're impatient and want to get to the bottom line. You don't want to hear all my reasons or feelings. In fact, I wish you would share more details with me. I wear a new outfit and ask you how it looks, and all you say is, 'It looks fine.' Can't you tell me any more about how you feel about it?"

Bob looked at me and rolled his eyes upward and then said, "But

I said it looked fine. What else do you want to hear?"

I interrupted Bob and said, "On a scale of zero to ten, with zero meaning it looks terrible—like it's out of the rag pile—and ten meaning it's super—it's outstanding—where does the word 'fine' fall?"

Bob said, "Oh, it's somewhere between an eight and a nine."

Jean looked surprised and blurted out, "How would I know that? That's the first I've heard that *fine* had any meaning at all!"

"This is what I mean, when I say you need to define your words. Bob, if you couldn't use the word *fine* and had to give a three-line description of the dress Jean is wearing, what would you say?"

Bob thought a few seconds and then said, "Well, I like it. The color looks good. The dress looks like you, and I like some of the detail around the waist. It fits well and I like the curves. It just seems to look like you. And the style is flashy."

I asked Jean, "How do you feel about Bob's response?"

"That really feels good. He really seemed to notice, and I enjoyed hearing his description. But I guess I'd like to hear more feeling words, too."

Bob said, "Well, I could do that, but when I'm with some of my other friends and we say fine, we know what we mean."

I said, "I can understand that. When you're with them you speak the same language, but when you're with Jean, you need to speak her language. She wants more detail, more description, more adjectives, and more feeling words. That's what registers with her. This is a good example of what I mean by speaking the other person's language. Which one of you tends to give more detail when you talk?"

Jean replied, "I'm the detail person. Quite often Bob asks me to get to the point and give him the bottom line so he understands what I'm talking about. I just want to make sure that he's going to grasp what I am sharing. I've always given a lot of details and feelings, but sometimes it's as if he doesn't hear my feelings. He ignores them."

Bob said, "I don't ignore what you're saying. I do see what you are getting at, but I don't always know what to do with those feelings. It's not that I always mind the detail, but I wish you would focus on the bottom line first, instead of going around the barn several times and then telling me what you're talking about. I like it straightforward and to the point."

"Bob, you're asking Jean to condense some of the details a bit and identify the bottom line right at the start. That helps you focus on her conversation better. That also means, since Jean enjoys detail, that when you share with her, you will need to give her more detail than you do now."[9]

Did you note the different words we each used? Reread the interchange and note the visual, auditory, and feeling words and who used them. All of us see, hear, and feel. But both you and your spouse have a dominant sense through which you prefer to communicate and receive communication. One of your primary missions as a husband or wife is to discover your spouse's dominant sense and center your communication in that area. As you learn to communicate in your partner's language, your relationship will change.

Who takes the initiative for beginning to alter your typical communication pattern? Consider what Stu Weber suggests in his book, *Tender Warrior:*

> Women speak a different language than men. It's not Spanish or Korean or Swahili. It's not Hindi or Hebrew. It's "Woman," and it's spoken all over the planet. Yes, I suppose men have a language of sorts, too, but that's not the issue here. The crux of the matter is that women speak their own unique dialect and it is incumbent upon Tender Warriors to learn that language and speak it with passion.
>
> I'm reminded of a cross-cultural snapshot one of my friends described to me. On a brief trip to Haiti, he found himself alone in a room with a young Haitian man who seemed wide-eyed with excitement about meeting an American. The Haitian obviously longed to open a conversation. His hands opened and closed. His eyes burned with a desire to weave his thoughts into understandable words. He seemed to have a thousand questions on the tip of his tongue. But my friend didn't speak a word of Creole and the Haitian didn't speak English. So eventually, after a few smiles, nods, vague gestures, and self-conscious shrugs, the two young men strolled awkwardly to different corners of the room, and they parted—almost certainly for the rest of their lives.
>
> That little experience paints a powerful analogy in my mind. You and I know men and women who live together ten, twenty, *fifty* years or more but never learn to speak one another's language. They sit in rooms together, ride in cars together, eat meals together, take vacations together, and sleep together when the

sun goes down. But for year after empty year they never learn how to get beyond vague gestures and a few surface phrases.

That, my friend, is a *man's* responsibility. He is the one who must take the initiative and learn how to speak "Woman." There it is in clear terms.

In 1 Peter 3:7 it says, "You husbands... live with your wives in an understanding way, as with a weaker vessel, since she is a woman; and grant her honor as a fellow heir of the grace of life."

Webster defines understanding as "gaining a full mental grasp." Not bad. Those are words we men ought to be able to grapple with. To understand is to gain a full mental grasp of the nature and significance of something. To understand is a mental process of arriving at a result. It's when you study and study an issue, turn it this way and that, and suddenly the wires connect, the light blinks on and you say, "Ah-ha! So *that's* the way it works!" There ought to be ah-ha's as we seek to comprehend the implications of womanhood. Men are commanded to understand, to comprehend, to apprehend the meaning of, to grasp the force of living with a woman. Understanding involves a discerning skill, a rational process, and a reasoned judgment.[10]

Speaking your spouse's language includes not only vocabulary but also the person's packaging. Packaging refers to whether a person is an amplifier (sharing great volumes of details) or a condenser (sharing little more than the bottom line).

If he's an amplifier, go for it. If he's a condenser, keep it brief. Neither men nor women want to hear a monologue of the reasons they need to fulfill a request.

Amplifiers give a number of descriptive sentences as they talk, while condensers give one or two sentences. In approximately 70 percent of marriages, the man is the condenser and the woman is the amplifier. Neither is a negative trait, but the amplifier wishes his or her partner would share more, while the condenser wishes his or her partner would share less. It is only when each of you adapts to the style of your partner that real communication occurs.

And don't spend time recounting all the times your partner didn't come through for you or did it wrong. You'll just reinforce the possibility they'll repeat what you don't want to happen. Always, always talk about what you want and present it in such a way that they catch in your request the belief that they can do it.

If your partner is an amplifier, give lots of information and detail. Keep it brief for condensers. You can always expand if the condenser wants more. But we also have to take into consideration someone's seeing, hearing, or feeling preference and this preference reflects how a person learns best.

THE EYES HAVE IT

A visual man (or woman) relates to the world around him in terms of how things look to him. This is how the person learns best and 70 percent of people are visual. When he imagines he visualizes, and when he remembers, he recalls a picture. He experiences life through his eyes. He is primarily a watcher—movies, TV, sporting events, people, art exhibits or museums, scenery. He probably prefers reading, collecting items to look at, taking pictures, and looking at you. He is often concerned with how he looks to others. A visual person talks about how things look rather than how he feels. Often a visual person tends to withdraw and brood when upset rather than talking through the problem. Is this anyone you know?

Visual people prefer face-to-face conversations over using the telephone and respond well to written messages. That's me! They want to see a letter firsthand rather than have it read to them. A visual person who travels wants a map nearby and prefers to study it personally rather than having it described by another.

How can you tell if a person is visually oriented? Listen to the words he uses. Here is a list of statements that are more typical of a visual person:

From my point of view...

I see what you're driving at.

That looks like a sure thing.

That's really clear to me.

What you're picturing is...

I don't know; I've drawn a blank.

Show me what you're getting at.

There's a clear pattern to this.

It's beginning to dawn on me.

What do all these words mean? If you are an astute spouse, you will begin to communicate in terms that your partner can best appreciate and receive.

Here are some phrases you can use in response to the visual person:

I'm beginning to see your point of view.

That looks good to me.

What you shared with me really lights up my day.

You know, I can just picture us on the beach in Maui.

Practice using visually-oriented words, especially if they are new to you. Write down a list of visual words—as many as possible—and look for ways to use them in conversation with your visually-oriented partner. If you usually say, "That feels good to me," change it to "That looks good to me" when you are talking with a visual person. You will probably feel awkward at first as you try out a new vocabulary. Continue to practice and you will soon feel at ease. This is the first step in requesting a change in behavior or in the relationship.

Don't expect your spouse to notice your change in vocabulary. He or she probably won't be consciously aware of a language improvement. But your visual spouse will feel more comfortable in relating to you, perhaps without even knowing why.

Men tend to be more visual than women; in fact, most men are visual persons. In our society, women tend to lean toward feelings. But both men and women can learn to strengthen the two senses that are subordinate to the dominant language. Over the years the visual trait has been and still is my strong suit. But I have worked on the other two areas and now enjoy a greater balance.

If you live with a visual person you must adjust to his dominant style of perception. For example, if you are planning to buy new chairs for the family room, you will want to discuss with your spouse how the room's appearance will improve in addition to how comfortable the chairs will be. If you want to escape to a quiet retreat with no phones and few people, emphasize to your visual spouse the scenic aspects of the location. The visual person is more responsive to certain aspects of lovemaking. A romantic decor, leaving the lights on, or making sure you wear certain apparel may be more important.

THE EARS HAVE IT

The auditory man or woman wants to hear about life. This is how this individual learns best and 20 percent of our population falls into the auditory category. This individual relates more to sounds than sights. Reading a book, the auditory person hears words silently rather than seeing pictures. If your partner is auditory, don't expect a new article of clothing, hairdo, room arrangement, or plant in the yard to be noticed. You need to tell this person more than you show him or her. This individual prefers talking about something to looking at it. Long conversations are important to the auditory spouses and they tend to remember what they hear better than others.

If you want to share feelings, the auditory person will best understand you if you verbalize how you feel. Auditory people hear equally what is said and not said, and they are astute at picking up tonal changes and voice inflections. Harsh responses may be upsetting to them. The telephone is an important part of their lives.

Auditory people fall into two different categories. Some feel compelled to fill the silent moments of life with sound: talking, playing the stereo, humming. But others prefer quiet. Why would an auditory person opt for silence? Because many of them are carrying on internal conversations and external sounds are an interruption. Sometimes a silent auditory person's intermittent spoken responses may not make sense to you because he fails to relate the ongoing conversation in his head.

Romancing an auditory partner must include saying, "I love you" again and again. But how you say it is as important as how often you say it. Discover the words, phrases, and tones that best convey your spoken love and use them often.

Here are some of the words and phrases an auditory person uses:

That sounds good to me.

Let's talk about this again.

Boy, that's music to my ears!

People seem to tune him out when he's talking.

Harmony is important to me.

I hear you clear as a bell.

Tell me a little more about it.

Give me a call so we can discuss the proposal.

Your tone of voice is coming through loud and clear.

What kind of responses should you use with auditory people? The same types of words and phrases as they use. Identify them, write them out, and practice them. A simple change from "Doesn't that look good to you?" to "Doesn't that sound good to you?" will make a difference to an auditory person. Instead of asking, "Would you like to go see that new movie with me?" ask "How does attending that new movie sound to you?" Asking auditory people to share their feelings may not provoke a response. But asking them to say what comes to mind when they hear the words *love, romance, sexy,* or whatever will tap into their auditory style. Now you're speaking their language.

You may say, "Changing the way we talk to one another sounds like a pointless game that requires a lot of work." Work, yes; game, no. Effective communication requires being sensitive to, and diligently accommodating, the uniqueness of your partner. By learning new ways to talk we climb out of our communication ruts and become more flexible. Changing your style of communication can make the difference between holding your spouse's attention and being ignored. That would seem to be reason enough!

After learning about these differences a woman told me she understood her husband better. She said, "I used to ask Grant if he couldn't see that I had too much work to do and I needed his help. But it was as though that didn't register with him. All he was concerned about was the noise level around the house. He wanted the kids to quiet down and the stereo softer. After I discovered he was auditory I realized that loud sounds bothered him more than the clutter I needed help with. I used to think he was just overly picky when a faucet or freeway noise bothered him at night."

Remember Herb and Amy? Go back and reread their brief dialogue and the problem may be a bit more obvious. But there's also a third group of people.

NOTHING MORE THAN FEELINGS

Some people tend to be very feelings-oriented, although it is more often true of women than men. (When it comes to learning, only 10 percent fall into this learning style even though many more are very feelings-oriented. Thus a visual person can still be very feeling.) Feelings-oriented people tend to touch a lot. They often desire to develop deep relationships. They crave closeness, love, and affection. They are generally "right-brain" people, operating more intuitively than logically or analytically. Physical comfort and bodily sensations are important parts of their language style.

Feelings-oriented people often show their feelings even though many of them do not verbalize them well. You can usually read happiness, sadness, anger, love, or delight on their faces or hear these emotions in the tone of their voices. And they are concerned about how others feel toward them. A feelings-oriented man who can effectively verbalize his emotions can be one of the easiest husbands to live with.

Feelings-oriented people are more spontaneous than auditory or visual people. This trait can be both positive and negative. On one hand they are free to create spur-of-the-moment, fun activities. On the other hand they may, for no apparent logical reason, change their minds and upset the schedule of a plan-in-advance spouse.

The feelings-oriented person often uses the following words and phrases:

I have some good vibes about this.

I have a sense about that.

I like to get close to you.

That person was so sensitive.

I'm so happy today. Yesterday I was unhappy.

I like being near you.

You will also hear words like *touch, tense, pressure, hurt, touchy, soft, smooth, handle,* and *relaxed* from a feelings person. Whereas the visual person says, "It looks good to me," and the auditory person says, "It sounds good to me," the feelings person will say, "It feels good to me," or "I'm comfortable with that," or "I understand how you feel."

If you were a car salesman, and wanted to relate to a feelings-oriented customer, you wouldn't say, "You really look good in that car." Nor would you say, "Doesn't it sound quiet inside?" Rather you would say, "Don't you feel comfortable and relaxed behind the wheel? What a sensation it is to drive this car on the highway." You communicate with a feelings person through his emotions.

Feelings-oriented people like to be known for their sensitivity. A wise spouse will notice this trait and comment on it often. Feelings people like to be touched often, especially when spoken to.

I switch forms of expression quite often when I'm counseling. I may see eight different clients during the day, but I try to speak each person's specific language—visual, auditory, or feelings.

What happens when two people with different perceptions marry (which is usually the case)?

If a visual woman marries an auditory man, the husband may not meet his wife's standards for dressing because he is less concerned with fashion. Also, the wife may tend more toward neatness and orderliness in the household because of its visual attractiveness. The auditory husband may forget the visible shopping list his wife gives him, but will have better success remembering verbal lists and instructions.

What if the husband is visual and the wife is auditory? He attempts to show his love by buying her flowers and gifts and taking her places. Then one day she says, "You don't love me," and he's floored. He points to all the things he has given her, but she simply says, "You never tell me you love me." To the auditory wife, words are more important than gifts.

The auditory wife may also err by limiting the expression of her love to her visually-oriented husband to mere words. He may appreciate his wife telling him of her love, but he will really get the message when his brain receives certain visual stimuli. Her attention to grooming and dress, neatness in the home, and pleasant sights rather than sounds will visually present her love.

Sometimes people come into my work area and rearrange my personal items. These people may think I won't notice, but I do. I have also made some people uncomfortable when, in a home or a doctor's office, I will take it upon myself to straighten a crooked picture on the wall. What does this say about me? Yes, I am more visually-oriented.

Some couples clash over buying new furniture. The visual spouse wants the room to look neat and new while the feelings person wants to feel good and comfortable in the room. The loving solution? Agreeing on furniture that is both neat and comfortable, meeting the needs of both partners.

The feelings-oriented person needs to respond to the visual spouse by talking about how he "sees" things. The visual partner, in turn, should learn to develop a "feel" for those things that are important to his partner.[11]

THE WORTH OF WORDS

Let's consider some of the words Bob and I used in talking together. They were *focus, eye to eye, see, picture, looked, detail, flashy.*

Let's consider some of the words Jean and I used. They were *feel, sense, handle, feeling, felt, enjoyed, grasp.*

Is there any significance to the difference in the selection of these words? Definitely.

When we understand these differences, we will then understand our partner's reactions, misunderstandings, annoying habits, and personality peculiarities. If our spouse's style is different from ours, then we approach them in their language style first and then lead them to understand what we are saying.

For example, if your wife is visual, don't demand that she open up and respond on a feeling level. First, she has to connect with you on a visual level to feel comfortable. If your feelings are shared gradually, in a visual style, your partner will begin to relate to you. It's not always the easiest for a visual person to express his or her feelings in words.

Explain to your spouse that you can see her feelings even if she is not expressing them. Ask how things look to her first rather than how she feels. In time you can ask, "How would you express that if you were to use my feelings words?" and she just may be able to do it.

If your husband is auditory don't expect him to notice right off your new outfit or that you've washed the car or cleaned the garage. He needs to hear about it first. If you want your spouse to share his feelings, remember they are triggered by what he hears. He's more tuned into words than feelings and he usually carries on inner conversations with himself.

Yes, it's true. You probably married a foreigner when it comes to communication. But any and all of us can learn to adapt and expand our ability to connect with our spouse. And you know what? It's worth the effort! And when you put your request for change into a presentation that matches the other person's uniqueness of gender, personality, communication style, and perceptual style, not only do you show respect for that person but you will be heard.

HOW'D THEY DO IT?

"I wanted more nonsexual touching. After listening to the *Language of Love* presentation I prayed and God gave me a word picture to use with my husband.

"Our marriage had gotten to the point where I didn't want my husband to touch me in any way. I'd curl up on my side of the bed and say 'night.' He would try to hold me and I'd turn away and find something I 'had' to do. It was bad for both of us. I knew as a wife it was my duty to have sex, and so we did, but I'd roll over and cry afterwards. I did a lot of praying that God would change my feelings. I didn't want to hate his touch. I didn't hate him. We could talk easily about anything as long as we weren't touching.

"God gave me a word picture. We are farmers and have an old diesel-run tractor. To start this tractor in the winter you have to push a button and hold it in to warm it up. Then it will start. I told him I was like this cold tractor. When he touched me in a sexual way it was like turning the key on the tractor. It may sound like it would start, you may want it to start, but it won't, and as soon as you quit turning the key it's over. But when you put your arm around me in church, hold my hand in the car, help me clear the table, kiss my neck and that's all, it's like holding in the little silver button and warming me up. Then when you 'turn the key'—I'll start! (He just cried—it was the first time he understood what I meant.) We agreed 'no sex' for one month. I began not to feel threatened and we began to enjoy each other's touch. It didn't happen overnight, but our marriage is stronger in all ways than ever before.

"Our marriage is better than ever. Our sex life is better, but our nonsexual marriage is much better."

TAKE ACTION

1. Describe how your listening habits and your spouse's listening habits could be improved.

2. What response could you give to your spouse that would enable him or her to improve their communication with you?

3. Describe how you and your spouse usually word your requests. How could these be improved?

4. Place your name or your spouse's by the following words if they apply.

   Condenser

   Amplifier

   Visual

   Auditory

   Feelings-Oriented

5. To what degree do you speak one another's language? Evaluate this on a scale of 0 to 10.

0	1	2	3	4	5	6	7	8	9	10
Non-existent					Average					Superb

CHAPTER TEN

Conflict: The Pathway to Intimacy

Gary J. Oliver

I had been to London several times as a single student but this was the first time Carrie and I had been there together. We were on our way to Amsterdam to begin a two-week tour of Europe and had two days to spend in London. That was the good news.

The bad news is we arrived just three days before the royal wedding was to take place. I had never seen London so packed. The city was jammed with people from all over the world. But even more interesting was the uncharacteristic spirit of enthusiasm and optimism in the air. People had been captivated by the magical courtship and romance of Prince Charles and Lady Diana and were excited about the wedding.

Three days later they walked down the aisle and stood in front of Robert Runcie, Archbishop of Canterbury. He looked Prince Charles and Lady Diana in the eyes and in a warm yet solemn voice said,

Here is the stuff of which fairy tales are made, the prince and princess on their wedding day. But fairy tales usually end at this point with the simple phrase, "They lived happily ever after." This may be because fairy tales regard marriage as an anticlimax after the romance of courtship. This is not the Christian view. Our faith sees the wedding day not as a place of arrival but the place where the adventure begins.[1]

Unfortunately, far too many people see their wedding day as a place of arrival and not as the place where the real adventure begins.

Marriage, especially in its first year, is a relationship that demands flexibility, adjustments, and change. Not necessarily major personality reconstruction but certainly numerous minor adjustments and fine-tunings. Unless people look at their marriage vows as a commitment to grow, they are in for some increasingly difficult times and will grow apart, never achieving the intimacy and trust they both desire.

One of the main problems that plagues marriages is unresolved conflict. It started long ago in the garden of Eden with Adam and Eve and it's been going on ever since. We don't understand it. Most of us don't like it. I've heard it said that there's only one thing people avoid more than change, and that's conflict. If you think about it, that's not too surprising, since conflict is frequently an inevitable part of the change process.

What do you think of when you hear the word *conflict?* Is your first reaction positive or negative? What do you feel like after you've experienced a conflict with someone you love? What is your first memory of conflict?

Most people haven't learned the value of conflict. We misunderstand its potential and interpret it as an attack. We view conflict as a rude and unwelcome interruption in our lives rather than a normal and necessary part of being in relationship.

Conflict is a major theme in the Bible. From Genesis to Revelation we find people in conflict with God, with themselves, and with each other. Conflict is the process we go through and the price we pay for intimacy. After over fifty years of combined experience in counseling, we have seen that intimacy is always achieved at the price of facing our differences and negative feelings, listening, understanding, and resolving them.

Conflict is a necessary and potentially valuable part of the change process. Unfortunately, most people don't understand the potential value of conflict, and by avoiding it they avoid growth. What's the opposite of growth? Stagnation, deterioration, and the discouragement that comes from remaining stuck.

In Romans 15 we are encouraged to "be of the same mind," to "accept one another," and to "admonish one another." This is especially applicable to marriage. Relationships involve people coming together. However, as we seek to "become one in Christ" we find that our differences can produce problems. They can lead to disagreements that at times result in conflict.

Our differences—when understood, appreciated, and allowed to be used by God—are those things God created for the great purpose of conforming us to the image of His Son or, as Proverbs puts it, to "sharpen" one another. What do you get when iron rubs against iron? Heat. Sparks fly. But if the pieces are rubbed in the right way, they inevitably sharpen each other.

This process of rubbing lives together day after day, month after month, year after year, becomes God's change-agent—His refining tool to make us better people, to rub off the rough edges of our personalities, to give us understanding hearts, to teach us acceptance, to help us change. This change will occur if we choose to learn from each other. But if we remain rigid, we will thwart one of the great purposes of marriage.[2]

Churches are not destroyed by differences. Families are not destroyed by differences. Marriages are not destroyed by differences. They are destroyed by the immature, irresponsible, and unhealthy ways we choose to respond to those differences. They are destroyed by our inability or unwillingness to take them to God and allow Him to use our differences for His glory.

GROWTH OR STAGNATION?

When we experience conflict we are faced with an important decision: How will we choose to interpret conflict? We can choose to interpret it positively or negatively. Our choice will determine to a great degree whether our love relationship will deepen and grow or whether we will get stuck and stagnate.

TWO WAYS TO INTERPRET CONFLICT

Choice #1: We can choose to see conflict as negative—something to be avoided at all costs. I know some people who believe that one sign of Christian maturity is that everyone must always agree. This distorted perspective interprets conflict as a sign of immaturity and carnality.

Those who believe that differences always lead to division tend to discourage individual uniqueness and creativity. They place pressure on others not to disagree. From their perspective, spirituality and maturity are in part determined by the degree to which everyone thinks alike.

Someone has said that where everyone always agrees and thinks alike no one thinks very much at all. Several years ago I saw a bumper sticker that read "Christ died to take away our sins, not our brains."

If we view conflict as negative, we are likely to experience emotions such as fear, anger, or frustration. We will either respond to those emotions by avoiding the situation or attacking the person we think is challenging us. If we choose to avoid, our response will lead to greater distance. It won't solve the problem, it will only postpone our need to deal with it. If we choose to attack, our response is likely to create a bigger problem and lead to division.

Negative Interpretation of Conflict
> motivated by fear, hurt, frustration, anger
> responds by avoiding or attacking
> results in division or distance

Throughout this chapter, let's become acquainted with another couple, Ken and Laura, who had experienced much marital conflict. As we discussed the different ways people can interpret conflict, Ken and Laura realized that almost always they both interpreted it negatively. Ken's pattern was to feel threatened, so he avoided conflict. That's how his dad had done it, that's how "gramps" had done it. "How often has this helped to solve the problem?" I asked Ken. "Well," he paused, "as I think about it I don't know that it has ever helped."

As you might have already guessed, Laura's response was the opposite of Ken's. At the point of conflict she would feel hurt and frustrated and so she tended to attack. "I just wish Ken would talk about issues for once in his life. Whenever there seems to be an issue he does his deaf and dumb act." What do you think Ken did when he felt attacked? Of course! He withdrew; he sought distance from Laura.

Choice #2: We can choose to see conflict through God's eyes as a great opportunity for increased intimacy, growth, and maturity. The process of growing into an intimate relationship involves conflict. Since many of us avoid it like the plague we don't grow, we don't change, we don't get close, we don't experience intimacy. We stay stuck in the rut of mediocrity.

Rather than deal with the issues, rather than speak the truth in love, it's easier to deny, repress, suppress, and ignore what we are feeling until the fear, hurt, and frustration become intolerable. Then we dump and do damage.

If we choose to see conflict from a positive perspective we are more likely to be motivated by love. This leads to a healthy confrontation where we risk speaking the truth in love. This results in increased trust, peace, love, understanding, and unity.

The positive response says:

1. There are issues that are important to me.
2. I care enough about you and our relationship to risk confrontation; I care enough about you and our relationship to speak the truth in love.
3. I don't lose when I'm proven wrong. I don't lose when I don't get my way.
4. I DO LOSE when I throw away an opportunity to learn, care, and grow.

Mature people don't avoid, suppress, repress, deny, or ignore conflict. Rather they see it as an opportunity. Once people come to see conflict that way, they are able to exchange their defensive and combative posture for a creative one. They don't feel threatened, they feel challenged.[3]

POSITIVE INTERPRETATION OF CONFLICT
>motivated by love and hope
>>responds by a confrontation of speaking the truth in love
>>>results in trust, peace, love, understanding, and unity

No one wins in a world where we don't speak the truth in love, where conflict is denied or avoided or both. No one grows where the truth is absent, where no one is pushed to be and do the best. Without conflict we remain relationally shallow. Intimacy can never develop. We will never become all that God has designed us to be.

Some of us avoid conflict because we are afraid of being proven wrong. Let's face it, nobody enjoys being wrong. Yet there are two ways we can interpret being wrong. If we view it as negative, if our value, worth, significance, and security are based on being right all of the time, then being wrong is catastrophic. It means that we're bad, we've failed, we're a loser. However, if we choose to look at the possibility of being wrong from a positive perspective, we can see it as an opportunity to learn, grow, change, and become more mature.

What's the price tag for our inability or unwillingness to face problems and learn how to resolve conflicts? It keeps us from:

knowing ourselves

knowing others

getting close to others

establishing or building meaningful and quality relationships

experiencing meaningful ministry

experiencing God's best for our lives

HOW CAN WE TURN THIS AROUND?

Is it possible to change some of these deep-seated, automatic, responses to conflict? Based on our work with thousands of couples the answer to both of those questions is a resounding yes!

Understand that conflict develops through predictable stages.[4] If you and your spouse can identify and understand the underlying patterns that lead to conflict, you are much more likely to make your conflict work for you rather than against you.

Remember, conflict arises because every human being is different. Stop for just a moment and think about your spouse. What are some of the ways in which you are different? Do you come from different ethnic backgrounds? Were you raised in different parts of the country? Did one grow up in the country and another in a large city?

How were your childhoods different? What were your parents like? How many brothers and sisters did you have? What were your birth orders? What are your personality-type preferences? Which ones are similar and which ones are different?

When Ken first met Laura, he was attracted to her fun-loving, extroverted style. She loved to talk with people and had a way of drawing him out. Laura was attracted to Ken because he seemed like "the strong, silent, and thoughtful type. He was so different from all of the other guys I had dated." So far so good. We call this the stage of *acceptable differences.* These differences are normal and healthy.

While they were dating Ken and Laura would bump into some differences but the excitement of romantic love felt so good they chose to gloss over them. For a while they successfully ignored them. However, after they were married they found themselves disagreeing more and more. The differences they had only partially understood and had chosen to ignore during courtship were becoming a problem. At this point they had left acceptable differences and entered stage two: *uncomfortable differences.*

For the first two days of the honeymoon everything went great. Eventually, however, their differences led to disagreements they could no longer ignore. Unfortunately, neither one of them grew up in a home where they had learned healthy styles of conflict resolution. It didn't take them long to develop a dance that only after several years they were able to identify. One variation of the dance went something like this:

1. Laura shares an emotion or feeling. Ken feels threatened or criticized and, in turn, challenges the "logic" of her feeling… or he hears what Laura says as a message that he needs to be responsible and tries to "fix" the problem.

2. Laura tries again.

3. Ken feels like he has failed to understand or help her and so he withdraws into "his responsibilities" to avoid his rising anger or discomfort.

4. Laura's frustration leads to anger that she expresses by criticizing Ken, trying to "draw him out." She continues to "push" Ken to get him to interact with her.

5. Ken starts criticizing her as a way to protect himself and in his anger he calls her names and shames her.

6. Laura feels put down and Ken feels rejected and unhappy with his own behavior, but he isn't willing to admit it or be vulnerable.

7. Ken or Laura "lose it" and attack each other with generalizations such as "you always" or "you never" or "you're just like your mother (father)."

8. The situation is so disappointing and painful that their fear of conflict and their belief that nothing good can ever come from conflict is reinforced and they simply work harder to stuff, suppress, repress, deny, and ignore problems until, once again, they grow to the point of threatening the relationship.[5]

In stage three the couple hits the wall of conflict. At this stage many men feel threatened by their own vulnerability and the increasingly assertive behavior of their wives. Some women experience physical abuse at the hands of their husbands. Unhealthy and out-of-control anger can take center stage, and the legitimate concerns and issues that led to the conflict are forgotten in the wake of the deeper fears and anxieties they have struggled with for years.

Ken and Laura did what many couples do. They cycled back to stage one and started the process all over again. They may have several hours or days of silence, they may kiss and make up and pretend that everything is "fine." Nothing is clearly identified or resolved. They've lost another opportunity to learn from their differences. At this point a light came on for Ken, "We've been doing this silly dance for years. And we always end up right back where we started."

"You're right," I replied. "Do you want to continue to do that dysfunctional dance?" I asked. They both blurted out an emphatic "No!" I went on to tell them that with help and over time they could learn to break through the wall of conflict and move to stage four to *achieve the understanding, growth, and resolution that produces change.* However, if they were to do this they would need to identify their dysfunctional styles of dealing with conflict and replace them with healthy styles.

Understand and appreciate the nature and value of conflict. Both Ken and Laura had an automatically negative interpretation of conflict. "I never dreamed that conflict could be constructive," Ken observed. He came from a home in which conflict was avoided. Laura came from a home where she saw all kinds of conflict but little

HOW CONFLICTS DEVELOP[6]

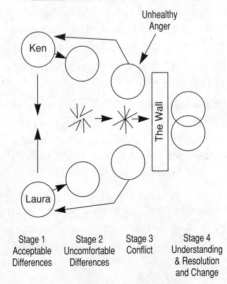

Stage 1	Stage 2	Stage 3	Stage 4
Acceptable Differences	Uncomfortable Differences	Conflict	Understanding & Resolution and Change

of it was healthy. I reached into my desk drawer and pulled out a handout I give couples on the "Twelve Principles of Healthy Conflict." I'll let you read them for yourself:

1. Conflict is a natural phenomenon and is inevitable. Cadavers don't have conflict. They are calm, cool, and laid-back. An occupational hazard of being human is that we will experience conflict.

2. Conflict involves both personal needs and relationship needs.

3. Most conflict is not dealt with openly because most people have not been taught effective ways of resolving conflict. When there is conflict most of us:

   > tend to see only one solution... ours.

   > tend to personalize it.

   > tend to interpret it as an attack.

   > tend to magnify negative implications of statements.

4. Conflict provides opportunities for growth in a relationship.

5. Unresolved conflicts interfere with growth and satisfying relationships. Problems don't magically disappear. They go underground and grow and develop into other problems.

6. As we understand the value of conflict we can allow it to serve a more positive and constructive role in our lives.

7. The more we try to deny, hide from, overlook, and otherwise avoid conflict the greater the problem becomes.

8. It is normal to feel defensive when challenged or criticized, thus conflict often involves anger.

9. Conflict isn't good or bad, right or wrong... conflict simply is. It is how we choose to respond to conflict that produces the growth or creates the real problem.

10. If we want conflict to serve a constructive role in our lives, conflict resolution must become a priority.

11. Constructive conflict involves a commitment to serve one another, encourage one another, and be vulnerable with one another. In the early stages it involves caring enough to be willing to take some risks.

12. Constructive conflict involves a commitment to stop, look, and listen, and then, maybe, speak.[7]

Whenever two people disagree there are always at least two levels of need. First of all there are some personal needs. Part of the reason we have conflict is that at times what I think or want differs from what you think or want.

On their honeymoon Ken wanted to get to the destination and then enjoy himself. His goal was to arrive at the hotel at the time they had planned. On the other hand Laura wasn't too concerned about when they got to the hotel. She wanted to enjoy the trip there. She thought it might be fun to explore some shops along the way, look for a quaint restaurant, and talk.

While Ken and Laura had different personal agendas they both wanted to nurture their relationship. They had personal needs but they also had relationship needs. Ken said, "I knew it was important for me to deal with this issue in a way that wouldn't seriously injure or destroy our relationship." That of course is the challenge of effective conflict resolution. How can we deal with issues in ways that take into account both our personal and relationship needs?

Learn how to identify your style of conflict. The least effective style is to cede or withdraw. In style 1 we say "I'll get out." We refuse to discuss the situation and stonewall our partner. This style is the least effective because we lose out on both our personal and relationship needs.

In style 2 we say "I'll get what I want or I'll get him or her." We go for "control." This was Laura's preferred style. She was bright, verbal, confident, assertive, and competitive. When she wanted something she went for it. She was usually able to do it in ways that were healthy and appropriate, that showed sensitivity and respect for the other person.

However, when her sense of significance or security was threatened she would go for the win. In this mode her motto was "Take no captives." In the win mode she was able to get her personal needs met but at the cost of the relationship. Over time she learned that, in any relationship, whenever one person wins what really happens is that both people lose.

Some people whose predominant style is 2 aren't as healthy as Laura was. They always have to be right. They need to see themselves as better, brighter, and more important than anyone else.

They are people who have become legends in their own mind. They have what psychologists call a narcissistic personality disorder. I heard one therapist say that a narcissist is like a cracked pitcher. No matter how much applause, praise, or recognition they get, the leaking container of whom they see themselves to be can never be filled.

While Laura's predominant style was 2, Ken's was 3. Style 3 says "I believe in peace at any price, so I'll capitulate or give in." For awhile Ken was able to do this. After all Ken was a man and the Bible teaches that men are to be peacemakers. Meeting his need for harmony was at times more important than getting his personal needs met.

It doesn't take much thought to see that the first three styles are unhealthy and can be destructive. They lead to circular arguments that produce more heat than light, that build more walls than bridges, that increase the hurting rather than the healing.

In style 4 we come to the first of the two healthy styles. Style 4 involves compromise and says "I'll meet you halfway." Some people use the word *compromise* as a synonym for *sell-out*. Webster defines it as an adaptation, adjustment of differences, or a settlement. In conflict it means that I am willing to bargain some of my personal needs for some of my relationship needs. Legitimate love always requires a bit of compromise. In my experience over 90 percent of our conflicts can be dealt with through compromise.

In style 4 we are able to reach a solution for the immediate problem. Ken and Laura frequently disagreed about what TV shows they felt the kids should watch. With some patience and encouragement they finally developed enough conflict resolution skills that they were able to decide whether their kids should or should not watch a particular program.

Style 5 is similar to style 4 but it goes an additional step. Style 5 invites us to move beyond compromise to collaboration. It says "I'll grow with you beyond this problem." In compromise we are able to solve a specific issue. As we talk, share, listen, and ask questions, as we better understand our spouse, child, or friend, we at times are able to go beyond the specific issue at hand and arrive at a solution that deals with the whole category of issues.

As Ken and Laura talked about their concerns with various TV programs their discussion expanded to movies. They began to clarify both for themselves and for each other the deeper values that underlie the opinions they expressed. Over the course of several conversations, some of them rather animated, they discovered that not only did they understand each other, they had arrived at a mutual policy regarding all movies and TV programs for their kids.

The following chart uses minus and plus signs to show the effectiveness of the five styles of conflict. Giving in is ineffective; and while control meets one's personal needs, it is a failure in dealing with relationship needs. When I capitulate I get some short-term relationship needs met at the cost of my personal needs. When I compromise I bargain some of my personal needs for my relationship needs. Clearly, the most effective method is collaboration, where we work together, take time to understand the issues behind the conflict, and leave the conflict not only having solved the immediate problem at hand but with a deeper understanding of and appreciation for each other's perspective. Study the chart below.

	PERSONAL NEEDS	RELATIONSHIP NEEDS
1) Cede	–	–
2) Control	+	–
3) Capitulate	–	+
4) Compromise	+	+
5) Collaborate	+++	+++

Now it's time to ask yourself, "What is my predominant style of conflict resolution?" What style was modeled for you in your family of origin? We've seen that Ken grew up with the capitulate style and Laura grew up with the control style. Which style are you most likely to respond in? If you are like most people, it is one of the first three styles: cede, control, or capitulate. Are you happy with your current style? If not, are you willing to make a commitment to change, to grow in your ability to effectively deal with conflict?

Identify the factors that usually precede your most frequent conflicts. This will help you deal more effectively with the conflicts once they arise. Most couples find that this simple process also helps clarify and reduce unnecessary conflicts.

Start by identifying frequent conflict issues and determine their seriousness. Many couples find that a majority of their conflicts center around sex, money, parenting, in-laws, leisure time, and holidays. Ken and Laura discovered that over three-fourths of their conflicts were in two categories: finances and leisure time.

Next identify the factors that make you most vulnerable to conflict. Ken found that he was most vulnerable when he had been working too hard and was under pressure to meet some deadline. Busyness and overcommitment increased the probability that he would engage in conflict.

Laura realized that she was more vulnerable when the kids had been particularly difficult or when when she and Ken hadn't had adequate couple time together. If you're not sure what your conflicts center around, ask your spouse, your children, or a friend. They'll be glad to tell you.

Next, ask yourself what are some of your behaviors that can sabotage constructive conflict? For example, does the volume of your voice increase? Do your attacks become more personal (i.e. you bring up past mistakes and failures or you start talking about your spouse's mother, or perhaps you engage in exaggerations and over-generalizations such as "you always," "you never")? Are you so consumed with communicating your point that you don't make a sincere effort to understand your partner's concerns?

As Ken and Laura answered this question they discovered that both of them had some unhealthy habits that contributed to their failure in resolving conflicts. Laura was the first to acknowledge "my biggest problem behaviors are that I interrupt Ken and at times complete his sentences for him, I have difficulty giving Ken time to think about an issue before discussing it, and I tend to want to solve a problem that we haven't clearly defined." Ken realized that, "I need to listen for Laura's heart and not just for the 'bottom line' and I need to stay with the conversation and not give in to my tendency to withdraw as soon as I get frustrated or uncomfortable."

WHEN CONFLICT STARES YOU IN THE FACE

We've seen that conflict is something that most people avoid, yet we all know conflicts are inevitable. Some conflicts can be dealt with quickly and easily and some take a lot more time and energy. Regardless of the severity of the conflict, however, I've found that constructive conflict resolution is always easier when you have a plan.

Over the past twenty years many men and women have found that the following seven steps have helped them make conflict work for them, rather than against them. I know that you'll find it worth your time to give them a try.

Acknowledge, discuss, and define the conflict. The first step is to acknowledge that there is a problem, set aside ample time to discuss each other's perception of the issue, and then work toward an agreed-upon definition. Frequently when people disagree the temptation is to try to solve a problem that's at best only partially defined and barely understood.

During this time, you may need to agree to disagree with the other person. Some issues can be taken care of in one discussion and some may take seven or eight. Disagreement may continue for a while. If you place pressure on yourself to "solve this thing" you will only increase the level of frustration.

Once you define the problem, and before going any further, commit this specific conflict as well as your desire to deal with conflict in a healthier and more mature manner to God in prayer. In 1 Thessalonians 5:17 we are instructed to "pray without ceasing." In James 5:16 we read that "The effectual fervent prayer of a righteous man availeth much."

It will also be helpful to make a mutual decision as to which style you both will use to reach a solution. In her practical book, *The Dance of Anger,* Dr. Harriet Lerner has listed twelve additional suggestions that are important to keep in mind. Her Do's and Don'ts are practical:

1. Do speak up when an issue is important to you.
2. Don't strike while the iron is hot.
3. Do take time to think about the problem and to clarify your position.
4. Don't use "below-the-belt" tactics.
5. Do speak in "I" language.
6. Don't make vague requests.
7. Do try to appreciate the fact that people are different.
8. Don't participate in intellectual arguments that go nowhere.
9. Do recognize that each person is responsible for his or her own behavior.
10. Don't tell another person what he or she thinks or feels or "should" think or feel.
11. Do try to avoid speaking through a third party.
12. Don't expect change to come from hit-and-run confrontations.[8]

Ask yourself, "What is my contribution to the problem?" Whenever there is a conflict we usually have little difficulty identifying the other person's contribution to the problem. It's amazing how clear many of us can be about how "they" need to change, what "they" could do differently, and how "they" could listen better.

It's easy for us to pray, "Lord, please change them. Please help them see things as clearly as I do. Please give them the same wisdom and insight you've given me." It's easy for us men to pray "Change my *wife*, O Lord" rather than, in the words of a popular praise song, "Change my *life*, O Lord."

Proverbs 25:12 (LB) tells us that, "It is a badge of honor to accept valid criticism." Those are sound words. Listen to what the other person has to say. Even if 90 percent of what they are saying is invalid look for the 10 percent that might be true. Look for even the 1 percent that God could use in your life to help you deepen and mature.

Identify and develop alternate solutions to the problem. By this time you know what doesn't work. Ignoring the problem won't make it go away. Make a list of what you've tried that hasn't worked. Then make a list of what you haven't tried.

Talk to some other individuals or couples who've been in a similar situation. What worked for them? What did they learn as they worked through their conflict? In Step 3 be careful not to ignore a potential solution just because you don't think it will work. Get as many ideas as possible on your list. Look them over. Talk about them. You may find that pieces of two or three different ideas come together to provide a solution neither one of you had considered.

Another valuable idea is to take into account you and your partner's personality-type preferences. "One of the conflicts Laura and I had for years had to do with our different sense of timing, especially when it came to her shopping," Ken said. At this point in their marriage Ken realized that their personality differences were a key part of this conflict. "I'm structured, precise, and organized. I probably glance at my wrist every ten minutes to check the time, whether I need to or not. Laura is, well, a sort of spontaneous, free-spirited person who owns a watch but isn't sure why."

Sometimes when they would be out shopping, they would come to a store and Laura would tell Ken, "I need to run in here for something." Ken would ask, "How long will you be?" and she would give him her usual answer of, "Oh, no more than fifteen minutes."

In Ken's mind that's what it meant, exactly fifteen minutes. In

Laura's mind it could mean up to two hours! When the fifteen minutes was up Ken would begin to get frustrated. Finally, when she did return, they got into it. He accused her of being thoughtless and she accused him of being rigid and inflexible. Ken concluded, "I guess for me shopping was a task, something that I had to endure. But for her it was fun. Something she enjoyed and looked forward to. We knew that one of us needed to change."

Ken and Laura made the wise decision to start with a fairly safe conflict. They agreed to work on their frustrating differences in estimating time. They narrowed it down even further to the times when they were together and Laura wanted to make a "quick" stop to pick up something.

As they walked through the steps Laura realized that what often caused her to take longer than she thought was that, once in the store, she saw some other things she forgot she needed and decided that, since she was already there, to go ahead and pick them up. This often took more time than she thought. Ken realized that he was much more rigid than he needed to be. When some of his stops took more time, Laura never made a big deal about it. But whenever she took more time he always mentioned it. Here is a list of six changes they decided they would be willing to make.

1. If Laura wants to make a quick stop, only pick up what she said she was going in for and nothing else.

2. Laura can make her estimate then add an additional five minutes as a buffer. If the errand takes a little longer, no problem. If she comes back earlier, all the better.

3. Ken can go into the store to pick up the item.

4. Ken can "mellow out" about Laura being exact in her estimate of how long an errand might take. If she is within ten minutes that will be considered the same as being on time.

5. If it takes more time than Laura thought, she will let Ken know why.

6. They can do the errand together.

Discuss and decide on a mutually acceptable solution. Ah, this sounds so easy. Over time it can become easy but in the early stages of changing your conflict patterns, it may be rather difficult. Don't be upset or disappointed. It's normal!

When it comes to step 4 be sure to set aside ample time for discussion and prayer. Find a quiet place with no interruptions. Take the phone off the hook. Remember that you are choosing to bargain some of your personal needs for some of your relationship needs. Ken and Laura found it helpful to read 1 Corinthians 13 out loud before entering into the discussion.

At this point in workshops I've had people raise their hands and ask, "But what if we can't agree on a mutually acceptable solution?" After a brief pause I usually smile and respond by saying, "Well, if you can't agree on a solution reach into your pocket, pull out a coin, ask the other person if they want heads or tails, and flip it."

This usually brings a lot of laughter but I'm quick to tell them I'm serious. It's better to try something that might work than something that is a proven failure. Remember that, "Crazy is to find out what doesn't work and to keep on doing it."

If the first solution you try doesn't work, then move on to the next option. It may take three or four attempts before you find something that works. But if you follow through with my suggestions I think that over time you'll find there are very few issues you can't deal with.

List the specific steps involved and who is responsible to do what. This is an important step that most people leave out. What are the specific steps involved in the solution? Who is going to do what? When will they do it? For how long will they do it? When will you let each other know that you have done what you agreed to do?

If your issue is finances, who is going to record the checks, and when will you meet each month to check your progress? If the issue is child care, who will be responsible to check out the different options? And when will you do it?

Just do it! You've run from it, hid from it, fought about it, cried over it, and now you have the opportunity to resolve it. You have defined the problem, considered your contribution to it, discussed possible solutions, agreed on where to start, clarified who will do what, and now's your chance to make it work. Or to find out it doesn't work. Either way you both win. You are one step closer to discovering what will work and resolving the conflict.

Once you've agreed on what you are going to do differently and decided who is going to be responsible for what part of the plan, then do it. Don't wait for the "best" time. Put your plan into action now. Failure isn't trying something and finding it doesn't work. Failure is continuing to stay stuck in the rut of what hasn't worked in the past and probably won't in the future.

Review it. When you've given your plan adequate time, it's important to get together and discuss the results. How well has this solution worked? Were there any surprises? How could we improve it? How did I change? How did my partner change? What did I learn about myself from this conflict? What did I learn about our relationship? What did I learn about God's faithfulness? What did I learn about what I can do differently next time?

For years Ken and Laura had experienced frustrating and futile fights over the same issue. Even though it hadn't worked they had stayed in a rut of responding in the same ineffective way.

"What changed?" I asked. Ken responded, "I guess you could say that she changed me one day when she said, 'Ken, you haven't yet realized that my fifteen minutes and yours are different.' As soon as she said that a light went on," Ken said. "That's it! I couldn't believe I had experienced so much frustration over something so simple." Laura's observation helped Ken realize that what he was doing wasn't working. As they talked about the problem Laura realized there were some things she could do differently.

Ken continued, "So now when Laura says she's going shopping I ask, 'Do you have a rough approximation of when you might be through?' Laura smiles and says, 'Oh, in about an hour or two.'" This humorous response takes the pressure off both of them. Ken jumped in, "We now have a plan. If I go with her, I can take a book to read. And often she's back much sooner than she used to be." After a brief pause he concluded, "Maybe we've both changed."

HOW'D THEY DO IT?

"My wife and I were accustomed to living on two average incomes when our first child was born and I began seminary. Both of us went to part-time work in order to adjust to our new family and the demands of school. Our reduced income also necessitated a move to a much less attractive house. In addition, it became necessary for us to be much more thrifty than either one of us had ever experienced. My wife is not naturally given to bargain-hunting, coupon shopping, or other cost-saving measures. Being naturally a bit more of a tightwad, I realized that I needed to encourage her to change.

"To encourage my wife to change her shopping habits, I did several things: 1) I prayed for her to be open to change and I prayed that God would show me what to do and say so that she would want to change; 2) I very tactfully passed on cost-cutting tips I was aware of or learned about; 3) I held up the virtues of cost-cutting and the practices of other thrifty women we both knew; 4) I praised her each time she came home with a bargain; 5) I set an example of thriftiness and cost consciousness; 6) I allowed her to challenge and exhort me in this area as well; 7) I trusted God to change her because I couldn't do it alone.

"The challenge of living on less, especially with school expenses and then a second child was sometimes intimidating. We found, however, that we were still able to tithe to our church and also continue to save, even while my wife was out of work following the birth of girl number two. My wife is now proud of her good management of the household finances and I'm proud of her as well. We both have a deeper appreciation for the way God blesses those who are good stewards of what He entrusts to them. We've been equally blessed by freedom from the love of money and things and the added generosity of others in times of special need. Responding constructively to a potential threat to our relationship has drawn us closer together and given us confidence for facing other challenges."

TAKE ACTION

1. What are some of the differences between you and your spouse?

2. Is it possible that God has allowed or brought him or her into your life for a purpose?

3. What might God be wanting you to learn through those differences?

4. Throughout the week, look for the positive side of differences. Ask yourself:

    What can I learn?

    How can God use this in my life?

continued on page 204

5. When conflict comes remember that you have a choice:

A. Review the assumptions of conflict.

B. Note the stages of conflict.

C. Remember to pray. Share your prayer need with a trusted friend. Start by asking God to help you become a listener.

D. Remind yourself that caring and confrontation go hand in hand. Get out your Bibles and read:

Romans 12:19-16

1 Corinthians 13:5-7

Galatians 5:14-15

Ephesians 4:15-16

CHAPTER ELEVEN

If You Married a Perfectionist or Controller

H. Norman Wright

*P*erfectionism—the very word strikes fear in the heart of the person who lives with one. But for the perfectionist partner, the word brings a sense of satisfaction, security, and longing. Why? Because perfectionism is their quest, their source of security, their calling in life. But it is an elusive calling. I have yet to meet a successful perfectionist.

Most of us would like to be successful. Some of us, however, turn success into a requirement. When this happens, we become preoccupied with the pursuit, not of excellence, but of perfection. The greater the degree of pursuit, the more often our joy is lessened. Perfectionism becomes a mental monster.

In order to prove they are good enough, perfectionists strive to do the impossible. They set unrealistic goals and sky-high standards. They see no reason why they should not achieve them. They strain to reach these goals and expect their spouses to live up to them as well. They're driven by "musts, shoulds, have tos, and never good enoughs." They overschedule, overwork, overdo, and come unglued when there are surprises or unforeseen changes. Soon they are overwhelmed by the arduous task they have set for themselves.

The standards of a perfectionist are so high no one could consistently attain them. They are beyond reach and reason. The strain of reaching is continual, but the goals are impossible. Perfectionists

believe their worth is determined by attaining these goals. They live
with the fear of failure and because of this they often procrastinate.
They take positive traits to the extreme and make them liabilities.
Neatness, punctuality, responsibility, and attention to details are usually assets, but a perfectionist contaminates them.

INSIDE A PERFECTIONIST'S HEAD

Perfectionism is not so much a type of behavior as it is an attitude
or a belief. Let's climb inside the head of a perfectionist and discover
what he or she believes.

One belief is that *mediocrity breeds contempt.* The thought of
being ordinary is intolerable. Even the garden planted or the lunch
served must be the best. Perfectionists have to have the best sex, the
best grammar and speech, the best-behaved children, the best communication in marriage, the best dishes. The standards they set for
their partners and children are unbearable. They frequently cause
others to give up. The perfectionist is not really competing with
other people, but reacting to the inner message, *You can do better.*

Often the perfectionist tends to do *all or nothing.* "Either I go on
a diet all the way or not at all."

Another belief is the importance of *going it alone.* It is a sign of
weakness to delegate or ask for assistance. So the perfectionist must
not ask for advice or opinions. This does little to promote intimacy
in a marriage. The partner ends up feeling isolated.

Perfectionists think there is *one correct way to complete a task.*
Their main job is to discover that one right way. And until they have
made that discovery, there may be a hesitation to begin. "Why make
the wrong choice?" This even keeps some people from committing
themselves in marriage, for they certainly do not want to make the
wrong selection.

IN SEARCH OF THE PERFECT PARTNER

As Christians we are called to pursue a life of excellence, but striving after perfectionism is not a spiritual calling nor a gift. When you
pursue excellence you can be just as thorough, careful, and meticulous as a perfectionist, but in the process you enjoy what you do.

You don't always have to be the best, you can accept and learn from failure, and your identity is not based upon your performance. (See the conclusion of this chapter for a comparison of excellence and perfection.)

A perfectionistic man or woman has great trouble finding an acceptable marriage partner. Perfectionists want perfect mates, not human ones. Sometimes they tend to reject potential partners, often delaying marriage for years. They have difficulty forming relationships close enough to lead to marriage. One man in his early forties told me he had dated hundreds of women looking for the perfect one. He is still single today. Some people simply give up the attempt to form close human ties and devote themselves to work, not realizing that it lies within their power to change their attitude toward themselves. Such is the case with many successful bachelors and career women.

A perfectionist often looks upon marriage as another achievement. A prospective mate is viewed through rose-colored glasses and seen as "perfect." But the fantasy soon fades, especially after marriage. A friend of mine, Dr. Dave Stoop, describes the situation graphically. He says the spouse is no longer a prince or a princess but has turned into a project! Now the focus of attention is on making the imperfect partner perfect!

IT'S A THIEF

Once married, perfectionists do not know how to enjoy themselves. They generally continue their perfectionist attitudes, demanding perfect order in their own lives as well as the lives of others. A woman becomes anxious if the house is not in order at all times, with eggs done to a split-second three minutes, toast to a precise shade of tan, clothes hung a certain way, and perfect children from her perfect husband. Her anxiety leads her to demand these things because anything less than what she considers "perfect" arouses her childhood patterns of self-belittlement.

I've seen married men and women who don't allow their partners to get to know them. They tend to retreat and live behind closed emotional doors. They're afraid they'll be found lacking in some way. Many a husband quietly accepts his perfectionistic wife's demands that he not wear shoes in the living room because she is afraid that he will leave marks on her perfect rugs. He endures her corrections of his speech, manners, and tidiness, but he never feels comfortable in his own home.

Let's consider the scenario of a young, perfectionistic wife who, after rejecting a number of men, finally marries with a "perfectly" orchestrated wedding and honeymoon.

Jane's home was a showcase. The furnishings, the decor, the magazines, every item was perfectly arranged. The drapes were evenly hung without the slightest sag. Each picture was placed at the same height, to the exact inch. Nothing was irregular in this house—except perhaps Jane whose perfectionism was evident in her surroundings. She constantly drove herself and her husband in order to maintain order and an immaculate house. Hank found it difficult to let down and relax in his own house.

Jane paid meticulous attention to details. She was precise in everything she did, but it was never enough. Nor were Hank's efforts good enough. She always felt her home could be better, her husband could be better, and she could be better. Whenever friends showered her with compliments, she beamed, but the satisfaction never lasted. *It could be better!* she would say to herself. She appeared successful in creating an attractive home, but actually she felt more like a "successful failure."

Unfortunately, the amount of time Jane spent maintaining this showcase was out of proportion to the result. Her standards were too high. Very possibly her parents' standards were high also, and she had been programmed to be a perfectionist.

Perfectionism is a thief. It offers rewards but it actually steals joy and satisfaction.[1] Jane went through her life feeling cheated and let down.

A marital perfectionist is weighed down with unrealistic expectations and distorted thinking:

"Our sex life ought to be perfect every time and stay that way. My spouse ought to be so tuned into me that he can do exactly what I need every time to please me."

"Disagreements should never be a part of our lives. We shouldn't ever get angry with each other. We must present to others that we're the perfect Christian couple."

"Our friends and fellowship group at church should be just as perfect as we are. If they don't believe what we believe or have the same values as we do, I'm not sure we should be involved with them. They could affect our image."

"As a couple we should do everything together. We need to have the same interests and hobbies and do them better than any one else."

Unfortunately, the list goes on.

HELP! I MARRIED A PERFECTIONIST!

How can you keep a perfectionist from making your own life crazy and stressful, and at the same time help him or her discover a balance and sense of enjoyment in life?

(If you, the reader, are a perfectionist I've suggested three resources at the conclusion of this chapter to help you develop a new freedom in your life.)

You have made a lifetime commitment to someone you love but it's difficult to handle the perfectionistic atmosphere. Perfectionists are difficult to work with and to live with. They're not team players.

A woman who had been married for ten years described what it was like living with her husband:

"Carl is just so critical and particular but not in a loud or angry way. He never raises his voice. But he looks at me, shakes his head, or rolls his eyes to show his disgust over what I've done. If not that, I get what I call the 'soft lecture.' He doesn't raise his voice, get angry, or sound firm. Rather, he talks in a soft, patient, condescending tone of voice implying, 'How could you have been so stupid?' Sometimes I get the silent treatment and some sighs. That's the signal for me to figure out what I've done wrong.

"There have even been times, believe it or not, when he has taken the fork out of my mouth because I'm eating too much, turned off the TV because I shouldn't be watching that program, or corrected my volume of talking in public. I'm tired of it. I'm tired of going along with what he's doing. I can't deny who I am and I can't live trying to figure out how to please him. Besides, I've heard this so much I've begun to doubt myself. I've even thought, *Maybe he's right. Maybe I need to do what he says. Maybe I am creating the problems.* But fortunately I came to my senses."

Perfectionists have a "corrector" tendency. There is a right and perfect way to do everything, and it's according to their gospel. When you're washing the dishes your spouse walks over and turns down the water because you're using too much. Your partner rearranges the canned goods in your cupboard according to his system of efficiency. Your partner makes unsolicited comments about your choice of ties and shirts with comments like, "I just want you to look your best and make a good impression." Your spouse follows you around the house turning out the lights even when you've just stepped out of the room for a few seconds. And then you hear continuously, "We're wasting money."

When you're married to a perfectionist it's easy to fall into the trap of blaming and berating yourself, walking on eggshells, getting down on yourself when your overly sensitive partner is offended by your constructive criticism, or resenting your spouse's continual intrusiveness into your life.[2]

LEARNING TO LIVE WITH A CONTROLLER

Perhaps your spouse isn't a perfectionist but just a controlling type of person. You probably feel the same pressure with this type of person as with a perfectionist.

Spouses use control to protect themselves from real or imagined concerns. Their use of control is part of their survival system. They believe "the best defense is control." They live in fear of the disastrous results and consequences of not being in control. They fear rejection, abandonment, hurt, disappointment, and losing control itself. They may also be addicted to the respect, power, or emotional rush they get from controlling others.

But what about *your* controller? Is he or she defending against some concern? If so, do you know what it is? How does knowing what concerns your controlling spouse affect your feelings toward him or her? How does it affect your spouse's power over you?

I have worked with numerous controllers in counseling. Their controlling tendency is an integral part of their personality. Some have even said, "I know I control. But why not? I have a lot to offer and I know what I'm talking about. Why waste time? I want to see things happen—fast and efficiently. And I can do that!" That's sad. It can destroy people as well as marriages.

Controllers use a variety of methods to get you to do what they want. One clever ploy is indebtedness. Their message is, "You owe me," and this pushes your guilt button. "If it weren't for the good words I put in for you with my friend, you never would have had that opportunity." "Marrying me has really salvaged your life."

Sarcasm is a favorite response. You feel its bite. And often the tone and nonverbals (which make up 93 percent of the message in face-to-face conversation) are the means intended to control you. Consider a statement like, "Oh sure, you remembered that we're going out to dinner tonight. Then how come you arrived here an hour late and looking like you've been cleaning out the garage? Sure you remembered." This emotional hook not only drags you in, but you can feel the irritation beginning to build. Your stomach churns and your pulse quickens. The more you explain, the worse it gets. The accuser's sarcasm and disbelief just increase. It is irritating to be labeled a liar.

HOOKS THAT HURT

One of the hurtful hooks of controllers is an *assumed agreement* with an underlying threat of criticism. "Karen, now stop and think about this for a minute. Then you'll see I'm right, and it's best to go along with this. Any intelligent adult could see this right away." You end up feeling trapped.

Another hook makes you the victim of a *forced choice*. "Fred, tell me which day you can clean the garage. I'd like to know now. Not tomorrow, but right now." You feel the pressure beginning to build. Later you probably feel anger toward your spouse, but also at yourself for getting pulled into the trap.

In another clever method, the controller *pretends to be talking about himself while making it clear he's talking about you.* He or she says such things as "I should have known better. Letting you use that equipment was a mistake. It's my fault for letting you use it, and now it's ruined."

Have you ever heard something like this: "You really shouldn't let your parents run your life like that, you know. At thirty-eight years old, you need to be your own person. When are you going to break loose from their control!" *Judgment statements* inform you that the controller knows what's best for your life, more so than you do.

Every now and then I read or hear a disclaimer made by an organization or television station: "The views expressed by this speaker are not necessarily the views of the management of this station." I've heard controllers voice similar *disclaimers*. They say "I don't mean to be critical but...," or "I don't mean to be telling you how to run your life, but..." Oh, but they do want to run your life! They know it, and you know it, but you don't know what to do about it.

Sometimes a controller's criticism is hidden so deep in a statement it's difficult to confront it directly. *Imbedded or implied criticism* is like that. Often it's expressed in the form of a question, but it's not just a question. The hook is in the delivery. There's usually a surprised or amazed tone of voice. "You aren't actually going to wear that to this fancy party are you?" The message is the controller doesn't like it, and you should know better.

Both controllers and perfectionists use absolutes such as *always* and *never*. They fail to give you the benefit of the doubt. You may have heard phrases like "If it weren't for you..." or "Because of you I...." These are *blame and shame* statements. Responsibility for whatever has gone wrong in the controller's life is thrust onto your shoulders, whether valid or not. And the more defensive you become, the greater their level of deafness.

Controllers are clever. They often use *blame-shifting* to get their point across. This way they don't have to shoulder any of the responsibility. "It doesn't bother me that you're not going to attend, but I think it is going to bother your parents. You know how they are!" Controllers just can't seem to come out straight and truthful. When you try to confront them by saying "Are you saying you're bothered too?" they will deny it forever. I've heard wives use this approach with their husbands. "Some wives would be upset if their husbands took the entire weekend off to go fishing," they say, and then when their husbands ask if they would be offended they quickly respond "Oh, no. Not me. But some wives I know would be."

Double implied messages are characteristic of controllers. Their message contains denial of what they're saying, but you know it's still true. "Oh, go on. Why should I mind that you can't call your old mother every day?"

WHAT CAN I DO ABOUT PERFECTIONISTS AND CONTROLLERS?

There are eight different steps you can take to enable you to survive and even begin to assist your partner in becoming more flexible and aware of life's joy.

1. Stop taking your spouse's words or deeds as personally as you have in the past. It's true your partner puts pressure on you and wants you to live up to his or her standards and appears not to accept you. But your spouse would do this to anyone. It's not a personal vendetta against you. And your husband or wife does not intend to hurt you. This is a lifestyle and a habit pattern. As one author put it:

> Reframe your perception of them so that they seem less like villains or slave drivers or thorns in your side and more like relatively harmless robots with their wires crossed. Instead of getting knocked off your feet by the emotional undertow of an angry tirade, think of those shouting, foot-stomping, name-calling perfectionists as if they were children throwing tantrums to vent the frustration they do not know how to deal with in any other way.[3]

Don't look at your spouse as bad or wrong. Being judgmental will just activate your anger. Think of it as just a different way of seeing and doing things. In a way, this is applying 1 Corinthians 13:7 to the situation: "Love... is ever ready to believe the best of every person."

Remember, as perfectionists and controllers were growing up they learned that this was how to survive in life.

Above all, don't accept their perception or portrayal of you. They're trying to change you because of their own need for control. If you discover an area of your life that does need change and correction, then take steps to do it for your own personal growth. Their flaw-picking suggestions need to be disregarded. But instead of throwing out all their criticisms, evaluate them carefully. In the midst of an ineffective methodology, you may discover a kernel of truth.

> A man who refuses to admit his mistakes can never be successful. But if he confesses and forsakes them, he gets another chance.
>
> **Proverbs 28:13, TLB**

Remember, you are not the problem.[4]

2. Bring your thoughts about your partner under control. You're probably making the situation worse than it is by what is taking place in your thought life. When people are under the tyranny of a perfectionist or a controller they tend to begin thinking in ways that magnify the problem. Most people in this situation tend to worry about what will happen if they don't live up to their spouse's expectations. They end up taking on some of the perfectionist's thinking patterns and live in fear of being criticized, rejected, or ignored. They're on the lookout for whatever could go wrong. They tend to jump to conclusions, minimizing their own ability and skills. They also tend to project past experiences with their partner into the future.

This is a time to go back to God's word for clarity, insight, guidance, and strength. Let the Scriptures assist you in stabilizing your thoughts. Look at these passages and what they say about worry:

Anxiety in a man's heart weighs it down, but an encouraging word makes it glad. **Proverbs 12:25, AMPLIFIED**

All the days of the desponding afflicted are made evil (by anxious thoughts and foreboding), but he who has a glad heart has a continual feast (regardless of circumstances). **Proverbs 15:15, AMPLIFIED**

Do not fret or have any anxiety about anything, but in every circumstance and in everything by prayer and petition with thanksgiving continue to make your wants known to God.

And God's peace be yours, that tranquil state of a soul assured of its salvation through Christ, and so fearing nothing from God and content with its earthly lot of whatever sort that is, that peace which transcends all understanding, shall garrison and mount guard over your hearts and minds in Christ Jesus.

For the rest, brethren, whatever is true, whatever is worthy of reverence and is honorable and seemly, whatever is just, whatever is pure, whatever is lovely and lovable, whatever is kind and winsome and gracious, if there is any virtue and excellence, if there is anything worthy of praise, think on and weigh and take account of these things—fix your minds on them.

Practice what you have learned and received and heard and seen in me, and model your way of living on it, and the God of peace—of untroubled, undisturbed well-being—will be with you.

Philippians 4:6-9, AMPLIFIED

With practice you can learn to turn your thoughts off and on. But to do so you must put things in their proper perspective. The more you practice control the greater the possibility of immediate control. We don't have to act in accordance with our feelings or negative thoughts.

Scripture indicates that our mind is often the basis for the difficulties and problems that we experience. "Now the mind of the flesh (which is sense and reason without the Holy Spirit) is death—death that comprises all the miseries arising from sin, both here and hereafter. But the mind of the (Holy) Spirit is life and soul-peace.... (That is) because the mind of the flesh—with its carnal thoughts and purposes—is hostile to God" (Rom 8:6-7, AMPLIFIED).

As a Christian, you don't have to be dominated by the thinking of the old mind, the old pattern. You have been set free. God has not given us the spirit of fear, but of power, and of love, and of a sound mind (see 2 Timothy 1:7). Soundness means that the new mind can do what it is supposed to do. It can fulfill its function.

What can you do? Let your mind be filled with the mind of Christ. There are Scriptures that place definite responsibility upon the Christian in this regard. In Philippians 2:5 (KJV), Paul commands, "Let this mind be in you, which was also in Christ Jesus." This could be translated, "Be constantly thinking this in yourselves, or reflect in your own minds the mind of Christ Jesus." The meaning here for the words "this mind be" is "to have understanding, to be wise, to direct one's mind to a thing, to seek or strive for."

The main thrust here is for the Christian to emulate the virtues of Jesus Christ as presented in the previous three verses. "Complete my joy by being of the same mind.... Do nothing from selfishness or conceit, but in humility count others better than yourselves. Let each of you look not only to his own interests, but also to the interests of others" (Phil 2:2-4, RSV).

In verses six through eight, another example of Christ's character is given—humility. This humility came about through submission to the will of God. The mind of Christ knew God and submitted to Him. A Christian following Jesus Christ must give his mind in submission to God. In 1 Peter 1:13, we are told to gird up our minds. This takes mental exertion, putting out of our minds anything that would hinder progress.

Every time you have any kind of a negative thought about your partner or yourself, challenge it. Give yourself the benefit of the doubt. If you're going to think about the problem, see yourself being capable and handling it rather than being a victim and seeing your spouse as a villain. Don't continue to empower your spouse with your thinking.

3. Find a healthy way to emotionally vent. You need to use methods that are different from those your spouse uses. Often perfectionists use tears, tantrums, or caustic comments, and you know what a controller does! But becoming a mirror image of your spouse won't solve anything. If you express your emotion openly and intensely, expect your spouse to either become defensive or shut down completely. Perfectionists tend to be hypersensitive to any criticism and are very uncomfortable with other people's emotional outbursts. Controllers have their own set of tactics which we already discussed. They won't hear you even if you're 100 percent accurate! What you say will be thrown back at you.

But burying your feelings is even worse for you emotionally, physically, and spiritually. And dumping on yourself because of how you feel is no solution either.

You need a safe, healthy outlet for what's building up inside. Express your feelings aloud in prayer—with no editing. Express them to a trusted friend of the same sex, a person who can listen and reflect back what you are feeling. Express them through writing unmailed letters to your spouse or keep a confidential journal. Read your letters out loud to an empty chair or into a tape recorder. But do release your feelings.[5]

4. Evaluate what you will and won't tolerate. As you learn to release your feelings you will discover that what your spouse does or says will not affect you as much. You may be able to assist your spouse in modifying some aspects of his or her perfectionistic style. But your new beliefs and responses will ease some of the pressure you once felt.

Expect resistance to your responses. I have suggested to some spouses that they share with their partners the following statement: "You may be uncomfortable with my request and response and resist what I am saying. I just wanted to let you know that it's all right to do that. I would expect that. You need some time to consider what I'm doing and saying. I'm not looking for an immediate response." A remark such as this takes pressure off you and lets your partner know that you're aware of their struggle. In a sense you're now directing their response because subtly you've suggested what they could do.

There may be times when a drastic measure is needed with either a controller or a perfectionist.

I don't have an answering machine at home. When I don't want to be bothered I simply unplug the phone. Sometimes you need to literally unplug yourself from your spouse's tactics so that you're not overwhelmed. How can you do that? You can leave the room or hang up the phone. With a controlling or extremely critical perfectionistic partner, it could mean saying, "You have a choice. You can back up and approach me with sensitivity and courtesy, and we will discuss what you want. If you continue in the same way, I will leave the room. If you pursue me, I will go next door to the neighbor's. Then when you want to change your approach, I will be willing to talk with you."

Do not respond to all of the perfectionist's remarks and suggestions. Ignore those that are not significant. If your partner uses the silent treatment, don't pursue, trying to dig out what's wrong. You might even commend them for taking some time for reflection.

To help determine what you will and won't tolerate, make a list of your partner's positive qualities and then another of the perfectionistic quirks that bother you. Evaluate each of them to discover which are essential for change and which you can live with. A husband shared with me, "I decided one day to look at Sarah's perfectionism. I asked myself what the negative is for each of her tendencies and then what was the positive. I was surprised to discover I was overlooking some real pluses and dwelling, as a perfectionist does, on the negative. Was that a revelation! I've even shared this with her and made it a point to verbally affirm and compliment the pluses. Sarah has appreciated this and is working on those things that bother me. It was worth the effort."

5. Don't bother telling your spouse that he or she should be less perfectionistic or less controlling. It's a waste of words. A perfectionist will probably interpret your comments to mean he has not measured up in the attempt to be a "good" perfectionist. This will lead to a reaction of hurt or frustration. He will feel unappreciated for his efforts and unfortunately may even try harder to win your respect and approval. Failure can't be tolerated. Too often perfectionists dig their heels in deeper, because to them perfectionism is not a malady or a vice but a virtue. Instead of mentioning the word *perfectionism* just suggest to your spouse exactly what change in behavior you would prefer.

The initial five steps have more to do with strengthening and pulling yourself together. This is vital so you will be able to relate to your perfectionistic (or controlling spouse) in both a healthier and more helpful manner. With the sixth step we move into some new approaches toward your partner.

6. Learn how to share your feelings with your spouse. This is a survival technique, otherwise you may lose your identity in this relationship. Perfectionists tend to dictate to you how to live your life. And if this is accomplished your life ends up being miserable. One way to express your feelings is found in the following fill-in-the-blank sentence: "When you_____, I feel_____. What I would like is for you to_____."

Examples of this could include:

"When you remind me to put the magazines in the rack when I leave the room, I really feel bothered and hovered over. Please wait until I'm through reading for that time period and I will put them away."

"When you tell me how much lipstick to wear, I don't feel accepted. I feel like you're trying to make me over so I don't embarrass you. I would like you to let me be me and decide how I would like to groom myself. If you do this I will feel more positive toward you."

"When you continue to check the way I'm cooking the meal, I feel like a child. I feel like my abilities are being evaluated by someone who is not an expert and it irritates me. Please let me do my job the way I do it. Then if you don't like the end result, we can discuss it to see what can be done, all right?"

Notice the formula in the above examples: You share your feeling, identify the unacceptable behavior, follow with a request, and then share what your partner will gain by responding to what you've said. It may help to identify the consequences if your request is unheeded. Some will be obvious, but it may help to clarify the natural consequences. And you need to be willing to follow through.

One of the reasons that perfectionists and controllers continue to respond in the way they do is that we reinforce it. We comply. Why shouldn't they continue? If it works that way, it can also be effective the other way as well. I'm not talking about grandiose threats but basic simple natural consequences. For example, "If you continue to check up on me when I'm cooking, I could end up making some mistakes and I'll be less inclined to try anything new." Only do this when you're calm, not during an altercation.

If you know that you're going to use this approach, you may want to identify in advance what you want to say and then stand in front of a mirror rehearsing it until you're comfortable.

Hopefully your partner will care how you feel. In taking this step, you're teaching them to be aware of how their behavior can affect your life. One wife shared with me that she began asking her husband to explain why it was so important that she do things a particular way. She said, "I asked him what it meant to him. Why was it important? I said, 'I'm not challenging you. I just want to understand you and your perspective more.' That seemed to diffuse some of Ben's defensiveness. And it was interesting. There were some things he didn't have a good reason for which gave him something to think about. And when he shared the reasons for the others, some of them made sense. I could go along with what he was asking now that I understood. I even asked him to let me know his reasons in the future and it would help me. It was really a helpful discussion for both of us."

Be sure to share your feelings of appreciation and affirmation when your spouse does what you like, especially nonperfectionistic responses. Approval and acceptance is his top need and if he's also an extrovert, he really needs to hear this expressed verbally and directly.[6] Compliment your spouse's personhood more than for what he or she does.

7. Establish boundaries. The violation of a person's boundaries can occur in many relationships but it is especially prevalent in a relationship with a perfectionist or a controller. Perfectionists become invasive and try to run your life for you. Thus you need to determine both what you are willing to do with their demands and how much. In a sense, you will need to teach your partner to respect you! This includes respect for what you think, how you feel, and what you do. Without this respect, you may end up like Jonah and the great fish—swallowed—especially your identity. By setting limits and boundaries you will help to change your partner's response.

When you are being blamed, confront. And you will experience blame because it's a byword of a perfectionist. Don't accept blame. Blame condemns, creates guilt, and breeds resentment.

"Honey, I would appreciate it if you would make your statement in a different way. I don't appreciate being blamed for this problem. Let's look at it from a different angle for a minute."

Watch out for "shoulds." You will be told what you should do, feel, and think. A wife shared the following in counseling: "For years I boiled inside with Randy's 'should' statements. But I've learned several ways to respond that get his attention. I either stop and say the word, 'should' back to him in a questioning way and sometimes he rephrases. Or I ask, 'Is that a request or a suggestion?' and he rephrases. When he does, I thank him and say I will think about it.

Randy is slowly getting the idea, but old habits change slowly."

When you talk with your partner, remember to take into account his or her personality style, learning style, and their manner of communication. Discuss your concerns in a way your spouse can relate to. If you tend to be general or vague, be specific. If you're an amplifier, and your spouse is a condenser, be specific, short, and to the point.

Be sure you concentrate on what you want, on solutions rather than your partner's mistakes.

Since you will commonly hear demands from your perfectionist or controlling partner presented in a way which denotes a necessity, the best way to respond is to rephrase it into a preference. You will hear, "I need that..." or "We must..." or "You must...." These demands usually have both an immediacy factor as well as an all-or-nothing aspect. That can drive you up the wall attempting to comply. But the good news is there's an easy way to comply with them. Counter them with a balanced comment like, "I *must* be there or you would *like* me there?" "You *need* me to accompany you or *would you like* me to?" In time your spouse may begin rephrasing these statements without your prompting.

You have probably discovered that your perfectionistic partner has a difficulty with tolerance. You may hear statements such as, "I can't stand...", "I just can't cope with...", "They'll be the death of me."

I think one of the best learning experiences for any of us is to hear ourselves on tape. I've had a number of counselees tape family or spousal conversations. When no other confrontation registered, sometimes the shock of hearing oneself leads to expressions of "I said that?" or "I sounded like that?" which begins the change process.

You can respond with expressions such as, "I know it's difficult for you but you can stand it. You have for several months now. Let's talk about a possible solution," or "I know you feel like you can't cope but you've been handling it pretty well. What can you do now?"

Some perfectionists tend to rate and judge others by elevating themselves and downplaying others or by comparing you with someone else. There's a purpose in this. It's not to hurt you but to build up themselves—but it's done at your expense. Don't let it continue. Confront it. Let your partner know about it, how you feel, and what you would prefer. Let them know you're not interested in being compared with others—or with them.

You could say, "Honey, you're comparing me to your mother and I cannot and won't be her. I love and value you for who you are. I would appreciate it if you'd do the same for me. Thanks for listening." When you are compared to your spouse you could ask, "Is there something I'm doing that is threatening you?" and it will cause them to think it through.

Will perfectionists give up comparing completely? Probably not, but you can help them reduce the frequency and intensity.[7]

Help your partner see options and solutions. Help him or her develop a different perspective.

Sometimes I've approached perfectionists in counseling by saying, "I'm not asking you to give up your perfectionistic style of life. I just want to help you learn some other ways of responding and relating to life and to others. When you learn that, you can decide which of the two options or lifestyles you prefer. If you like your own best, then keep it. But at least you'll have a larger repertoire to draw from."

Or I'll say, "It's strange but of all the perfectionists I've ever met, I've never met one that's successful in being one. Where do you fall in this category?"

They've all been open to considering a different approach that can be successful. Remember what was said earlier about Dr. Glasser's teaching? People won't change until they make some kind of a value judgment on what they're doing.

Sometimes I've had perfectionists list the advantages of being a perfectionist. Once that's been completed we look at the disadvantages. Usually they list far more disadvantages than I can suggest. That's taught me that many people are aware that what they are doing isn't working, but they're afraid to give it up because that's all they know. And how can they be assured that a new approach is any better?

Remember that your spouse is harder on him or herself than you. You're just not always aware of it. There will be many occasions when your partner needs your listening ear with no suggestions, your empathy, and at times your assistance. The simple question, "Would you like to hear a suggestion?" can do a lot to enable the two of you to work together.

8. Resolve the issues. For this to occur it will mean learning to bargain and negotiate. It involves a continuous process of adjustment and learning to be compatible and you will probably end up being the catalyst or instigator. As you make requests of your perfectionistic partner, let him or her know that you're willing to change as well.

Each will need to compromise but that means the ability to suggest alternatives. That may be your style. For a perfectionist, it's not. To them it means giving up control. It means failure. It's important to discover the goals that each of you wants and then verbalize them so the perfectionist can hear them. Both of you will get some of what you want but not all of it. And the solution will be imperfect but fulfilling.[8] Most couples find it helpful to agree to some ground rules. Here is one set of rules a couple in counseling devised. And it works.

We will attempt to control the emotional level and intensity of arguments. (No yelling, uncontrollable anger, hurtful remarks.)

We will take time-outs for calming down if either of us feels that our own anger is starting to elevate too much. The minimum time-out will be one minute and the maximum ten minutes. The person who needs a greater amount of time in order to calm down will be the one to set the time limit. During the time-out, each person, individually and in writing, will first of all define the problem that is being discussed.

Second, the areas of agreement in the problem will be listed. Third, the areas of disagreement will be listed, and fourth, three alternate solutions to this problem will be listed. When we come back together the person who has been the most upset will express to the other individual, "I'm interested in what you've written during our time-out. Will you share yours with me?"

Before I say anything I will decide if I would want this same statement said to me with the same words and tone of voice.[9]

This last suggestion may sound strange inasmuch as you are hoping to change a perfectionist. But you shouldn't expect your proposal to bring perfection. It will never happen. Expect change. Expect growth. It will be small and slow. Encourage it. Believe in your partner's capability to be flexible and adapt. Your partner doesn't believe it, so someone needs to. And that person is you!

Remember, by responding in a new way, you set the stage for a new relationship, and it gives your partner the opportunity to discover a new way of responding. There will be discomfort at first. The perfectionist or controller won't like it initially. But give the person time.

The Difference between Working toward Perfectionism and Excellence

EXCELLENCE SEEKERS

They accept who they are. They are aware of their strengths and their limitations. They believe that they are worthwhile and valuable because of how God sees them but accept that they are still fallible human beings. They can fail and still feel good about themselves. They accept the possible.

They set goals and standards that are realistic and in line with their strengths and limitations. They are more likely to achieve their goals.

In a challenge, they focus on their strengths and on doing as well as their abilities allow them to do.

Challenges are welcomed and they try new ventures, take risks, but learn from their experiences and mistakes. Procrastination because of fear is not an issue.

When tackling new tasks, they feel relaxed, excited, and clear about what needs to be done. They enjoy entering uncharted waters.

They gain satisfaction and good feelings about themselves from their efforts. They appreciate doing a job well. In numerous situations, they can be less painstaking or results-oriented. An excellence seeker can enjoy the process of doing something as well as the end result.

These people lead balanced lives. They are able to relax, get along with others, and have fun. They can engage in and enjoy activities at which they do not excel.

PERFECTIONISTS

They are self-absorbed and overly aware of their flaws and deficiencies. Virtues are minimized and they work hard to conceal their inadequacies. They are usually on the defensive. They must win and be infallible in order to believe they have any worth or value at all. They strive for the impossible.

They demand a higher level of performance that is impossible and unrealistic for them to achieve. Naturally this sets them up for failure.

When facing a challenge (which they usually see as a problem), they focus on their deficiencies. Their focus is on how not to do poorly or make any mistakes. They live with the fear of failure.

New experiences and risks are avoided. They live with the fear of looking foolish or incompetent. Energy is directed toward avoiding situations where they might make mistakes. Thus they procrastinate.

The new and unfamiliar create tension and unpredictable situations are avoided. They may devote so much energy to worrying about something new ahead of time that they feel exhausted before they even begin. This contributes to mistakes. Criticism is seen as a personal attack. They're very sensitive to this.

They rarely if ever see what they do as good enough. They constantly say, "I could and should do even better," and they get little satisfaction from their accomplishments, for, large or small, it's never good enough. They use, "I must ..., I should ... and I ought to ...."

There is no balance since they are always striving. Guilt and anger are their companions and this affects their relationships with others. They don't get along the best with friends and family since the unrealistic standards they have for themselves are projected onto others. And they don't have fun or do things just to do them.[10]

HOW'D THEY DO IT?

"My husband had no concept of organization. He's a perfectionist and if something couldn't be done perfectly then he wouldn't do it at all, or he'd leave a job half complete. Needless to say, we had a lot of half-finished projects, a lot of messes, and a lot of tasks never started!

"I'm not a nag and I didn't pester him about the unfinished projects, but I did pick up the tools and materials left lying around and put them in big piles. I also have a drawer (big drawer) in the kitchen that I called his tool drawer. Anything I found lying around I put into that drawer. That way if anything was missing he could find it either in a pile or in the drawer.

"This caused a lot of arguments because he said it was his house too and he should be able to have his items wherever he wanted. (My husband is a carpenter and some of these items included big boards on which he would write notes or phone numbers or lists of materials he needed. I started burning the boards in the fireplace.) All this was after many requests for him to write on tablets and put things away.

"I started buying him organizational tools—a small handheld computer and tablets, and we worked on writing lists of things he needed to accomplish in a day. He prioritized the list. If he didn't have the materials needed to start a job then it went to the bottom of the list.

"I showed him it was OK to do a job as good as you could; it didn't have to be perfect and it didn't have to be better than anyone else could do it. He began to feel good about starting something, completing it, and crossing it off his list.

"I praised him when he began a job, during the job, and of course after it was complete he got lots of praise. Most of the time the finished project was better than anyone else could have done it.

"Praise was very important to him and I found he needed to hear me praise him to other people. I would tell the person what his next project was going to be and how excited I was about his plans. I guess he just needed a system to get him organized. He could see that if he didn't get organized his stuff was going to get burned or he was going to have a pile in the backyard as big as the house. He needed to know his projects were appreciated and we didn't expect perfection."

TAKE ACTION

1. Who leans toward being a perfectionist in your marriage?

2. Who leans toward being a controller in your marriage?

3. If these are concerns, what have you tried in order to handle the issue? Describe the results.

4. Which of the eight steps mentioned would help you at this time?

5. Which of the examples mentioned are you willing to use?

6. Describe three steps that you will take to improve the level of perfectionism or control in your marriage.

CHAPTER TWELVE

How to Change Your Spouse

Gary J. Oliver

Throughout this book we've talked about the importance, value, and necessity of change. We've discussed the high cost of not changing. Through many different examples we've shown the ways couples can influence and change each other.

This chapter is designed to give you a practical, step-by-step plan for applying the principles and ideas you've just read. Sometimes after reading a book, I find myself saying, "That sounds great, but how can I do it?" This chapter is intended to answer that question.

How do we encourage change in a constructive way? Is the desired change really for our spouse's good and the health of our marriage, or is our motivation self-centered? If we cannot *change* some personality trait, how do we help our spouse at least *modify* their behavior so we don't go crazy? How can we encourage flexibility and growth while avoiding manipulation, threats, anger, criticism, accusations, nagging, or withdrawal? What are some healthy and appropriate approaches that encourage change?

Those of us who long to change our spouses must put ourselves in their shoes. How does it feel to have someone trying to change us? What makes people so fearful of change or locks them in defeating patterns or irritating behaviors?

Learning how to help a partner change and grow is a new skill for most people. Like all skills it takes time and practice. At this point you might be saying, "OK, there are a few changes I'd like to see my spouse make. Who wouldn't like a spouse to change something? But where do I start?"

In the following pages we will present some proven keys to effectively changing your spouse. They aren't magic. They won't work overnight. But if you follow each one of the steps we describe, you will likely see some growth, some change, and some increased sensitivity in your spouse. Over a nine-month period, Ron and Erin, a couple who had come into the office discouraged and defeated, experienced meaningful and lasting change. Hundreds of other couples have as well. You can, too! As I explain these principles for effecting change, I'll show how Ron applied them in his relationship with Erin. At the end of the chapter I'll tell you how well they worked.

EXAMINE YOUR MOTIVES

The change process starts with asking yourself some questions. "Ron," I said, "before you pick up the binoculars or magnifying glass to better see what you'd like to have Erin change, I challenge you to grab the mirror and take a good look at yourself." Here are the questions I challenged Ron to ask himself: Why do I want my spouse to change? What is my motivation? Is my spouse's behavior or trait immoral or unbiblical? Or is it something that is inconvenient or uncomfortable for me? Am I being fair and realistic in my request for change?

Many of us desire more perfection than we can reasonably expect in life. We each need to ask, "Am I expecting too much?" If you want a good marriage, a happy family, a successful profession, you will experience some discouragement and dissatisfaction. A big part of the maturing process is coming to terms with the limitations of yourself and others.

Many of the frustrations we experience in relationships come from our inability to accept people just the way they are. A part of us needs to make the people we love into something we want them to be. We become discouraged, disappointed, and feel like failures when they insist on being themselves and doing things we don't want them to do.

Oswald Chambers wrote:

One of the hardest lessons to learn comes from our stubborn refusal to refrain from interfering in other people's lives. It takes a long time to realize the danger of being an amateur providence, that is, interfering with God's plan for others. You see someone suffering and say, "He will not suffer, and I will make sure that he doesn't."... Is there stagnation in your spiritual life? Don't allow it to continue, but get into God's presence and find out the reason for it. You will possibly find it is because you have been interfering in the life of another—proposing things you had no right to propose, or advising when you had no right to advise. When you do have to give advice to another person, God will advise through you with the direct understanding of His Spirit. Your part is to maintain the right relationship with God so that His discernment can come through you continually for the purpose of blessing someone else.[1]

Are you a change junkie? I've worked with people who are hooked on the challenge of trying to change the other person. They didn't marry their partners; they married reclamation projects. They don't particularly care about their spouses becoming conformed to the image of Christ, to become who He designed them to become. They want to make their partners into someone convenient and comfortable for them to live with.

Do you always demand that things go your way? Has your mate altered more of his or her distinctive features for you than you have? Does such an imbalance add up to a control that shouldn't have been in your relationship to begin with? Are you really committed to preserving your spouse's God-given distinctions to the same extent you want yours to be protected?

In Ephesians 5:27 Paul writes that a husband is to love his wife in a way that will result in her growth and maturity so she will have "no spot or wrinkle or any such thing; but that she should be holy and blameless" (NAS). When Paul talks about holiness he's referring to character. When he talks about being blameless he's referring to conduct. God has called us to treat our spouses in ways that will lead to holy character and blameless conduct.

Many attempts at changing our spouses involve little thought, reflection, or prayer. They are often knee-jerk reactions to small irritations or contradictions to the way we would normally do things. We need to make sure our desire for change isn't due to our inability to accept people for who they are. Ron had to evaluate how much of his desire for Erin to change came from his need for perfectionism and control.

After some prayer and discussion with Erin and other friends, Ron decided his desire for Erin to be on time was not selfish or unrealistic. This desired change would not only decrease his frustration, it would also increase Erin's effectiveness. It would be a win-win change for both of them.

IDENTIFY DESIRED CHANGES

Next, pinpoint your primary area of concern. Exactly what is it you would like to change?

Start by making a list of all of the things you *value* about your spouse. Ask the Lord to bring to mind all your spouse's talents, gifts, positive traits, and strengths. When you have completed your list, put it in your Bible. After a couple of days, pull out the list, read over it, and make sure you haven't forgotten anything.

Now make another list. Write down some of things you'd like to see your partner change. Go ahead and be as thorough as you can be. Once the list is complete, rank the items you have listed starting with those that are the most reasonable and might be easiest for your partner to change. Then ask yourself the following questions about each item on your list:

- How important is this issue? Is it a "high-ticket" or a "low-ticket" item? On a scale of one to ten, with one being low and ten being high, how does this rate? (A low-ticket item is anything between 1 and 5. A high-ticket item is something 6 and above.)

- Is this desired change one of personal comfort or convenience or is it something that is damaging my life, health, testimony, marriage, or family? Is it a minor irritation that I can learn to live with or is it central to our relationship?

- Do I want to change something that God may want to use to challenge me, strengthen me, and help me grow?

- Is it something my spouse really can change? There are some things that, because of their nature or importance to the person, are non-negotiable. It is unfair and unrealistic to ask an introvert to become an extrovert, or a morning person to magically become a night person. It is realistic to ask people to clean up their own messes or to respect other people's time.

Low-ticket items aren't necessarily insignificant. Most of the behaviors that frustrate men and women aren't big things. They are little things that occur frequently. Like a squeaking door or the little drops of water dripping from a shower in the night, these little irritations dripping through your relationship can lead to big frustrations.

In April 1990, NASA launched the celebrated $1.5 billion Hubble telescope. Only two months after its launch the telescope was found to have an improperly-ground mirror that blurred its view of extremely distant objects. The slight flaws of less than an inch in the mirror rendered it ineffective and forced a multi-million-dollar repair mission.

In our bedroom we have sliding glass doors on our closet. My natural tendency is to leave them open. Leaving them open seems more energy efficient since you don't have to waste energy opening them. For primarily aesthetic reasons, however, my wife Carrie prefers to have the doors closed. It's not a high ticket item for me. I don't really care if the doors are open or closed. So, why not change? If I know that closing the closet doors brings joy to my wife, if I know that that little act of thoughtfulness says "I love you" to her in her love language, I'll close those doors every time.

Some changes Carrie and I made were big and some were little, like the closing of the closet doors. Some of them took much more time than others. All of them were reasonable and have improved our marriage and family relationships.

How can you know if the change you desire is unreasonable? One woman wrote that you are definitely asking too much if what you want to change involves "a new hair color, a possible jail sentence, or any procedure performed under anesthesia."[2]

CREATE AN ENVIRONMENT FOR CHANGE

How you implement this next step is critical. How you request change may be more important than your actual words. If your spouse walked up to you and, in a very matter-of-fact tone of voice, said "I want you to change this about yourself," how would you interpret it? I asked over fifty couples to list their possible interpretations, and here is a small sample of their responses:

I want you to be different.

You should be different.

I don't like you the way you are.

I like you the way you are, and I would find you even more enjoyable to be around if you would be willing to...

I would like you to be totally different than you are.

I'd like you to become someone else.

I want you to do what I do, like what I like, think like I think, believe what I believe.

I don't really give a rip what you want, here's what I want; if you want to be a biblical spouse, you'll do it.

Isn't that amazing?

One of the best ways to create an environment conducive to change is by *loving* your partner, by *knowing* him or her, and by taking time to *communicate* in the other person's own language.

In order for our spouses to be open to our suggestions for growth and improvement, they need to know they are accepted just the way they are. Do you like it when you feel like a reclamation project? Do you like feeling that your spouse's love is conditional? How do you like the message that if you perform right you will be loved, but if you don't jump through the right hoops at the right times you won't be loved?

In our surveys and interviews many couples said it was easier to receive requests for change without defensiveness if they knew they would be loved even if they didn't change. If you have first established an atmosphere of love and acceptance, your request for change is more likely to be seen as a suggestion and not as a threat. Change is much more likely to occur in an already healthy relationship. Once we trust our partners to love us unconditionally, we are usually less stubborn about improving our already lovable selves.

PRAY FOR YOURSELF, FOR YOUR PARTNER, AND FOR PATIENCE

I remember a plaque that hung on the wall of my Grandma Jackson's living room when I was a child. It read, "Prayer changes things!" Prayer not only changes things, it changes people. And not only does prayer change those we pray for, it can also change us.

If you want to see change in your spouse, you must allow adequate time for your request to be absorbed, evaluated, and understood by your spouse. Change takes time. A change that appears easy and simple for you may be very difficult for your spouse. If you pray for your marriage on a daily basis, you'll find it easier to be patient.

The process of change often entails two steps forward and one step back. If you reinforce the backward steps by comments such as, "See, I knew you couldn't change," and ignore the steps forward, you will soon extinguish any hope that change is possible. Some people are easily discouraged and give up too soon, convinced that change means moving Mount Everest when in reality a bit of mole-hill modification is all that is needed. We must remember that new skills and behaviors are very fragile. Even after instituting change, it is easy to return to the certainty and security of old patterns. It may take months or even years for a new behavior to become an established part of who we are. Regular and consistent prayer will make an enormous difference throughout the process.[3]

IDENTIFY METHODS THAT HAVE
FAILED TO EFFECT CHANGE

Think over your many years of marriage and ask yourself, "What hasn't worked?" It sounds like such a simple and logical question, but most of us never ask it. We've worked with hundreds of people who have spent years learning what doesn't work yet they continue to try the same old, ineffective approaches.

Most of us know that tactics such as complaints, demands, ultimatums, nagging, whining, and moaning do nothing but make our spouse more resentful and resistant to change. Yet we keep on using these tactics. Probably the worst tactic is nagging, which Webster defines as a "critical, persistent, faultfinding harping." When one person was asked what it felt like to be nagged he replied, "Nagging feels like being nibbled to death by a duck." Imagine that!

As Ron evaluated his past efforts to change Erin, he realized most of his requests for change had been knee-jerk reactions born out of his frustrations and sense of futility. "I guess I've nagged her, criticized her, and shamed her," he admitted. I asked, "How effective has that been?" He laughed and replied, "Not very effective. In fact, all I've accomplished is to increase her discouragement and my frustration."

Earlier in the book I shared my favorite definition of crazy. "Crazy is to find out what doesn't work and keep on doing it."

Many of us have spent years behaving crazily, continuing to do things in ways that not only don't solve the problem, but often make the problem worse or create new problems.

Make a list of some of the ineffective ways you've tried to get your partner to change. If you get stuck, ask your spouse, who is certain to be an expert on the subject.

IDENTIFY METHODS THAT HAVE WORKED

You'll be surprised to discover there are some things that have worked to encourage change. Ask yourself: When does my partner listen to me? When is my spouse most open to change? What have I said or done in the past that has been received well?

ENCOURAGE YOUR SPOUSE

My father-in-law is a hard-working Nebraska farmer. Every year his fields produce a high average of bushels of corn per acre. What is the secret of his success? Every spring he spends many hours cultivating his fields. After he has planted the seeds of corn, he continues to weed, water, and watch for bugs or diseases. Throughout the spring and summer he invests hundreds of hours cultivating and caring for his fields. This creates an environment in which the corn is free to flourish and grow.

Just as a good farmer will spend many hours cultivating his field, we need to spend time cultivating our relationships. One way to do this is to regularly encourage our partners.

There are few things more powerful than regular and consistent encouragement. If you consistently mix three parts encouragement with one request for change, you may be surprised at the results. You are much more likely to see the desired growth.

If you hope to change what you don't like, start by encouraging what you do like. What are you thankful for? What about them wouldn't you change? Praise them, thank them, give credit where credit is due. Notice the little things.

When we came to this step Ron observed, "I'm the kind of guy who doesn't praise or encourage very much. If people do something right they don't need to be complimented. That's what they were supposed to do." Ron realized he only remarked upon those things Erin and the kids did wrong. But as a farmer, he knew the importance of cultivation. "I can't believe I've missed something so basic and essential."

BEAR IN MIND YOUR PARTNER'S UNIQUENESS

Does your partner's gender or personality type give you any clues for effectively communicating your desire for change? As Ron thought about how to approach Erin, he considered her preferences. Like many women, relationships were important to her. Rather than being a "bottom line" person who went for the immediate solution, she enjoyed the process of getting there. She had a greater need for closeness and intimacy than he did. She enjoyed hearing the details of his day and what his plans were. She appreciated being included in the decision-making process. And then, of course, there was the topic of shopping. While Ron would rather have a spinal tap than go shopping he knew this was something they could do together that would communicate both his love for her and his openness and willingness to change.

Ron considered Erin's personality type. On the Myers-Briggs Type Indicator she preferred extroversion. While as an introvert he might prefer bringing up the subject and then not talking about it for a few days, Erin would prefer to process it out loud, immediately.

Ron also knew that Erin valued harmony and relationships. Rather than merely giving her logical reasons for his request, it would be more effective to explain how he felt when she was late and what it would mean to him if she were more time-conscious.

When it came to organizing the outer world Ron was more structured than Erin who was spontaneous and flexible. This had initially drawn him to her; now it was one of his greatest sources of irritation.

"I decided that I first needed to compliment Erin on her spontaneity and flexibility and let her know how valuable those characteristics were," Ron said. "Then I needed to tell her there are times when those strengths are a problem." Ron realized that what came naturally for him might take some work for Erin. I reminded him, "Just as you have wanted Erin to be patient with your attempts to be less driven and more flexible, you need to be patient with her attempts to be on time."

COMMUNICATE CLEARLY WHAT YOU WANT AND WHY

If you have any hope of seeing your partner change, you must express a carefully thought-through concern in a way that communicates you value your spouse. You need to communicate what you want to see changed and why.

Be honest about your feelings. Speak the truth in love. Address the behavior, not the person. It's not your spouse you object to but a behavior that frustrates you. Spend more time helping them understand rather than creating guilt.

Connie described her marriage as a desert, meaningless and empty. She was bitter toward her husband, because he hadn't comforted her adequately when their baby daughter had died several years before. "There are times when I'd like Warren to just listen to me without trying to solve everything and then, maybe, just hold me close."

"Have you ever told him that?" I asked. "Well," she paused, "I guess I haven't." She continued, "But if he had any sensitivity at all you'd think he would know that."

Over a period of several weeks I helped Connie find some creative ways to communicate her needs and expectations to Warren. Since Warren was a morning person, she knew that it would be best to approach him before nine o'clock at night. From the Myers-Briggs Type Indicator she knew Warren preferred making decisions based on logic, and so she prepared a list of reasons for her concern.

At our next session she was thrilled. "I just can't believe it. Warren was open to what I said and is more than willing to work on it." All he needed was a little clear communication, some direction, and some encouragement.

A healthy request for change does not say, "I want you to be a totally different person from who you are." It does say "I love you and I appreciate you. And because of who I am, there are some things that may not be important to you but that are a real source of frustration to me. Here is what I'd like you to consider changing, and here is why."

REQUEST CHANGE, DON'T DEMAND IT

Many people make the mistake of *demanding* change rather than *requesting* change. Which approach are you most likely to respond to positively? When Ron wanted to change Erin, there were two ways he could phrase his request:

He could say, "I'm sick and tired of your thoughtlessness in always being late."

Or Ron could take into account that she is, by nature, less structured than he is, and that being a mother and wife is a full-time, stress-filled job. He could say, "Erin, one of the things that attracted me to you was your spontaneity and flexibility. However, I am frustrated and embarrassed when we arrive late for something. I feel like everyone is looking at us and I'm being a bad example to others. It would mean a lot to me if you would be willing to work on being on time. And if there is anything you can think of that I can do to help you, I want to know."

When you ask your partner for a change do they hear you saying they are wrong, inferior, a failure, dumb, or stupid? Or do they hear that there is much about them that you value, but there is something that, for whatever reasons, rubs you the wrong way, and you would appreciate it if they would be willing to consider doing it differently?

BREAK YOUR LARGE GOAL INTO SMALLER ONES

Discouragement can set in if your spouse feels you expect a miracle overnight. How do you respond to a request that seems impossible? If you are like most people you either give it a half effort or you don't try at all. Why put a lot of effort into something you know you won't be able to do, at least to the satisfaction of your spouse?

Ask yourself, *How can I break the large goal into smaller ones?* Karen wanted to pursue a career in nursing, but Scott insisted that "no wife of mine will ever work." While Karen's goal was to become a nurse, she started by volunteering at the local hospital. This didn't threaten Scott's breadwinner status.

When the hospital offered some continuing education courses, Karen took advantage of them. As her experience and education grew the hospital offered her a part-time position. Scott saw that Karen was happier as she was learning and growing, and, quite frankly, he was proud of her. And with the kids getting older, he realized they would be needing more money for their education. So Scott encouraged Karen to go to nursing school and pursue her dream.

Ron realized he expected Erin to suddenly change and be exactly on time (or even early) for everything. I asked him, "If you could pick one situation you would most like Erin to be on time for, what would it be?" His immediate response was, "Church. I hate being late for church."

Now the immediate goal was not Erin being on time for everything. It was Erin being ready for church on time. This was a more realistic and achievable request. And since Ron understood why it was so difficult for her to be ready on time, he asked her for two or three specific things he could do to help. He also decided to compliment her for any steps in the right direction. "I decided to compliment her when we got any place under ten minutes late. The first time she was ready to leave on time I was so enthusiastic I almost had to be pulled off the wall." When Erin realized Ron wasn't expecting perfection, just progress, she was more encouraged to work toward the goal.

BEWARE OF SOUNDING CRITICAL

There is a fine line between expressing a concern or criticism and sounding critical. And gender differences play an important role here.

While all of us dislike being criticized, many men see criticism as an attack on their adequacy. Men can be threatened by conflict because they assume it will involve an admission of failure, inadequacy, or incompetence.

When a man's power and competence is questioned he may feel his value and worth is at stake. Many men grew up with the myths that real men have all the answers, real men aren't weak, real men don't lose. I've had several women tell me, "My husband acts as if because he's the man of the house he always has to be right. If he is wrong, he's afraid no one will ever respect him again and the world will end."[4]

LISTEN TO YOUR SPOUSE'S RESPONSE

After you have shared your concerns with your spouse, take time to listen to the response. If you have aroused defensiveness, don't respond to the defensiveness. Most of us react in that way when we feel criticized. Listen carefully, try to summarize in your own words what you are hearing, and invite them to clarify it.

As you listen to your spouse don't focus on what you want to say next. Just listen. Try to understand your spouse's response. Is your concern still warranted? Maybe some new information will modify or change the way you see things. You may need to be open to change yourself. I've heard many spouses say, "Once I knew I had been listened to, heard, and my point of view understood, it was easier for me to change."

Ask if there is anything you can do to make it easier for your spouse to follow through with your request. When Ron asked Erin this, he discovered that while her lateness was at times due to her inattention to time or inefficiency in organizing her day, at other times it was due to the overwhelming tasks facing a mother of three healthy children. Erin explained, "When we are getting ready for church on Sunday morning, your only job is to get yourself ready and be out in the van. I have to prepare breakfast, clean up, lay out the kids' clothes, herd them around to make sure they are on track, get myself dressed, and get all of us in the van." The light dawned for Ron. He realized that unless he was willing to make some changes and help out, his expectations were both unrealistic and unfair.

CONTINUE TO CULTIVATE YOUR RELATIONSHIP

Offer your full and frequent encouragement at every opportunity until the desired change is achieved. Remember, the change process may take many months. Look for opportunities to nourish, cherish, comfort, build, and encourage.

Set aside at least one night a month when just the two of you go out on a date. Look for little opportunities during the week to be together. Run an errand together. Make time for a one-minute phone conversation during the day just to see how your spouse is doing. Ask if there is anything special you can pray about that day. Carrie and I have found that even a half-hour talking over a cup of cappuccino (without the kids) can bring us closer together and energize the rest of the week.

What says "I love you" to your spouse? How can you be and

become the person your partner would have you to be? The best way to encourage your spouse to change is to model the process. Focus on how God might have you change and grow.

Finally, when you believe the change has taken place... celebrate!

DOES IT WORK?

When Ron and Erin first came in for counseling they were frustrated, discouraged, and tempted to give up. Somewhere between their wedding day and their oldest child becoming a teenager, they had lost touch with each other and become "married singles."

As we worked together they realized they weren't as far apart as they thought. There were many things about each other they loved and appreciated. But they had become stuck in the rut of focusing on what they didn't like rather than celebrating what they did like.

What happened with Ron's attempt to change Erin's tendency for being late? I'll let Erin speak for herself: "For years Ron had attempted to shame, blame, and humiliate me into being more prompt. I felt unappreciated and misunderstood. After awhile I just turned him off. But when he took the time to approach me in a new way, to communicate his love for me as well as his desire for change, and when he took the time to listen to what it was like from my perspective, I guess for the first time I really understood and had hope."

After only five months of working together on Sunday mornings, Ron and Erin were consistently at church not just on time, but five minutes early. The change didn't take place overnight, and there were plenty of setbacks. But a real change did take place. As Ron began to look at things through Erin's eyes, he became more motivated to make some changes in his own life. Erin used the Twelve-Step plan, developed by Alcoholics Anonymous, to help change Ron's workaholic tendencies. That took a bit more time than Erin's learning to be more prompt, but Ron was delighted by the changes Erin helped him make.

As Ron and Erin learned to understand their gender and personality-type differences, some of the little things that had bothered them suddenly seemed unimportant. Erin commented, "As we learned how to change each other we grew in the ability to understand and appreciate each other. As a result, there were fewer things we wanted to change."

Is Ron and Erin's marriage perfect? No. Do they still have problems? Yes. But now they have hope, a track record of success, and some specific tools they can apply to specific problems. Ron summarized his feelings: "I never dreamed our marriage could be this good. It has taken time and work, but it's not nearly as painful as the hopelessness and helplessness of being stuck."

Changing your spouse is not only possible, it is an essential part of a healthy marriage. If you find yourself becoming increasingly unhappy in your marriage, don't pretend nothing is wrong. Asking for change may be a risk, but keeping your frustration and unhappiness to yourself is a time bomb. Speak up!

God wants to see us grow and mature. Growth is impossible without change. Those who are not open to change are not open to growth and condemn themselves to a lifetime of mediocrity, stagnation, and hopelessness. Remember that change:

is a process

takes time

can be painful

involves mistakes

involves failure

involves small steps

can be confusing

provides hope

produces maturity

results in healthy relationships

Chuck Swindoll writes:

When you boil life down to the nubbies, the name of the game is change. Those who flex with the times, refuse to be rigid, resist the mold, and reject the rut—ah, those are the souls distinctively used by God. To them, change is a challenge, a fresh breeze that flows through the room of routine and blows away the stale air of sameness.

Stimulating and invigorating as change may be—it is never easy. Changes are especially tough when it comes to certain habits that haunt and harm us. That kind of change is excruciating—but it isn't impossible.[5]

TAKE ACTION

1. Are you committed to being the person God would have you to be? Do you want to grow? Are you open to change? If you are feeling particularly brave, ask your spouse the following question: "If there was any one thing about me that you could change, what would it be?" Then be open to listening and discussing the answer.

2. In your daily prayer time ask God this question: "Lord, if there was any one change You would like to see me make this year, what would it be?" Once again, be open to what He says. And remember, He may speak to you through His Word, your spouse, a friend, or even an enemy.

3. Write the following quotes on change on three-by-five-inch index cards, and put them in a visible spot. For the next thirty days, read them once a day and see what they inspire in you.

Welcome change as a friend; try to visualize new possibilities and the blessings it is bound to bring you. If you stay interested in everything around you—in new ways of life, new people, new places and ideas—you'll stay young, no matter what your age. Never stop learning and never stop growing; that is the key to a rich and fascinating life.

Alexander De Seversky

There is a certain relief in change, even though it be from bad to worse! As I have often found in traveling in a stagecoach, that it is often a comfort to shift one's position, and be bruised in a new place. **Washington Irving**

He who rejects change is the architect of decay. The only human institution which rejects progress is the cemetery.

Harold Wilson

CHAPTER THIRTEEN

How'd They Do That?

H. Norman Wright and Gary J. Oliver

As we said at the conclusion of chapter 1, this final chapter contains the stories of husbands and wives who have influenced and helped to change their spouses. We trust these stories will be helpful and encouraging to you.

❦

"It took me several years to try something new, and I couldn't believe how well it worked. Whenever Jim had a Saturday off, I wanted us to make the most of the day. But he would sleep until 10:00 or 11:00. He gets enough sleep during the week, so I tried to talk to him about getting up earlier on the weekend, but usually we just ended up arguing.

"I decided to quit talking and take some action. For two Saturdays in a row I planned an activity that took me away from the house until 1:00. When Jim got up he was surprised that I wasn't there and that I didn't mention his sleeping in any more. I just decided if he wanted to spend his time that way I wasn't going to waste my time waiting around and stewing over the situation.

"The third week I hung around the house for a while, and to my surprise Jim was up by 8:30 and asked, 'What do you want to do today?' That night I cooked his favorite meal and put a card next to his plate that said, 'In appreciation for the super question you asked me this morning.'

"Once in a while he sleeps in, but most of the time he's up at an earlier hour, and Saturdays are good days for us."

ॐ

"I had been frustrated for some time with the lack of communication between my husband and me. Part of the problem was that his work took him away all week, and he was home only on the weekends. But when he was home, his interest was in sex, not talking. I felt a lot of resentment.

"He also complained about me being away at church on Sunday morning, but that was a must for me. I'm a believer, and at that time he wasn't. I finally went to a marriage counselor for some suggestions. He sent me home with a book filled with suggestions to spark romance, and also a series of cassette tapes on the role of sex in marriage by Dr. Ed Wheat. I read and listened, and it finally dawned on me that if I wasn't getting my husband to talk to me, I'd better approach the communication problem in a new way.

"The next weekend was my husband's birthday, so I dropped the children off at my parents' house, and Saturday night I took him to a very romantic restaurant. He seemed to enjoy it. When we came out of the restaurant we were next door to the Marriott Hotel. I stopped Terry, looked him in the eye and said, 'Let's not go home tonight. Let's go in, get a room, and go up and take a bubble bath together.' He stopped in his tracks and just looked at me. When the shock wore off, he stammered, 'Well, we can't!' I asked, 'Why not?' 'Well... I didn't bring my toothbrush.' At that point, I smiled, reached in my purse, and took out his toothbrush and a room key. I handed them to him and said, 'Let's go!' And we did. It was great.

"That night we talked for six hours. The next morning I skipped church and stayed in bed with my husband. That's where I felt the Lord wanted me to be that day. That night turned our relationship around. I guess there's something to this idea of meeting your partner's needs. It sure changed Terry's response to me."

ॐ

"How do you get your wife to be a better cook? My wife tried, but she cooked food the way her mom did, and it was the same basic stuff day after day. I like to eat and enjoy different foods. But I was concerned that I would devastate Trudy if I complained, so I had to think of some creative way to help her improve.

"The answer came in an unusual way. Somebody dropped off a cookbook at the office that was loaded with recipes. It would take years to try them all! I bought a copy of the book, took it home, and showed it to Trudy. I said, 'I looked through this book and it really looks interesting. I don't know if we'd like everything, but what if we tried one new dish every two weeks? Then we could evaluate whether the recipe is good or not. If it is, we can have it again sometime. If not, we can cross it out. How do you feel about it?'

"We've been using the cookbook for over a year. Trudy is becoming an excellent cook, and I tell her so. The twenty dollars I spent was worth it."

&

"My husband and I had been married for less than a year. Since we had married a little later than most couples, Ted already owned his own well-furnished home. In the master bedroom, we had a large two-shelf stand, and on the top was a massive stereo with speakers and all the other components. I found it a bit unsightly and suggested we put the speakers and components on the lower shelf so I could decorate the top shelf with plates, vases, or plants. Ted didn't go for the idea and had his logical reasons for why the stereo should stay where it was. We discussed it several times, but he didn't even want to give it a try.

"One day I decided to take a chance and move everything to the lower shelf. I spent some time arranging the top shelf in a new way. I tested the stereo to make sure it sounded all right.

"When Ted came home and finally went into the bedroom, he saw the change, as well as a note that said, 'This isn't permanent; it's one of my wild experiments. Tell me what you think about it and test the sound. If you think it's OK and would like to keep it this way, we can. But if not, I'll be glad to put it back the way it was. Thanks for your input.'

"When he came down, he looked at me, smiled, and said, 'Well ... I like it. Let's give it a try.' That's all I was asking for, the opportunity to try it."

&

"I've tried to change my husband in two areas. First, my husband has a tendency to gain weight. It's not that he overeats constantly, although he does really enjoy good food. His whole family struggles with weight. When we first got married, I nagged him about not overeating and losing ten pounds. The nagging did little to motivate him and even hurt him, because he didn't feel fully accepted by me.

"Realizing that my behavior was not producing anything but bad feelings, I tried a new approach. First, I worked hard to make good meals that were low in fat. I made only enough for two servings, so there weren't mounds of food sitting on the table begging to be eaten. I never bought junk food. My husband loves popcorn, and that became his snack food.

"Second, my husband is an excellent athlete who enjoys exercising when he has the time. He especially enjoys competitive sports. Although membership at a gym is expensive, I fully support him doing this. Although he isn't fond of fast walking, I frequently ask if he will walk with me. He calls these 'love walks.'

"Last winter, he decided he wanted a Nordic Track. For months we looked through the paper trying to find a used one, but finally I encouraged him to buy a new one. I'm glad we did it—he's gotten a lot of use out of it. Now his weight doesn't fluctuate twenty pounds every year, and he's in good physical condition.

"The second area of change was in my husband's education. My husband worked full-time during his college years, and it was impossible for him to finish his degree. Work always took priority over studies.

"After we had been married a while, he was thinking about a job change but didn't feel confident that he was marketable without a college degree.

"We looked into a college program especially designed for working people. It was an intensive and expensive program that guaranteed a degree in a little over a year. At first my husband didn't want to do it. The money, the time, and the stress seemed overwhelming.

"I had taught some college courses and assured him I would help him every step of the way. I explained that we could finance his education if we kept to a strict budget and put off having children for another year. I promised to do most of the household chores and other responsibilities so he would have time to study.

"He entered the program. I typed papers, brainstormed projects with him, helped him do library research, quizzed him at test time, and cheered him on through the entire year.

"He graduated summa cum laude! He has a degree and a good job. I don't believe he would have pursued this degree at this point in his life if we hadn't been married. My very presence in his life motivated him, because we were building a future together. I also think that my practical support eased the stress and struggle of that year. I'm thrilled to see his success."

❧

"My husband and I married right out of college and have been together for thirty-two years. When we married, I'm sure both of us had an ideal of what marriage would be—but we had our first child within nine months, and four more children soon followed. We were so busy just meeting the practical realities, I can't remember consciously trying to change my husband.

"The challenges of our life together and our strong personality differences seemed to bring about change more than intentional efforts have.

"For instance, I am a morning person—he is a night person—and that is still true. He likes to process things before he shares, and I am more verbally extroverted—in this area we have learned much about each other. Neither of us has changed here, but we try to accommodate each other's preferences. (I took on the habit of ending things I say with a question, however, in order to get an immediate response.)

"So after many years of marriage we find ourselves more appreciative of our differences and more patient with the things that are difficult. We've blended our ways, but we haven't really changed each other."

❧

"Adjusting to marriage was a difficult process for my wife and me. The first three years were miserable and we felt more like adversaries than allies. We were both on a crusade to change one another and it wasn't working. Then we decided to try an idea that we read about. We each made a list of all of the things that bothered us about each other. They weren't easy to read. In fact, reading them was more difficult than hearing them. We each read some things we had never heard before.

"The next step was different but great. We put our lists in the fireplace and burned them. As we watched them burn and crumble into dead ashes, we just sat there in silence, holding hands and thinking. It had been a long time since we'd had a positive time together like that.

"We then made individual lists of all the good things we could think of about each other. It wasn't easy since our focus had been on the negatives. But by the next day our lists were finished. We shared our new lists with one another and then we made a commitment to read this list and affirm one another daily for at least one of these positive traits. But it didn't end there. We posted the lists in the bedroom and continue to add to them as we discover new positive traits. Now when either of us suggests a change for the other we're more open to considering it since it's expressed in the context of a positive relationship."

❧

"My husband loses his temper every now and then, and when he does he begins yelling. That's what they do in his family, but it's not my background or style. He kept telling me it was normal, and that everyone does it. I couldn't accept that line of thinking, but nothing I said seemed to have any effect on him.

"One day we got into an argument and the yelling started. We were in the kitchen and our tape recorder was on the table, so I just reached over and pushed the record button. Our argument continued and even escalated. At one point I said, 'I wish you wouldn't yell at me. It's difficult to talk with you.' He yelled, 'I'm not yelling!' I stopped, reached over, rewound the tape, turned it on, and left the room while he sat there and listened. I don't know if it was hearing himself on the recorder or the shock of what I did, but it worked. We've even been able to talk about the yelling in his family. We're now able to resolve some of our differences."

❧

"For years I'd put up with his verbal abuse—put-downs, yelling, cursing. I loved him, we were both Christians, we didn't believe in divorce, and the other times he was a good husband. But it was getting to be too much, and I was down on myself and scared much of the time. I started getting some counseling for myself, and it really helped.

"One day I had some errands to run after school, and I got home a bit late. John had gotten home early for some reason. He was so angry. He didn't even wait until I got in the house before he started in on me. He gave me the third degree—where was I, why didn't I think to do the errands earlier. Then he started in on what I hear so much of the time—he feels the kids are more important than he is,

I'm neglecting him, and he gets the leftovers. He went on and on. Usually I try to explain and give him good reasons for where I was, but I finally realized, Why bother? It won't register. He won't hear me and I'm not even sure he wants to let me off the hook.

"Defending myself hasn't worked, so I took a step forward and said, 'John, I will not put up with your tirade and your yelling. Now stop it.' He did—probably because he was so shocked. Fortunately, I knew what his next approach would be, and before he could say what he's said so many times, I said, 'And John, I'm not having PMS nor is this something I've been told to do in counseling. I will not accept how you respond to me anymore. It won't work on me any longer, and every time you begin berating me, I will respond in this way. I deserve to be treated with respect, and not only do I know that, I know that you love me and would feel better about yourself if you treated me better.'

"John went into the family room and spent the entire day and evening there. He even skipped dinner. In the past I would have caved in and gone after him, but this time I didn't. He seemed to be in a better mood the next day, and we were able to talk about our situation. We've made some good progress."

🍂

"'There will be times you may need to give a non-angry but caring ultimatum to your spouse. And if you ever do, you must be willing to carry though with it.' I remember reading a statement like this and saying, 'Never, never in a thousand years could I get away with giving Fred one more ultimatum.' I'd tried over the years and all it had gotten me was some bumps and bruises. But finally I came to the place where I couldn't tolerate his drinking anymore. So one day during a calm time in our marriage, I said to Fred, 'I love you and I'm concerned for you and your happiness, but I am not willing to live in the same house with you if you continue to drink. You've tried drinking as part of your life so you know what it does. Now it's time to try experiencing life without drinking. If you go for professional counseling and join AA, I will stay with you. And that's what I prefer doing. If you choose not to, I will separate from you.' After that I gave him a note stating the same information and then left the room.

"Two hours later Fred came in and said he would try it. We've had our setbacks and ups and downs, but he's continued and it's working. I was scared to death that he wouldn't try, and then I'd have to move out. I didn't want to, but I would have. I just couldn't stand seeing Fred throw his life away like that. I love him too much."

§♣

"For years I wanted my husband to read more, not just for me but for his own growth and enjoyment. It's not that he didn't know how to read or didn't enjoy it. Every time I would suggest reading or point out a book he'd say, 'Well, some day. I'm too busy now.'

"So I thought about how I could be creative. I don't know if what I did was legal, but I never asked. I knew that Herb always read in the bathroom and would leave his *Sports Illustrated* magazine there. I went out and bought two books. One was a novel by Tom Clancy and the other a Christian book by Patrick Morley called *The Man in the Mirror.* I made a photocopy of the first chapter of each book. He always folded down the page in his magazine where he left off, so one day I slipped in the first chapter from Tom Clancy's book. He went into the bathroom that evening and didn't come out for a long time. When he did emerge, he smiled and said, 'OK, where is it?' I replied, 'Where's what?' 'The book. I know you did it. I'm hooked. I've got to read the rest.' So I gave it to him.

"About two weeks later I could see he was just about finished, so I slipped the chapter from *The Man in the Mirror* into his novel (he was no longer reading the sports magazine), and when he found it and read it, he sat down and told me what Patrick Morley said in the first chapter. About three weeks later Herb floored me. He came out of the bathroom and asked where his chapter was. He'd finished the book and was ready for another. He said he liked the variety between novels and personal growth books and suggested that I keep selecting some since he never got around to going to the bookstore or the library. So that's what I do for him now. Once in a while he doesn't care for the selection, but we've both agreed that it's all right not to select a winner each time. Every now and then I read the same book so we can discuss it."

§♣

"I was concerned over my husband's financial priorities. I felt he was selfish and unfair with me in this area, although he never would agree with me that he was. We could not seem to communicate about this problem. The situation really intensified when my mother-in-law could not live alone any longer and had to come live with us.

"We had our R.V. parked at a resort, so I went away for the weekend all by myself. For most of Friday night I cried, and then about 4:00 Saturday morning I took the problem to the Lord. I knew I couldn't talk to my husband about it as he would get hostile. I felt the Lord told me to write him a letter.

"I prayerfully wrote the letter to him and told him all the things I was feeling. Then I called him and told him to bring Mom and come for dinner on Sunday.

"When he arrived, I gave him the letter and told him when he was ready to discuss the matter with me to let me know. When he read the letter I could see he was doing some serious thinking. He told me that most of what I said in the letter was true, but not all of it. He said after he prayed about it all, we could discuss it.

"We never really discussed it, but the problem cleared up almost overnight. I told him I could see he had made a big change in this area. We had been married for thirty-six years at the time, and this had always been a problem. I thank our heavenly Father for recommending this method of communication to us.

"This event made us stop and think when we had to discuss a touchy situation. We'd ask ourselves what would be the best way for us to deal with it. It made me see I had not asked for the Lord's advice in this situation years ago, causing me years of needless stress."

❧

"When my wife and I first got married, I let her do the grocery shopping. She spent enough to feed us for a month; but she usually did this weekly! We were both in college, and I had a part-time job that only paid $50.00 a week.

"I told her I would like to go along to help her when she shopped for groceries. I could carry the groceries, and I told her that two people could get through the aisles picking out items quicker than one. I also made a shopping list ahead of time.

"Over the twenty years, I have done more shopping than she has, but we both have continued to shop together whenever possible. She gets the help, I get the satisfaction of knowing the budget is met, and we both have time together. I guess I discovered that she needed my support and guidance in this area since it wasn't her strength. Instead of scolding or lecturing, which wouldn't have worked, I chose this other course of action. And it has given us more time together for an outing."

&

"My husband wanted me to be more hospitable and have people over more often for dinner or dessert. I knew it was a sore point for awhile, but one day he exploded. He also had shared his frustration to others in front of me which embarrassed me greatly.

"I thought about what was preventing me from doing this for my husband. Why was it a hassle? I came to the conclusion that my standards for the house were too high. Everything had to be too perfect (like my mom's house always was). My parents rarely had people over, and his mom had people over a lot.

"The other reason was a fear of rejection.

"I also deduced that one of my husband's gifts was hospitality, and I was squelching it.

"After realizing all this, I took several steps. I chose to make an effort to be more hospitable and called some people to set up times when they could come over. I did this because I really wanted to please my husband.

"I also lowered my standards on the house and dinner.

"He really appreciated my effort, and it drew us closer together and closer to those we invited over. I ended up having a really good time and found out it wasn't that much work. It just took some time and planning, and God always blesses us in the process."

&

"My husband was not a 'touchy, huggy' person but this was something I deeply wanted.

"I showered him with verbal 'I love yous' and always touched, hugged, and kissed him (even when he would turn away.)

"He has become more showy and says he loves me and the children often. My husband had a difficult childhood. He was abandoned when he was eight years old. He was placed in fourteen different foster homes over the years. When he was in high school, he was placed in my sister's home as a foster child.

"My family is a loving and showy family. When my husband and I got married, I learned that it was difficult for him to trust people and to physically or verbally show his love. Through my faith, I have been patient and consistent in showing him and telling him that he is important and valuable to me. Over the years he has learned to show and verbalize his love for me and our children through hugs, kisses, and verbal and written 'I love yous.' Sometimes he didn't want my affections, but I persisted and now if I don't do it he wonders what's wrong."

&

"When I first met my husband he had an extreme disregard for his personal appearance. I was drawn to him because we found each other intellectually stimulating and because we had similar emotional needs and similar goals for a close relationship. While we had great times together, I was sometimes embarrassed to be seen with him in public.

"I am fortunate that my great emotional need enabled me to temporarily overlook his outward appearance and accept and love him on the basis of the wonderful person he is, and to accept his love for me. As time went on, I began a little campaign to improve his appearance. One of the major detriments to his appearance was his hair. It was the outgrowth of a short haircut, and with his thick, wavy hair it had turned into an unruly bush devoid of style. I never once said, 'I hate your hair,' or 'I sure wish you'd get a haircut.' Instead, when I saw a hairstyle I thought would look good on him, I would say, 'I bet that hairstyle would look really good on you. I like that style.' I also told him how nice his dark, thick, wavy hair was. I don't think he had ever before considered it to be an asset. Eventually, of his own accord, he got his hair cut. I told him how much I liked it without making too big of a deal out of it and making him feel self-conscious. Then I began to work on the clothing. If he wore a sweater I liked, I'd tell him. If it didn't match the pants, I wouldn't correct him. Instead I would say, 'A brown pair of pants would look great with that sweater.' I also either bought him entire outfits, or, when I purchased something individually, I would tell him specifically what I had bought it to go with. He never deviates from the original outfit or my suggestions.

"Today my husband is a very attractive person—inside and out. Often when I show someone a picture of my husband, they'll say, 'Oh, he's really handsome.' I always tell him when this happens.

"I realize how much he cares for me because my opinions are obviously important to him. As he looks back, he is amazed that I loved him, in spite of his looks, and cared enough to help him improve himself. I think this is also a testimony to his love for me in spite of my many shortcomings. How could I let such things as unruly hair and mismatched clothing stand in the way? One of my husband's favorite movies is *Beauty and the Beast.* I see him wiping tears away each time we watch it. How privileged I am to be married to a handsome prince who considers me to be his 'Beauty.'"

☙

"My husband, being a man of God, was in tune to God's direction and leading in his life and our marriage. I have always believed any change needed to come from God, not me. My responsibility was to pray for him and our marriage, not to change him.

"One time in his life he was going through a difficult time. His abusive father basically disowned him and told him never to come home again. When my husband spoke of his father it was always very critically, constantly putting him down.

"One day as we were walking, my husband started telling me all this negative stuff about his father. I stopped, looked him in the eye, and asked him to tell me one positive thing about his father. We stood looking at each other in silence for almost five minutes. He said, 'I can't think of anything.' I said, 'I'll tell you one that I can see,' and I shared it with him. I told him to think about that one positive thing for a day, and then tomorrow to share with me two positive attributes. We did that for a week until he had seven positive qualities he saw in his dad.

"My husband has developed into a very positive person, looking for the good in people. He is an encourager to many in his ministry. He often reminds me to think and look for the good in others. By the way, the relationship between father and son has been restored."

☙

"I wanted my husband to be more empathetic and less critical. I would tell him over and over how a situation or action made me feel. Whenever our family went out to bowl or golf, etc., my husband always told everyone how to improve and what they should do differently. He perceived this as being very helpful and constructive. None of us perceived it that way. We saw and heard it as critical, demeaning, and implying, 'You aren't good enough.' It ended up taking the fun away from the activity.

"Over the years I said to my husband, 'If we want help, we'll ask.'

Also, 'We are all trying our best,' and, 'It doesn't have to be great to be fun.' It helped us to realize where he's coming from, believing that if you can't win, improve, or do something well, it can't possibly be fun. We have told him that his helpful suggestions crush our desire to continue the activity.

"I think he finally is starting to realize there may be more than one way (his way) to perceive something. Unfortunately because change has come slowly our sons (ages eighteen and fifteen) have become somewhat like their father."

&a.

"I wanted my husband to be more godly and to become a Christian. But trying to conform to my husband's lifestyle caused me to have some mental health problems. When I realized I could not live a lifestyle that went against my beliefs and standards, I informed him I was returning to church, and he could decide to come or not. I told him if he didn't we would probably stay married but would live our separate lives. He chose to go to church and was saved. I feel God has changed him more than I have, although sometimes God and I have our arguments about the best way to change him.

"With God in the center, our love has deepened and when the feelings haven't been there the commitment has.

"I don't know if my husband wanted me to change, but when I was having my emotional problems, he really affirmed me and told me, 'I will love you no matter what and will never leave you. You may leave me, but I will always love you.' His words made me want to continue living and get better. I also made a commitment at that time to give the best to my marriage and make it work.

"It has helped us to carry each other's burdens. When the going is rough for one, the other just gives a little more. We have also seen how we have to rely on the Lord in that same way."

&a.

"The longer we were married, the more I wanted to change the way we made major decisions together. Sometimes we strongly disagreed when facing difficult decisions, and my husband would end up making the final decision without my approval. For example, several weeks prior to the birth of our second baby, my husband accepted a job which allowed him to be home only during the weekends. The new job required us to eventually move our family, selling our home and buying one in another state. I would have to quit my manage-ment job of many years and look for a new job. Until we were able to move the family, I'd have the full burden of caring for a new baby and preschooler along with a very demanding career. I did not think that the decision to take the new job was a good one for our family.

"At first I was resentful and angry, but I knew this would destroy our marriage. After several months, I knew I had to give this up to the Lord and ask for forgiveness for harboring bitterness. I knew I could not change my husband on my own, so I prayed that the Lord would soften his heart to be more aware of my concerns. I also prayed that God would give me strength and grace to accept what-ever was in store for us, even if it was not what I wanted. Then I began to demonstrate love and support for my husband and partici-pated in the effort to sell our house and relocate our family.

"My husband noticed a major change in me and my attitude. The anger and resentment was gone, and he saw that I had forgiven him. I stressed that the most important thing was our being together as a family.

"Soon his determination to continue with that new job changed to a determination to seek what was best for the whole family. After one very long year of being apart because of the job, we decided together to stay in our current house and start our own company. He left the job and launched a very successful business.

"Now, before we make any decisions, we pray and seek the Lord together. We allow God to work in us both so that we move togeth-er in one mind and one spirit."

§⋅

"For years my wife was reluctant for us to pray and worship togeth-er. Each of us would maintain a separate devotional life, but we would miss the intimacy which comes from joining together in fel-lowship with the Lord. I very much wanted her to feel comfortable sharing her spiritual life with me.

"I frequently prayed for God to help us, and I tried to encourage her and let her know how much I wanted us to share our spiritual lives together. The point of change came as God began to work a change in my own life. I started to honor my wife in new and signifi-cant ways, both in my words and actions. I would let her know how in awe I was of her as a woman, a mother, and as my wife. I also demonstrated a greater sense of vulnerability.

"My wife began to feel comfortable sharing with me in prayer and worship, and she came to realize how much I needed her to experience my own growth in Christ. We have since joined together almost daily in Bible reading, worship, and prayer. The effect on our relationship has been astounding. God has brought us into a powerful and beautiful communion with Him, and as husband and wife we have experienced a new level of wonderful intimacy."

Perhaps these stories will encourage you to believe that change and growth are possible. It happened for these couples, and it can happen for you. Reflect on your marriage and you may discover changes that you were not aware of until now. Just remember that there is hope for growth and change in your marriage, especially if you work together as a couple and give your concerns and desires to Jesus Christ. His presence and direction in our individual lives and marriages will be the stabilizing factor.

We would like to hear from you. We know there are many more stories of changes among you who have read this book. And these stories can bring hope and encouragement to others. Please write us at the following address:

H. Norman Wright and Gary J. Oliver
c/o Family Counseling and Enrichment
17821 17th St. Suite 190
Tustin, CA 92680

APPENDIX A

What to Do When Your Spouse Wants to Change You

So far we've talked about how you can change your spouse. But what happens when your spouse wants to change you? Now that's a different story. It's one thing to want to change something about someone else. It's something else to have someone want to change you!

First of all, be encouraged that your spouse wants to change something about you. When your partner no longer cares about you or what you do, your marriage is in a danger zone. Dissatisfaction and frustration are much more promising than apathy.

The best time to decide how you want to respond to your spouse's request for change is *before* he or she talks with you. Be open to your spouse's suggestions. Remember that you can't grow without trying out new ideas, values, and experiences. And some of these are going to be suggested to you by your spouse.

Change provides an opportunity to learn and grow. Look at changes you have made in the past. Are you glad you changed? Was it as painful or humiliating as it first appeared? What did it cost you to make the change? What would your life be like if you hadn't changed? Over the long haul, what is going to cost you more, changing or not changing?

Here are some practical and proven guidelines to follow when your spouse asks you to change.

1. Before you say or do anything, pray. Ask God for the ability to focus on what your spouse's concerns are, on what your spouse is trying to communicate, rather than on the actual words.

2. Listen carefully. Don't argue. Arguing will stop the conversation and you won't learn anything.

3. Don't react. Take time to respond. Don't attack, defend, or raise your voice. God can use what feels like criticism, even painful and unfair criticism, to show you something in your life that needs changing.

4. Beware of reflexive defensiveness. When someone suggests a change, we commonly respond by asking questions such as, "Is the suggestion or criticism deserved?" "Is it totally accurate?" "Is this person as spiritual as I am?" These questions aren't helpful. Rather, we should ask, "What can I learn from this person's concern?" "Is there even a small piece of truth here that God can use to help me grow?"

As a young man, one of my greatest failures was not being open to change. When I was a young Christian, I selected Philippians 1:20 as my life verse: "According to my earnest expectation and hope, that I shall not be put to shame in anything, but that with all boldness, Christ shall even now, as always, be exalted in my body, whether by life or by death" (NAS).

There have been times in my life when that verse hasn't characterized my life. There were times when God tried to speak to me through the suggestions and criticisms of others. On a couple of occasions I was too busy "serving" Him and too insecure to listen to what He had to say. I didn't understand that God could use for my own good people who seemed like critics and enemies. I ignored such people, defended myself, and in time fell flat on my face. In over twenty years of counseling, I've worked with many who have made the same mistake.

The pain of those experiences taught me an invaluable lesson. God can use anyone to get our attention and point out a blind spot, a weakness, or something as simple as an annoying habit. If we can benefit from listening to friends or enemies or people we don't know very well, we are especially wise to listen to what may be God's voice speaking through our spouses.

5. Almost every request for change contains a valuable piece of information about yourself and the person making the request. What insights can you gain from this request for change? What is it about this particular criticism that you can agree with? Try to find and seize the one element of truth you can use.

If your first response to a request for change is to criticize or argue with the other person, practice substituting understanding for argument. One measure of love is the degree to which we set aside our preferences for those of our spouses. That's why the Bible says, "in honor, preferring one another."

6. Someone once said that digging for the facts is much better exercise than jumping to conclusions. When your spouse requests a change, choose to dig for the facts behind the request. Asking questions buys you time, provides you with additional information, and communicates to the other person that you value them. Ask questions such as these to help you clarify a request for change:

How long has this been a problem?

When else have I done this?

What do you think I could do differently?

7. Summarize what each of you has said. Make sure you clearly understand what your partner is asking. Then, if you agree that the request is reasonable and realistic, talk about some ways in which you might be able to make that change.

APPENDIX B

Marriage Type
Identifier

Used by Permission of Author, David L. Luecke
The Relationship Institute
700 Lovers Lane
Waynesboro, VA 22980

T he Marriage Type Identifier is composed of eighty multiple-choice questions indicating personality preferences. There are no wrong answers. No answer is better than any other. About half the spouses who use this instrument will agree with your selections. Of course, about half will also disagree.

This instrument measures preferences, not intelligence or competence. A coffee drinker is not necessarily better or worse than a tea drinker, but it can be useful for your spouse to know which you prefer. Similarly, one "marriage type" is no better or worse than another, but couples can benefit from understanding each other's personality preferences.

The Marriage Type Identifier is provided to enable couples to experience directly the relational differences described in this book. However, the results of this kind of instrument tend to be subjective and are not always consistent or conclusive. Actual preferences can be confused with what you think you should prefer. Preferences can be altered by mood, specific circumstances, and social expectations. If results do not seem to fit, make adjustments according to your own self-awareness, self assessment, common sense, and feedback from your spouse and others. The Marriage Type Verifier is also designed to help.

Since you must answer every question, get ready for some frustration. Both answers to a question may seem equally good or equally bad. You may not be able to decide with conviction. Don't agonize over a question. Your first, most spontaneous response is probably the one to use.

Put your answers on a separate sheet of paper if you and your spouse are both using the instrument. Do the same for the scoring procedure.

Do not put your answers directly on the Scoring Sheets. An awareness of patterns in your responses is likely to influence your choices. Transfer your answers to the Scoring Sheet after you have completed all the questions.

MARRIAGE TYPE IDENTIFIER (MTI)

1. You are more likely to choose a spouse that
   a. feels good to be with
   b. fits into your life and future

2. It is more important for children to
   a. develop initiative for life goals
   b. be well protected, nourished, and nurtured

3. You are more likely to complain that your partner is
   a. unreasonable
   b. insensitive

4. Visiting with friends and building outside relationships is a
   a. high priority
   b. low priority

5. You would usually prefer to talk about
   a. good restaurants
   b. good investments

6. Your partner is more likely to describe you as
   a. head in the clouds
   b. feet on the ground

7. In conflict, you are more likely to want others to
   a. calm down
   b. open up

8. If you hurt your partner's feelings, you are more likely to
   a. feel bad and regret it
   b. think about it and forget it

9. In general, you tend to go with
   a. what feels good   b. what has a future

10. You would probably prefer to talk about
    a. ideas and theories   b. people and places

11. Your emotions are usually
    a. hidden and unknown   b. open and expressed

12. When you are down and hurting, you are more likely to
    a. share your pain and feel your way out
    b. rationalize and think your way out

13. You tend to prefer to work with your
    a. hands   b. imagination

14. You are more likely to buy when you are convinced
    that a product is
    a. a good investment   b. practical or enjoyable

15. You are more likely to
    a. reflect analytically   b. react spontaneously

16. When it comes to family life, you are more likely to be better at
    a. personal relationships   b. household management

17. In a new situation, you are more likely to
    a. look and listen   b. process inwardly

18. You tend to have more to say when talking about
    a. possibilities for your future   b. experiences of today

19. In family conflict, you are more likely to
    a. define the issues   b. conciliate differences

20. When working on a project with your spouse, you are more
    likely to contribute
    a. excitement   b. efficiency

21. When inspecting a new gadget, you tend to wonder
    a. would you enjoy it?   b. what are its possibilities?

22. When your partner is down or hurting, you are more likely to try to
    a. understand in depth   b. respond with caring actions

23. You are more likely to be persuaded by an appeal to your
    a. intellect   b. feelings

24. Others tend to look to you mostly for
    a. emotional support   b. practical help

25. You are more likely to choose a job that
    a. you enjoy   b. offers future possibilities

26. You are more likely to be the one who
    a. conceives a new project   b. works out the details

27. Your friends are more likely to describe you as
    a. intellectually independent   b. emotionally intimate

28. You are usually more comfortable dealing with
    a. personal problems   b. mechanical problems

29. You tend to
    a. focus on immediate details   b. focus on the "big picture"

30. When left to yourself, you are more likely to think about
    a. dreams of the future   b. present pleasure

31. When working on an interesting project, you tend to be
    a. practical and methodical   b. enthusiastic and energetic

32. Others are more likely to see in you
    a. depth of feeling   b. depth of thought

33. Life is for
    a. enjoying   b. understanding

34. You tend to explore your world with your
    a. inward processing and reflection
    b. five senses

35. In family conflict, your concern is that others
    a. fight fair   b. make peace

36. When it comes to family life, your contributions tend to come from your
    a. heart   b. head

37. You are more likely to
    a. accept life as it is   b. yearn for what might be

38. If you had to choose, you would probably prefer to
    a. postpone enjoyment of future rewards
    b. enjoy today

39. It would probably bother you more to
    a. mess up a project   b. hurt someone's feelings

40. It is more important for children to
    a. feel loved and accepted   b. experience the real world

41. You tend to pay more attention to
    a. your physical surroundings
    b. your inner world of thoughts and feelings

42. You are more likely to trust
    a. what adds up in your mind   b. what you can see and touch

43. When working with your spouse, you are more likely to build
    a. efficiency   b. harmony

44. When an argument is developing, you are more likely to
    a. find common ground and reconcile differences
    b. try to win

45. When making a decision, you pay more attention to
    a. practical details   b. anticipated possibilities

46. You are more likely to complain that your partner is
    a. unimaginative   b. unobservant

47. You are more likely to feel best when you do what
    a. you think is right   b. pleases people you care about

48. Others are more likely to see you as
    a. sentimental   b. logical

49. You are more likely to be troubled by
    a. immediate problems   b. anticipated problems

50. When walking outdoors, you are more likely to
    a. be preoccupied with your inner world
    b. see, feel, smell, and enjoy your surroundings

51. If a child came to you crying, you would probably first
    a. ask what happened   b. ask what hurts

52. You are usually more comfortable dealing with
    a. people   b. things

53. When it comes to money, you tend to
    a. spend and enjoy   b. plan and invest

54. In general, you are more likely to
    a. anticipate tomorrow   b. enjoy today

55. Others are more likely to see you as
    a. efficient   b. social

56. When your partner is upset, you are more likely to explore
    a. feelings   b. facts

57. You would be more likely to select a new home based on
    a. present enjoyment   b. future investment

58. When it comes to food, you tend to
    a. eat to live   b. live to eat

59. When conversing, you tend to be
    a. brief and to the point   b. talkative and social

60. In general, you are more likely to be
    a. sensitive   b. consistent

61. When it comes to food, you are the type that
    a. tastes, smells, and savors   b. satisfies hunger

62. In general, your energy tends toward
    a. future possibilities   b. present enjoyment

63. In an argument, you tend to
    a. stick to the facts   b. get out the feelings

64. Working with others, you tend to
    a. try to keep others happy   b. try to get the job done

65. Your spouse is more likely to see you as having
    a. common sense   b. vision

66. When beginning a new venture, you tend to think about
    a. how will it work   b. how does it feel

67. You tend to argue with
    a. logic   b. feelings

68. You are more likely to want your partner to be more
    a. open and expressive   b. rational and logical

69. You are more likely to
    a. focus on details and miss the big picture
    b. focus on the big picture and miss the details

70. Planning a vacation, you are more likely to
    a. suggest a concept, itinerary, or activities
    b. tend to preparation and details

71. When disciplining children, it is more important to be
    a. fair and consistent   b. patient and understanding

72. When your partner tells you about a personal problem,
    you tend to
    a. show that you understand and care
    b. try to find ways to solve it

73. Your first opinion of a person is likely to be based on
    a. what the person says or does
    b. your hunches about inner values or motives

74. When in conflict, you are more likely to
    a. mull over underlying issues   b. have it out and forget it

75. When inspecting a new household gadget, you tend to wonder
    a. how does it work?   b. who will like it?

76. Your spouse is more likely to seek the benefit of your
    a. personal warmth   b. clear thinking

77. You are more likely to be bothered by
    a. your partner's irritating habits
    b. underlying flaws in your marriage

78. You are more likely to express your love with
    a. words   b. actions

79. In a family argument, you are more likely to take the role of
    a. umpire   b. harmonizer

80. You would prefer to think of your home as a
    a. social center   b. personal castle

Scoring Instructions

Scoring Sheets are provided on the following pages. Use the Sample Scoring Sheet as a guide. Draw another scoring sheet on a separate sheet of paper, if needed, for a spouse.

1. Record your responses by placing a check by the appropriate number under "a" and "b."

2. Add the "a" and "b" columns and record the total below in the boxes indicated by the arrows.

3. Add the numbers in the boxes so that you have a total number indicating the strength of each preference: "Sensing"— "Intuiting" and "Thinking"—"Feeling."

4. After you have completed your scoring sheets, determine your "marriage type" by following the steps below.

Determining Your Marriage Type

1. When it comes to "sensing" or "intuiting," my highest number indicates that I prefer to experience the world primarily through
_____.

2. When it comes to "thinking" or "feeling," my highest number indicates that I prefer to make decisions based on
_____.

3. Combining my two preferences noted above, I can identify my marriage type as:

   TYPE ONE: Sensing—Thinking

   TYPE TWO: Sensing—Feeling

   TYPE THREE: Intuiting—Thinking

   TYPE FOUR: Intuiting—Feeling

You have now identified your marriage "type." If you had a tie or sense a doubt that you are identified correctly, go on to the Marriage Type Verifier.

Scoring Sheet
(INSERT THE SCORING SHEET HERE)

MARRIAGE TYPE VERIFIERS
(From *Marriage Types* by David L. Luecke)

The Type Verifiers are designed to help you determine if you have identified your "marriage type" correctly. They can also help you understand yourself and your partner by reviewing some of the characteristics of your "type."

Read the twenty statements describing your type and circle the number by each one that fits at least in a general way. Total the number of statements marked at the bottom. At least ten items will be checked to indicate a significant type preference.

If the verifying statements under your "marriage type" do not adequately fit, or if you want additional verification, read through the statements under each of the four "marriage types" checking statements that apply and totaling the number of checks for each. The "marriage type" with the most checks should be the same as the one you identified above from the Scoring Sheet.

If the "marriage type" with the most checks is different from the one you identified on the Score Sheet, you may need to explore further. You can ask your spouse to review the statements in the Verifier with you and give feedback on the way you see yourself. Or you may proceed following your own self-awareness and best hunch as to where you fit. No one ever fits any "type" exactly.

TYPE ONE
Sensing and Thinking

Circle the number by each item that fits you at least in a general way. Add the total at the bottom.

1. You make decisions with logic more than feeling.

2. You are usually content to take life as it comes without speculating about how things could be different.

3. You prefer detailed descriptions; you don't want to be left to your own imagination.

4. You tend to experience life in the present rather than anticipate the future.

5. You do not waste words; you tend to be brief and to the point.

6. You are better at subjects dealing with hard facts (geography or accounting) than those dealing more with theory (psychology or sociology).

7. You understand organizations better than individuals.

8. You have difficulty expressing your feelings.

9. As a parent, you are a better provider than a nurturer.

10. You mostly take people at face value without speculating about inner motives or values.

11. You often like to withdraw from dealing with people into your favorite project or hobby.

12. You experience and enjoy life rather than speculate about it.

13. You prefer to experience life more than to change it.

14. You stick with what is familiar, tried, and true; you are often uncomfortable with new and speculative changes.

15. If you think it important, you can find some satisfaction performing routine, even repetitious tasks.

16. When others are upset, you are more likely to try to fix the problem quickly than to explore feelings in depth.

17. You are better at household maintenance than dealing with personal family relationships.

18. You prefer to work with things rather than with people.

19. You are more likely to be truthful than tactful.

20. You pay more attention to your senses than to your inner world of thought and feeling.

_____ Total circled

Type Two:
Sensing and Feeling

Circle the number by each item that fits you at least in a general way. Add the total at the bottom.

1. You prefer activities that are personal rather than intellectual.

2. You are able to tolerate routine and repetitious tasks in the service of something or someone you care about.

3. In general, you are content with what is, rather than yearning for what might be.

4. You tend to worry more than necessary about hurting the feelings of others.

5. You like to please others; one of your favorite pleasures is giving pleasure to others.

6. You prefer to live and enjoy life rather than analyze it.

7. You combine practicality with common sense; people come to you when they want a task done reliably and well.

8. You preserve traditions and rituals; you remember birthdays, anniversaries, and other special days.

9. Your responsiveness to needs and attention to details often means you work harder and longer than others.

10. Warm, harmonious relationships are more important than organization or efficiency.

11. You understand and enjoy quality in things that appeal to the senses such as food, music, arts and crafts, decorating, etc.

12. You are better at observing the appearance and behavior of others than understanding their inner world.

13. You enjoy things more than theories.

14. You are better at work that requires precision than work requiring inspiration or imagination.

15. Life is best for you when you are doing something you enjoy with people you like to be with.

16. People are more likely to come to you for practical assistance and personal warmth than for answers to theoretical questions.

17. You look for practical ways to help hurting people feel better fast rather than explore dynamics for long-term solutions.

18. You respond to the physical appearance or condition of others rather than assess underlying motives or character.

19. You show your warmth and caring by deeds more than words.

20. You would rather enjoy today than anticipate tomorrow.

_____ Total circled

TYPE THREE:
Intuiting and Thinking

Circle the number by each item that fits you at least in a general way. Total the items marked at the bottom.

1. You prefer dealing with the concept rather than the details.

2. You can be absorbed in your own thoughts and interests at the expense of your relationships.

3. You analyze life rather than simply enjoy it.

4. You think and act independently; you do not automatically follow established procedures.

5. You are more likely to be thinking about the future than experiencing and enjoying the present.

6. You like to develop better and more efficient ways to do things.

7. When something seems right, you push ahead without worrying very much about the reactions of others.

8. You are better at understanding ideas and theories than understanding people.

9. Projects that interest you often take priority over home and family.

10. A well-ordered and efficient household can be more important than emotional warmth or harmony.

11. You are more energized by ideas than by emotions.

12. Figuring out how a toy works can be as interesting as playing with it.

13. Conclusions that seem logical to you often seem puzzling to others.

14. You tend to be uncomfortable when others working with you become personal or emotional.

15. You like to find a way when others say, "It can't be done."

16. You enjoy innovation but lose interest with repetitious, routine tasks.

17. You can enjoy a good debate but not many people are willing to argue with you.

18. You provide for your family's future better than you enjoy your family today.

19. You would often like to withdraw into the world of ideas, books, or imagination.

20. Although at times you may talk a great deal, you reveal little about your own inner world of feelings.

_____ Total circled

TYPE FOUR:
Intuiting and Feeling

Circle the number by each item that fits you at least in a general way. Total the items marked at the bottom.

1. Efficiency is not satisfying without harmonious relationships.

2. You enjoy dreaming and planning future possibilities to share with those you love.

3. You experience a tension between wanting to think independently and wanting to be accepted by others.

4. You can be unrealistic about goals when you become impatient with details.

5. You are more likely to work with inspiration than perspiration.

6. People come to you for understanding and personal support.

7. You respond to hurting people more with insight and understanding than with deeds.

8. You tend to feel vaguely dissatisfied with your relationships, often yearning for something new, different, or better.

9. You tend to take up the problems of others as if they were your own.

10. You decide about others more on the basis of your hunches than by their actual behavior.

11. You feel responsible when close friends or family are unhappy.

12. You frequently feel restless, yearning for a life that is more fulfilling.

13. You prefer working with people than with things.

14. You like working with others as a team rather than having a boss or being the boss.

15. You put a high value on personal independence; you want variety and freedom in what you do.

16. You are likely to be the "idea person" while others work out the practical details.

17. Enjoyment of life is in the future—rarely in the present experience.

18. Warm, intimate family relationships are more important than a well-ordered household.

19. You like to find new and creative ways to help, teach, or pleasure others.

20. Although you may be successful and well-liked, you are nevertheless seen as a nonconformist in some ways.

_____ Total circled

At least 10 numbers will be circled to indicate a type identity. If you remain uncertain, mark the statements that apply under all types in the Verifier and compare all four scores. The more statements that apply, the more likely you are to fit that type.

Comparing your Identifier results with your Verifier scores should enable you to identify and confirm the Marriage Type that best describes you. Of course, as noted, no "type" fits anyone exactly. If the results of these instruments remain ambiguous, and you remain uncertain of your type, make a provisional determination that you can continue to test as you explore each type through further resources.

NOTES

ONE
Can You Change Your Spouse?

1. Steve Wilke, Dave Jackson and Neta Jackson, *When We Can't Talk Anymore* (Wheaton, Ill.: Tyndale, 1992), 11.
2. Joseph Cooke, *Free for the Taking* (Old Tappan, N.J.: Revell, 1975), 127.
3. James Fairfield, *When You Don't Agree* (Scottdale, Penn.: Herald Press, 1977), 195.
4. Jeanette C. Lauer and Robert H. Lauer, *Till Death Do Us Part* (New York: Harrington Park Press, 1986), 153-4, adapted.

TWO
Roadblocks to Change

1. Cecil Osborne, *The Art of Understanding Your Mate* (Grand Rapids, Mich.: Zondervan, 1970), 19.
2. Taken from a message given on "Back to the Bible Broadcast."
3. Adapted from a quote by Joseph Shore in Lloyd Cory, *Quotable Quotations* (Wheaton, Ill.: Victor Books, 1985), 55.
4. Tim Hansel, *Holy Sweat* (Dallas: Word, 1987), 54-55.
5. Michael P. Green, ed., *Illustrations for Biblical Preaching* (Grand Rapids, Mich.: Baker Book House, 1989), 38.
6. Charles Swindoll, *Come before Winter… And Share My Hope* (Portland, Ore.: Multnomah Press, 1985), 331-32.

THREE
Creating a Climate for Change

1. Michele Weiner-Davis, *Divorce Busting* (New York: Summit Books, 1992), 124-31, adapted.

2. Aaron Beck, *Love Is Not Enough* (San Francisco: Harper and Row, 1988), 155-58, adapted.
3. Michael E. McGill, *Changing Him, Changing Her* (New York: Simon and Schuster, 1982), 140-48, adapted.
4. McGill, *Changing Him, Changing Her*, 147-65, adapted.
5. Nick Stimeti, Barbara Chesser, and John DeFrain, *Building Family Strengths* (Lincoln, Neb.: University of Nebraska Press, 1979), 112, adapted.
6. Billie S. Ables, *Therapy for Couples* (San Francisco: Jossey-Bass, 1977), 3, 218.
7. Beck, 207-8, adapted.
8. McGill, *Changing Him, Changing Her*, 149-66, adapted.
9. McGill, *Changing Him, Changing Her*, 29-38, adapted.
10. Ed and Carol Neuenschwander, *Two Friends in Love* (Portland, Ore.: Multnomah Press, 1986), 108.

FOUR
We Are Different, Aren't We? (Part 1)

1. Michael McGill, *The McGill Report on Male Intimacy* (San Francisco: Harper and Row, 1985), 94-95.
2. McGill, *McGill Report on Male Intimacy*, 74.
3. H. Norman Wright, *Understanding the Man in Your Life* (Dallas: Word, 1987), 27-31, adapted.
4. Joe Tanenbaum, *Male and Female Realities* (San Marcos, Calif.: Robert Erdmann Publishing, 1990), 54, adapted.
5. Tanenbaum, 111, adapted.
6. Tanenbaum, 96-97, adapted.
7. Joan Shapiro, M.D., *Men, A Translation for Women* (New York: Avon Books, 1992), 71-84, adapted.
8. Tanenbaum, 82, adapted.
9. Tanenbaum, 40, adapted.
10. Jacquelyn Wonder and Priscilla Donovan, *Whole Brain Thinking* (New York: William Morrow and Company, 1984), 18-34, adapted.
11. Tanenbaum, 87-89, adapted.
12. Tanenbaum, 90.
13. Tanenbaum, 48, adapted.

FIVE
We Are Different, Aren't We? (Part 2)

1. Cris Erott, *He and She* (Berkeley, Calif.: Conari Press, 1992), 14-15, adapted.
2. McGill, *McGill Report on Male Intimacy*, 176.
3. H. Norman Wright, *I'll Love You Forever* (Colorado Springs: Focus on the Family, 1993), 138-40.
4. McGill, *McGill Report on Male Intimacy*, 276-77; Erott, 16-17, adapted.
5. McGill, *McGill Report on Male Intimacy*, 266.
6. Tanenbaum, 60-63, adapted.
7. John Gray, *Men Are from Mars and Women Are from Venus* (New York: Harper-Collins, 1992), 27.
8. Dorothy C. Finkelhor, *How to Make Your Emotions Work for You* (New York: Berkeley Medallion Books, 1973), 23-24.
9. Shapiro, 101-2, adapted.
10. Carol Staudacher, *Men and Grief* (Oakland, Calif.: New Harbinger, 1991), 155.

11. Barbara DeAngelis, *Secrets about Men Every Woman Should Know* (New York: Delacorte Press, 1990), 234-42, adapted.
12. McGill, *McGill Report on Male Intimacy,* 269, 276.
13. John Gray, *Men, Women, and Relationships* (Hillsboro, Ore.: Beyond Words Publishing, Inc., 1990), 116, adapted.
14. Gray, 115-17, adapted.
15. Erott, 18, adapted.
16. Shapiro, 104-9, adapted.
17. Erott, 18-19, adapted.
18. Georgie Witkin-Lanoil, *The Male Stress Syndrome* (New York: New Market Press, 1986), 129.
19. Erott, 52-53, 70, adapted.
20. Tanenbaum, 100, adapted.
21. Joel D. Black and Diane Greenbert, *Women and Friendship* (New York: Franklin Watts, 1985), 260, adapted.
22. Wright, *Understanding the Man in Your Life,* 70-71, 75-77, adapted.

SIX
It Takes All Types

1. This quote was shared in a seminar and attributed to Sydney J. Harris, source unknown.
2. David Keirsey and Marilyn Bates, *Please Understand Me* (Del Mar, Calif.: Prometheus Nemesis Books, 1978), 1.
3. Charles R. Swindoll, *Standing Out* (Portland, Ore.: Multnomah Press, 1979).
4. Adapted from A. H. Buss, and R. Plomin, *A Temperament Theory of Personality Development* (John Wiley & Sons: New York, 1975), 237.
5. The best way to determine your personality is to take the full MBTI from a qualified professional. You can start by asking your pastor or a local Christian counseling center, or the Association for Psychological Type (APT), P.O. Box 5099, Gainesville, FL 32602, (904) 371-1853, or Dr. Gary J. Oliver at Southwest Counseling Associates, 141 W. Davies, Littleton, CO, 80120.
6. LaVonne Neff, *One of a Kind* (Portland: Multnomah Press, 1988), 24-26.

SEVEN
How'd You Reach That Conclusion?

1. Otto Kroeger and Janet M. Thuesen, *Type Talk* (New York: Delacorte Press, 1988), 26.
2. David Stoop and Jan Stoop, *The Intimacy Factor* (Nashville: Thomas Nelson Publishers, 1993), 77.
3. Stoop and Stoop, 77.
4. Stoop and Stoop, 90.
5. Kroeger and Thuesen, 29-31.
6. Gary L. Harbaugh, *God's Gifted People* (Minneapolis: Augsburg Publishing House, 1988) adapted.
7. David L. Luecke, *Marriage Types* (Waynesboro, Va.: The Relationship Institute, 1989), 8-28.
8. David L. Luecke, *Prescription for Marriage* (Waynesboro, Va.: The Relationship Institute, 1989).

EIGHT
You're Either an "In-y" or an "Out-y"

1. Mark A. Pearson, *Why Can't I Be Me?* (Grand Rapids, Mich.: Baker Book House, 1992), 111.
2. Adapted from Earle C. Paige, *Looking at Type* (Gainesville, Fla.: Center for Application of Psychological Type, 1983), n.p.
3. Pearson, 106.
4. Paige, n.p.
5. Jonathan and Wendy Lazear, *Meditations for Parents Who Do Too Much* (New York: Simon & Schuster, 1993), n.p., October 22 selection.
6. Adapted from: M. Carlyn, "An Assessment of the Myers-Briggs Type Indicator," *Journal of Personality Assessment,* 1977, 42(5), 461-473

NINE
Learning to Speak Your Partner's Language

1. Seneca, quoted in Taylor Caldwell, *The Listener* (New York: Bantam, 1960), vi.
2. David Burns, *The Feeling Good Handbook* (New York: William Morrow and Co., 1989), 445-45, adapted.
3. Gray, 36-37, adapted.
4. Gray, 71-72, adapted.
5. Gray, adapted.
6. Deborah Tannen, *You Just Don't Understand* (New York: William Morrow and Co., 1990), 59, adapted.
7. Tannen, 77, adapted.
8. Gray, 250.
9. H. Norman Wright, *Holding onto Romance* (Ventura, Calif.: Regal Books, 1992), 144-47, adapted.
10. Wright, *Holding onto Romance,* 119-21.
11. Wright, *Holding onto Romance,* 156, adapted.

TEN
Conflict: The Pathway to Intimacy

1. David A. Seamands, "The Royal Romance and Yours," quoted in *Asbury Seminary Herald* (September-October 1981).
2. Jack and Carole Mayhall, *Opposites Attack: Turning Your Differences into Opportunities* (Colorado Springs: NavPress, 1990), 16-17.
3. Adapted from Warren Bennis, *Why Leaders Can't Lead: The Unconscious Conspiracy Continues* (San Francisco: Jossey-Bass Publishers, 1990), 158.
4. These four stages of conflict are adapted from Gary J. Oliver, *Real Men Have Feelings Too* (Chicago: Moody Press, 1993), 222-26.
5. Adapted from Richard L. Meth and Robert S. Pasick, *Men in Therapy: The Challenge of Change* (New York: The Guilford Press, 1990), 198.
6. Oliver, 223.
7. Oliver, 222.
8. Harriet Goldhor Lerner, *The Dance of Anger* (New York: Harper and Row, 1985), 199-201.

ELEVEN
If You Married a Perfectionist or Controller

1. H. Norman Wright, *Making Peace with Your Past* (Grand Rapids, Mich.: Revell, 1985), 103-7, adapted.
2. Miriam Elliot and Susan Meltsner, *The Perfectionist Predicament* (New York: William Morrow and Co., 1991), 262-63, adapted.
3. Elliot and Meltsner, 263.
4. Elliot and Meltsner, 264-67, adapted.
5. Elliot and Meltsner, 267-68, adapted.
6. Steven J. Hendlin, *When Good Enough Is Never Enough* (New York: G.P. Putnam's Sons, 1992), 205-10, adapted.
7. Hendlin, 216-18, adapted.
8. Elliot and Meltsner, 278-82, adapted.
9. H. Norman Wright, *So You're Getting Married* (Ventura, Calif.: Regal Books, 1989), n.p.
10. Elliot and Meltsner, 52-53, adapted.

TWELVE
How to Change Your Spouse.

1. Oswald Chambers, *My Utmost for His Highest: An Updated Edition in Today's Language,* ed. James Reimann (Grand Rapids, Mich.: Discovery House, 1992) November 15.
2. Judith Stone, "Changing to Please a Man: How Much Is Too Much?" *Glamour* 1985 (October 1987) 44.
3. For more information on prayer I would encourage you to pick up the exceptional book by Richard Foster, *Prayer: Finding the Heart's True Home* (San Francisco: Harper and Row, 1992).
4. If you would like to better understand some of the factors that influence men, how they respond in relationships, and how they can more effectively understand and deal with their emotions I would encourage you to read *Real Men Have Feelings Too* by Gary Oliver.
5. Swindoll, *Come Before Winter... and Share My Hope,* 331.

SUGGESTED READINGS

Elliot, Miriam and Meltsner, Susan. *The Perfectionist Predicament.* New York: William Morrow and Co., 1991.

Harbaugh, Gary L. *God's Gifted People: Discovering and Using Your Spiritual and Personal Gifts.* Minneapolis: Augsburg Publishing House, 1988.

Kroeger, Otto and Thuesen, Janet M. *Type Talk.* New York: Delacorte Press, 1988.

Luecke, David L. *Prescription for Marriage.* Waynesboro, Va.: The Relationship Institute, 1989.

Luecke, David L. *Marriage Types.* Waynesboro, Va.: The Relationship Institute, 1989.

Neff, LaVonne. *One of a Kind.* Portland, Ore.: Multnomah Press, 1988.

Pearson, Mark A. *Why Can't I Be Me?* Grand Rapids, Mich.: Baker Book House, 1992.

Seamands, David. *Freedom from the Performance Trap.* Chicago, Ill.: Victor Books, 1991.

Stoop, David. *Hope for the Perfectionist.* Nashville, Tenn.: Thomas Nelson, 1989.

Stoop, David and Jan. *The Intimacy Factor.* Nashville, Tenn.: Thomas Nelson Publishers, 1992.

Ward, Ruth McRoberts. *Self-Esteem: Gift from God.* Grand Rapids, Mich.: Baker Book House, 1984.

Wright, H. Norman and Oliver, Gary J. *Kids Have Feelings Too.* Wheaton, Ill.: Victor Books, 1992.

TEACHING KIT

A complete curriculum teaching kit is available to accompany this book. It is possible to teach the content of the resource in marriage seminars, Sunday school classes, retreats, small groups, etc. The kit contains the structure, outline, time sequence, and learning activities, as well as many transparency patterns which allow you to make professional level transparencies to use as you teach.

For information on ordering this unique teaching kit, either call Christian Marriage Enrichment at 1-800-875-7560 or write us at 17821 17th St. #190, Tustin, CA 92680.